Industrial Evolution

New Edition

Karl Bücher

VERNON PRESS

www.vernonpress.com
Vernon Press is an imprint of Vernon Art & Science Inc.

In the Americas:
Vernon Press
1000 N West Street,
Suite 1200, Wilmington,
Delaware 19801
United States

In the Rest of the World:
Vernon Press
C/Sancti Espiritu 17,
Malaga, 29006
Spain

Library of Congress Control Number: 2014932229

ISBN 978-1-62273-005-6

Contents

Prefatory Note

THE writings of Professor Bücher, in their German dress, require no introduction to economists. His admirable work *The Population of Frankfurt in the Fourteenth and Fifteenth Centuries*, published in 1886, gave him immediate celebrity with economic historians, and left him without a rival in the field of historical statistics. In his treatment of economic theory he stands midway between the "younger historical school" of economists and the psychological Austrians.[1] A full list of his writings need not be given.[2] But I may recall his amplified German edition of Laveleye's *Primitive Property*, his little volume *The Insurrections of the Slave Labourers*, 143-129 B.C., his original and suggestive *Labour and Rhythm*, discussing the relation between the physiology and the psychology of labour, his investigations into trusts, and his co-editorship of Wagner's *Handbook of Political Economy* (the section *Industry* being in his charge) as indicating the general direction and scope of his researches. The present stimulating volume, which in the original bears the title *Die Entstehung der Volkswirtschaft* (The Rise of National Economy), gives the author's conclusions on general industrial development. Somewhat similar ground has been worked over, among recent economic publications, alone by Professor Schmoller's comprehensive *Grundriss der*

---

[1] A few facts and dates regarding Professor Bücher's career may not be uninteresting. Professor Bücher was born in Prussian Rhineland in 1847. He completed his undergraduate studies at Bonn and Göttingen (1866-69). His rapid rise in the German scholastic world is evident from his academic appointments: special lecturer at Gottingen (1869-72), lecturer at Dortmund (1872-73), at Frankfurt Technical School (1873-78), and at Munich (1881); Professor of Statistics at Dorpat, Russia (1882), of Political Economy and Finance at Basel (1883-90), at Karlsruhe (1890-93), and at Leipsic (1893 to present) From 1878 to the close of 1880 he was Industrial and Social Editor of the *Frankfurter Zeitung*.

[2] This may be found in the Handwôrterbuch d. Staatswiss.

allgemeinen Volkswirtschaftslehre, Pt. I. But the method of treatment and the results of the present work allow it to maintain its unique position.

Chapters I. and II. outline the prominent features of primitive economic life in the tropical zone. These realistic accounts of the "pre-economic stage of industrial evolution," preceding the dawn of civilization, ably emphasize the kinship of economics and ethnology. In chapter III. he presents brilliantly and concisely the suggestive series of economic developmental stages of household, town and national economy, based on the industrial relation of producer to consumer; and Chapter IV. offers a masterly survey of industrial systems—domestic work, wage-work, handicraft, commission work (house industry), and the factory. With these chapters may be classed Chapter V. *The Decline of the Handicrafts*. The remaining chapters analyze more specifically, from the viewpoints of the individual and society, some of the great processes of industrial evolution: union and division of labour; the intellectual integration of society as effected by the press; the formation of social classes; and the further adjustment of labour through internal migrations of population. At the same time they enrich economic terminology with many telling expressions.

"The worst use of theory is to make men insensible to fact," Lord Acton remarked in the opening number of the English Historical Review. Our author, with his store of minute facts, his keen analysis and his broad and refreshing generalizations, has known how to avoid the snare. His historical attitude is indicated by his advice that "our young political economists" be sent on journeys of investigation to the Russians, the Roumanians and the southern Slavs rather than to England and America. In the following pages, which in their present form I trust do not entirely obliterate the pleasing style of the original, his attention is, of course, devoted primarily to economic rather than to social and other considerations.

The volume has had in Germany an unusually influential circulation, and has recently been translated into French, Russian and Bohemian. As the preface notes, it has done extensive service as a general introduction to "economic thinking." Its use for this purpose, through the medium of special transcriptions, has already been remarked at some American universities. The hope may be indulged that its merits will now receive wider recognition, and in some measure impart to the reader the stimulus felt by the writer during a two years' attendance on the author's lectures in 1895-97. Editorial annotations, it may be added, have been confined to the narrowest limits.

In translating it I have had the valuable assistance of my colleague, Dr. G. H. Needier, Lecturer on German, University College, to whom I wish to express my deep obligations. My thanks are also due Professor Bücher for his patient answers to the many queries sent over the water to him, to Professor Mavor for varied aid during the work of revision, and to Mr. H. H. Langton and Mr. D. R. Keys for help in correcting proofs.

For the convenience of the general reader a short supplementary bibliography of recent works in English is appended.

S. M. W.

UNIVERSITY OF TORONTO,

April 9, 1901.

Haddon, *Evolution of Art* (1895); Lloyd Morgan, *Animal Life and Intelligence* (1891), *Habit and Instinct* (1896); Keane, *Man Past and Present* (1899); Spencer and Gillen, *The Native Tribes of Central Australia* (1899); Mackenzie, *An Introduction to Social Philosophy* (ad ed., 1895); Giddings, *Principles of Sociology* (1896), Gumplowicz, *Outlines of Sociology* (trans. 1899); Loria, *Economic Foundations of Society* (trans. 1899); Ashley, *Economic History* (2 pts., 1888-92), *Surveys Historic and Economic* (1900); Gomme, *The Village Community* (1890); Cunningham, *Growth of English Industry and Commerce* (2 vols., 1890-92), *Western Civilization* (1898); Booth, *Life and Labours of the People* (9 vols., 1889-97); Mayo-Smith, *Emigration and Immigration* (1890); Weber, *The Growth of Cities* (1899); Hobson, *The Evolution of Modern Capitalism* (1894).

Prefaces to the First and Second German Editions

(April 1893 and November 1897.)

THE lectures in this volume were originally delivered before audiences that were not composed of specialists exclusively. Each lecture is complete in itself; the same trains of thought are indeed occasionally repeated, but in a different setting. Yet it will readily be perceived that the different parts have an inner connection, and supplement each other both in subject and method. The fundamental idea running through them all is expressed in the third. As need scarcely be remarked, the lecture is not printed in the summary form in which it was delivered. I trust that the gain ill accuracy and fulness of statement has not been at the expense of clearness.

The lectures are dominated by a uniform conception of the orderly nature of economic development, and by a similarity in the method of treating material. In both respects this accords with the practice which I have consistently followed ever since the inception of my academic activity and which during continued scientific work has become more and more clearly and firmly established. With the present publication I accede to the wish expressed by many of my former auditors in the only form at present possible, a form of whose insufficiency I myself am fully conscious.

In preparing a second edition one thing was clear: the book must be expanded in the direction in which it had been most effective. At its first appearance I had hoped that the little volume might exert some influence upon the method of treating scientific problems; and indeed there has appeared in recent years quite a series of writings by younger authors (some of whom were seemingly wholly unacquainted with my book), in which the results of the investigations here published are taken into account. This is outwardly evidenced by the use of the concepts and the technical expressions that I introduced into the lit erature of the subject, as if they were old, familiar, scientific furniture. It is perhaps justifiable to infer from this that the book has exercised some influence upon academic teaching.

But it seems to have found its chief circulation in the wider circles of the educated public, particularly among college students, who have used it as a sort of introduction to economics, and as a preparation for economic thinking. That naturally decided me to keep their wants very particularly in view in revising the book. In order to avoid misconceptions, however, I wish to state expressly that the employment of the book for this purpose requires the concurrent use of a good systematic treatise on the principles of political economy.

The better to meet the need of the larger class just mentioned, I have given some of the lectures of the first edition a simpler form, expanding them where necessary, and eliminating needless detail. Extensive alteration, however, has been confined to the lecture on the Organization of Work and the Formation of Social Classes. Here uniformity of treatment seemed to recommend a division into two chapters (VIII and IX), and such extensive additions as would serve to round off each independently of the other. The lecture on the Social Organization of the Population of Frankfurt in the Middle Ages has been omitted because it disturbed the greater uniformity aimed at for the complete work, and because, as a purely historical account, it is better suited to a collection of sketches in social and economic history, for which opportunity may perhaps be found later.

On the other hand three unpublished lectures have been added (Chaps. I, V, and VII). The first of these deals with the pre-economic period, and is intended to furnish the substructure for the system of economic stages which is developed in the third chapter. Its main features were sketched as early as 1885, in a lecture I delivered at the University of Basel on the beginnings of social history.

The second agrees in the major part of its matter, and also to a large extent in its form, with the report upon handicrafts that I presented at the last general meeting of the Social Science Club in Cologne. It seems advisable to give it a place in order to afford the reader at one point at least an insight into the great changes that are in progress in the field of modern industrial life. The third [entitled "Union of Labour and Labour in Common"] is an attempt to lay before a wider circle of readers, in the form in which I finally presented it to my university classes, a chapter from the theory of labour to which I have given considerable attention.

All the lectures in this volume, both old and new, were originally sections of university lectures. Every lecturer knows what a wonderful compilation his note-book is, how from semester to semester certain portions must be removed and reconstructed, how some parts are never approached without an inward struggle, and how finally the remaining difficulties are surmounted and the whole given a form satisfactory alike to teacher and students. To the lecture-room first of all belong the fruits of the scientific labours of the German university professor; but he also naturally wishes to submit what he has laboriously accomplished to the critical judgment of specialists; and for my part I feel in such cases the further need of testing the maturity of my conceptions by seeing whether they can be made intelligibly acceptable to a wider range of readers. So that all the lectures that have been taken over from the first edition were actually delivered before a more popular audience, while Chapters I and VII are essays in the same style. In the extent of their subject-matter, however, they all reach far beyond what can be offered directly to students in a university lecture.

In conclusion I may allude to two attacks that have been delivered by historians against some parts of the third and fourth lectures. The blame surely does not rest with me if these gentlemen have failed to perceive that this work treats of economic theory, not of economic history. He who, in the outline of a period of development extending over thousands of years, expects a minute and exhaustive presentation of the actual condition of any particular people and century, need blame only himself if he is disappointed. In the first edition I expressed myself clearly enough, I think, regarding the logical character of the economic stages. In the present edition I have taken occasion, however, to give the passages in question such a form that in future they cannot with good intentions be misunderstood. Though for the central idea of my theory of development it is altogether immaterial whether I have in every particular characterized the economy of the Greeks and Romans correctly or not, or whether the guild handicraft of the Middle Ages was chiefly wage-work or chiefly independent hand-work ("price-work").

Preface to the Third German Edition

IN the present edition, bearing in mind the way in which this book came into existence and has since expanded, I felt strongly impelled to mark my appreciation of the recognition it has gained, as indicated by several editions and by translations into French, English, Russian, and Bohemian, by preparing additional chapters to remove a number of gaps still noticeable in the last issue. If I have not yielded to the temptation, it is chiefly for the reason that a larger bulk would necessarily prejudice the wider circulation of the volume.

The most disturbing want has been met by the insertion of a new chapter on the economic life of primitive peoples (Chapter II). The chapter differs from the more detailed one in volume 3 of the Yearbook of the Gehe Stiftung in its more summary form and in the addition of some not unimportant facts.

All the other chapters have been carefully revised and many slight improvements made. More extensive alterations are confined to Chapters I, III, VII, and VIII. May the book in its present form satisfy its old friends and add new ones to the number!

CARL BÜCHER.
LEIPZIG, Oct. 15, 1900.

Chapter I. Primitive Economic Conditions

A LL scientific investigation of industry starts with the assumption that man has a peculiar "economic nature" belonging to no other living creature. From this economic nature a principle is supposed to spring, which controls all his actions that are directed to the satisfaction of his wants. This is the economic principle, the fundamental principle of economic activity. This principle reveals itself in man's endeavour always and everywhere to attain the highest possible satisfaction with the least possible sacrifice (labour) — the "principle of least sacrifice."

According to this view all man's economic actions are actions directed toward an end and guided by considerations of profit. Whether or not the final impulse to economic labour is to be sought in the instincts of man. (the instinct of self-preservation and of self-interest), the satisfaction of these instincts is always the result of a series of successive mental operations. Man estimates the extent of the discomfort that would arise from the non-satisfaction of a want felt by him; he measures the discomfort that the labour necessary to meet the want can cause him; he compares the discomforts with each other, and resolves to undertake the labour only when the accompanying sacrifice is less than the sacrifice of remaining unsatisfied. Moreover, upon undertaking the labour he again chooses the least burdensome among the various possible methods of procedure, and thus has a further series of considerations, estimations, comparisons, and judgments to enter upon.

In fact the whole science of political economy proceeds on the assumption that economic actions have behind them a rational motive and call into play the higher mental faculties; and it has evolved a kind of psychology of labour, by means of which it seeks to explain those actions in their typical progress. Economic activity is, therefore, something especially human; indeed the question whether the lower animals display similar activity, seems never to have been broached. The economic nature of man is something absolute, inseparable from the very character of man.[3]

Yet even among civilized mankind, from whose manifold activity the principle of economy has been deduced, indications are not wanting to show that the economic nature must be characteristic of different individuals in different degree. Between the industrious and the indolent, the provident and the improvident, the sparing and the spendthrift, there are innumerable gradations; and if we only observe the conduct of the child towards his possessions, we are easily convinced that the "economic nature" must be acquired anew by each human being, and that it is a result of education and custom, in which individuals differ no less than in their whole physical and mental development.

Having once reached this point, we shall scarcely be able to postpone the question, whether indeed that "economic nature" does not, for mankind in general, signify-something acquired rather than something given by nature; and whether we must not assume at the beginning of human evolution a period of purely instinctive satisfaction of wants reaching over many thousands of years, such as we are accustomed to take for granted in the case of the lower animal.

The answer to this question can be gained only by proceeding inductively. The picture of primitive man that we make for ourselves must be not an imaginary one—no Robinson Crusoe story such as is so often encountered in the deductions of the "classical" economists. Its lines must all be drawn from reality; they must show us the actuality of the assumed conditions under which uncivilized man lives and the impulses under which he is conceived to act and later also think. Civilized man has always had a great inclination to read his conceptions and feelings into the mind of primitive man; but he

---

[3] "The elements of economic character are firmly rooted in the physical and intellectual organization of man, and change just as little as his outward character does, at least in the periods which come within the scope of the history of mankind."—Wagner, *Grundlegung d. polit. Oekonomie* (3. Aufl.), I. P- 82. [As for animal sociology, it can hardly be said to have advanced as yet beyond animal psychology.—ED.]

has only a limited capacity for understanding the latter's undeveloped mental life and for interpreting, as it were, his nature. To be sure, aboriginal man in actual existence can nowhere now be found. Great as is the number of primitive peoples that have gradually come within our ken, none of them stands any longer at the lowest stage of savagery; all show traces of the first step in civilization, for all know the use of fire.

Many writers, it is true, have imagined, under the stimulus of evolutionist theories, that they had succeeded, now here, now there, in discovering populations preserving the original animal state down to the present. As late a writer as Sir John Lubbock is inclined to deny to several tribes of the South Sea Islands a knowledge of fire. O. Peschel has been at pains to prove that the instances adduced by Lubbock are incorrect;[4] and with him we may regard as valid the assertion that upon the whole earth the tribe that has not made use of fire is yet to be found. Even the prehistoric cave discoveries, which show us men of the Ice Age along with the bear, the aurochs, and the reindeer, show traces of the use of fire. Fire indeed is a powerful influence in the direction of civilization. It enlarges man's sphere of sustenance, teaches him to harden the points of the wooden arrows and spears, to hollow out the tree, and to frighten away the wild beasts.

Other investigators have imagined they have discovered human beings who lived together in small groups in trees, had fruits for food, and used only stones and cudgels as weapons and instruments, after the fashion of the higher apes. Frederick Engels[5] is of the opinion that by this assumption alone can we explain the continued existence of man alongside the great beasts of prey. Lippert.who investigates the case more carefully, finds, it is true, that in the myth of the Egyptians the tree plays a certain role as an abode of spirits; but he is prudent enough not to conclude from this that the ancestors of the Egyptians dwelt in trees, — more prudent than the philologist Lazarus Geiger, who discovered a relic of tree-dwelling

---

[4] *Races of Man* (New York, 1888), pp. 137 ff. I know, indeed, that the American writer Teale (quoted by Lippert, *Kulturgeschichte der Menschheit*, I, p. 52) has contradicted him in one instance. Mundt-Lauff has also, according to Peschel in "Natur" for the year 1879, p. 478, denied the use of cooked food by the Negritos in the Philippines, but his assertions again have been refuted by A. Schadenberg in the Ztschr. f. Ethnologie, XII (1880), pp. 143-4- [No ethnologist would now claim fireless tribes as known in actual existence.—ED.]

[5] *Der Ursprung der Familie, des Privateigentums u. des Stoats*, p. 7.

in the hammock used by the South American Indians. It is true that in Sumatra, Luzon, New Guinea, the Solomon Islands, and among the Gaberi negroes in Central Africa, huts have been found built in between the branches of large trees;[6] and the same is reported of individual forest tribes of South America.[7] But so far as these products of primitive architecture are not mere temporary protective structures that are supplemented by permanent dwelling-places upon the ground, they are by no means the most unfinished of habitations, and the peoples using them prove by many kinds of implements, utensils, and domestic animals, and some of them even by the agriculture they carry on, that they no longer stand at the first dawn of civilization.

After what has been said there can be no object in searching out uncivilized peoples and beginning with a description of them, after the example of Klemm who opens his General History of Civilization with the Forest Indians of Brazil, although it is not to be denied that these stand at a very low cultural stage indeed. In the same connection other investigators cite tribes standing at no higher stage: the Bushmen in South Africa, the Batuas in the Congo basin, the Veddahs in Ceylon, the Mincopies in the Andaman Islands, the Negritos in the Philippines, the Australians of the continent, the now extinct Tasmanians, the Kubus in Sumatra, and the Tierra-del-Fuegians. To whom to adjudge the palm for savagery might be difficult to decide. O. Peschel[8] finds individual elements of civilization among them all, even among the Botokudos, whom he himself considers still nearest the primitive state.

The assumption of such a primitive condition, in which, armed with no other resources than are at the command of the lower animal, man has to join in the struggle for existence, is one of the necessary expedients of all sciences that aim at a history of man's development; and this is true of sociology and especially of political economy. We must, however, abandon the attempt to exemplify the primitive condition by any definite people. On the other hand, there is more prospect of scientific results in an endeavour to collect the common characteristics of the human beings standing lowest in the

---

[6]Nachtigal, *Sahara u. Sudan*, II, pp. 628 ff. Finsch, *Samoafahrten*, pp. 271 f. Ratzel, *Völkerkunde*, I, pp. 101, 105, 245, 386; II, p. 83. [Its different arrangement precludes citation from the admirable English edition: *The History of Mankind*, 2 vols., London, 1896-97.—ED.]

[7]Waitz, *Anthropologic d. Naturvölker*, III, p. 393.

[8]*Races of Man*, pp. 149 ff.

scale, in order, by starting with them, to arrive at a picture of the beginnings of economic life and the formation of society. But in this it
is by no means necessary to confine ourselves to the above-mentioned
representatives of the lowest manner of life; for every delimitation
of that kind would challenge objections and contract the field of
vision. Moreover the various elements of mental culture and material civilization are by no means so mutually dependent that all must
necessarily develop at an equal pace, and thus we find among almost
all primitive peoples characteristics that can have sprung only from
the most ancient mode of life. The collection of these characteristics,
and their combination into a typical picture, must, however, be our
first task.

Hitherto the process has usually been made too simple by de-
riving the characteristics of primitive man from civilized economic
man. The many wants of man in a state of nature, so it has been
argued, demanded for their satisfaction exertions beyond the capacity of the individual; protection from wild beasts or from the
unchained elements could likewise be attained only by the labour of
many. Accordingly writers have spoken of a collective carrying-on
of the struggle for existence, and thus have had "primitive society"
and a sort of communistic economy complete.

But man has undoubtedly existed through immeasurable periods of time without labouring. If so disposed, one can find plenty
of districts upon the earth where the sago-palm, the plantain-tree,
the breadfruit-tree, the cocoa and date-palm, still allow him to live
with a minimum of exertion. It is in such districts that tradition is
fondest of placing paradise, the original home of mankind; and even
modern research cannot dispense with the assumption that mankind
was at first bound to such regions of natural existence and only by
further development became capable of bringing the whole earth into
subjection.

Of unions into organized society we find, moreover, hardly a
trace among the lowest races accessible to our observation. In little
groups[9] like herds of animals they roam about in search of food, find
a resting-place for the night in caves, beneath a tree, behind a screen
of brushwood erected in a few minutes to shelter them from the
wind, or often in a mere hollow scooped in the ground, and nourish
themselves chiefly with fruits and roots, though all kinds of animal

---

[9]Comp. on this point E. Grosse, *Die Formen der Familie und die Formen
der Wirtschaft,* p. 37.

food, even down to snails, maggots, grasshoppers, and ants are eaten
also. The men as a rule are armed simply with bow and arrow
or with a throwing-stick; the chief implement of the women is the
digging-stick, a pointed piece of wood, which they use in searching
for roots. Shy when they come in contact with members of a higher
race, often malicious and cruel, they lead a restless life, in which the
body, it is true, attains the maximum of agility and dexterity, but
in which technical skill advances only with extreme sluggishness and
one-sidedness. The majority of peoples of this type know nothing
whatever of pottery and the working of metals. Even of wood, bast,
stone, and bone they make but limited use, and this use leads in
no way to a stock of utensils arid tools, which indeed it would be
impossible to carry about, because of their nomadic life, bearing as it
does the character of one continuous search for food.[10] These peoples

---

[10]In order to supplement this general account by a few details I will here
introduce a portion of the description of the Negritos in the Philippines published
in the work by A. Schadenberg, cited above. I give for the most part his own
words:—The women among the Etas bear easily and quickly. Until able to walk,
the child is carried by the mother, generally on the left thigh, in which case it
assumes a sort of riding posture; or upon the back, as soon as it is able to hold
itself on. The mother nurses it for about two years. At about the tenth year
puberty comes; the Negrito youth is then tattooed, and from the moment when
this decoration of his body is finished he is independent. He accordingly looks
about him for a mate, who has in the majority of cases been selected for him
beforehand and who, if possible, belongs to the same "family." The members
of a "family," which generally numbers twenty to thirty persons, are under the
control of an elective chieftain, who decides upon the camping-places and the
time for breaking up. The family life is patriarchal in character. The father
has unlimited power over the members of his family; he can chastise them and
even barter away his children; the woman occupies a subordinate position and
is treated as a chattel. The Negritos carry on bartering with the Tagalas; in this
way they get supplies, chiefly of iron, in exchange for honey and wax. By means
of the iron thus acquired they prepare part of their weapons, which consist of
hunting-knives, arrows, bows, and spears. The Negritos are also very clever at
throwing stones, in which they are greatly assisted by their keenness of vision.
A stone in the hand of an otherwise unarmed Negrito is thus an offensive and
defensive weapon not to be despised. Their clothing is very scant, hardly more
than a breech-clout. Domestic utensils for permanent use are scarcely found at
all among the Etas; sometimes a clay vessel got by barter with the Malays, and as
a rule a piece of bamboo from three to four metres in length for holding drinking-
water. Their toes are prehensile, and are of great assistance to them in climbing.
In the matter of food they are not fastidious; it is both animal and vegetable
in character—roots, honey, frogs, deer, wild-boar, etc. A Spanish ecclesiastic
describes them as follows: "The pure Aitos or Negritos lead a secluded life; they
have no fixed dwelling-place and do not build huts. The father, the mother,
and the children are all provided with arrows, each having his own, and they set

have been designated "lower nomads" but it can scarcely be proven that actual hunting forms their chief means of sustenance. They all make use of vegetable food as far as it is at all obtainable, and with those who live in a warmer climate this food seems to predominate. Stores of such fruits and roots they do not gather, though a region of plentiful supplies attracts a greater number of members of the tribe, as a rich feeding-ground draws together many lower animals; when it is exhausted-they scatter again. And similarly as to the mollusks and insects which they consume; each individual at once swallows what he finds; joint household life is as little known as is a house. It is only when a large animal has been killed or found dead (the fondness for meat in a state of decay is widespread) that the whole group assemble,[11] and each devours as much as he can; but the method of hunting these animals strongly resembles the procedure of the wild beast stealing upon its prey. With, their imperfect weapons these peoples are hardly ever in a position to kill an animal instantly; the chief task of the hunter consists in pursuing the wounded game until it sinks down exhausted.[12]

Regarding the constitution of the family among peoples of this

---

out together upon the hunt. When they kill a deer or a boar, they halt at the spot where the animal has fallen, scoop a hole in the ground, place the animal in it and then build a fire. Each one takes the piece of the animal that suits his taste best and roasts it at the fire. And so they go on eating until they have filled their bellies, and when thus satiated they sleep on the earth which they have hollowed out, as pigs do when they have gorged themselves. When they awake they go through the same operation, and so on until all the meat is devoured; then they set out upon the hunt again." They observe no fixed times for sleeping and eating, but follow necessity in both cases. They age early; at forty or fifty the mountain Negritos are decrepit, white-haired, bent old men. — Compare further the descriptions of the Botokudos by Ehrenreich, Ztschr. f. Ethnol., XIX, pp. I ff; of the Bororos by K. v. d. Steinen, Unter d. Naturvolk. Central-Brasil., pp. 358ff.; of the Bushmen by Fritsch, as above, pp. 418ff.; of the Veddahs by P. and F. Sarasin, Die Weddas von Ceylon; of the Australians by Brentano, Ztschr. f. Sozial-u. Wirtschaftsgeschichte, I, pp. 133-4,

[11] From the custom prevalent among some of the lower tribes of proclaiming the finding of food by means of loud calls, Lippert, as above, I, p. 246, concludes that "the consideration due to the family" is expressed in this way. In this connection it is to be observed that many animals (for example, our domestic fowl) have the same custom. True, he lays stress upon the fact that no one thinks of collecting stores of provisions. Therefore, we are, further, not justified in agreeing to the proposal that has recently been made from several sides to designate these peoples as *gatherers of stores* (*Sammler*).

[12] Comp. G. Fritsch, *Die Emgeborenen Sud-Afrikas,* pp. 324, 425; Pogge, *Im Reiche d Muta Jamwo,* pp. 328-9; Wissmann, *Im Innern Afrikas,* pp. 260, 341; Martius, *Zur Ethnographie Amertkas, zumal Brasiltens,* pp. 665 ff.

class, there has been much discussion. Of late the opinion seems to be gaining ground that there exists among them a fellowship between man and wife that extends beyond a mere sexual relationship and is of life-long duration; while upon the other hand it cannot be denied that in case of a scarcity of food those loose groups easily split up, or at least individual members detach themselves from them. Only between mother and child is the relationship particularly close. The mother must always take her little one along with her on the march; and for that purpose she usually fastens it in some way on her back, a custom that is very general among all primitive peoples, even where they have gone over to agriculture. For several years the child must be nurtured at the breast or from the mother's mouth, but it soon acquires skill in procuring its food independently, and often separates itself from the community in its eighth or tenth year.

All the tribes involved in our survey belong to the smaller races of mankind, and in bodily condition give the impression of backward, stunted growth. We are not on that account, however, justified in regarding them as degenerate race fragments. The evidence rather goes to show that the more advanced races owe their higher physical development merely to the regular and more plentiful supply of food which agriculture and cattle-raising for centuries past have placed within their reach, while the peoples here in question have always remained at the same stage. Subject to all the vicissitudes of the weather and the fortune of the chase, they revel at times in abundance and devour incredible masses of food; still oftener, however, they suffer bitter want, and their only article of clothing, the breech-clout, is for them really the "hunger-strap" ("Schmachtriemen") of German story, which they tighten up in order to alleviate the pangs of gnawing hunger.[13]

How from this stage of primitive existence the path leads upward is manifest in countless typical examples furnished by ethnology. In addition to the collection of wild fruits and roots, the woman takes over the cultivation of food-plants. This she carries on at first with the customary digging-stick, later with a short-handled hoe. The man continues his hunting and fishing, which, in rich hunting-grounds and with more perfect weapons, he can make so productive that they furnish the greater part of his food. At times

---

[13]On the Bushmen comp. Fritsch, as above, p. 405; on the Australians, Peschel, *Races of Man,* p. 332; on the Botokudos, Ehrenreich in the Ztschr. f. Ethnol., XIX (1887), p. 27.

he supplements these by cattle-raising. In the procuring of food each sex has its sharply defined sphere of duties to which with advancing technical skill there are added in each case various industrial arts, which as a rule retain their connection with the original production and occupation. Among advanced primitive peoples all economic activity may be traced back to combinations of these elements; but in its details such labour is entirely dependent upon local natural conditions. We should therefore not be justified in any attempt to construct stages of development intended to hold equally good for negroes, Papuans, Polynesians, and Indians.

But wherever we can observe it, the method in which primitive peoples satisfy their wants reminds us continually in many of its features of the instinctive doings of the lower animals. Everywhere their existence is still far from settled, and even the unsubstantial huts they erect are for the majority only temporary structures which, however much they vary from place to place and from tribe to tribe, always remain true to a type, and remind us of the nests of birds, which are deserted as soon as the brood is fledged.

When Lippert finds the fundamental and controlling impulse to cultural development in *material foresight*, he undoubtedly makes an advance upon earlier investigators; but the phrase itself is not happily chosen. It is utterly impossible to speak of foresight, in the sense of providing for the future, in connection with primitive peoples. Primitive man does not think of the future; he does not *think* at all; he only *wills,* that is, he wills to preserve his existence. The instinct of self-preservation and self-gratification is the prime agent of development, compared with which even the sexual instinct takes quite a secondary place.

Wherever it has been possible for Europeans to observe men in primitive conditions for any length of time they tell us of the incomparable dulness and mental inertness which strike the beholder; of their indifference to the sublimest phenomena of nature, their complete lack of interest in everything that lies outside the individual self. The savage is willing to eat, sleep, and, where necessary, to protect himself against the greatest inclemencies of the weather: this is his whole aim in life.

It is therefore entirely false and contrary to numerous well-accredited observations when Peschel straightway ascribes to savages a peculiar wealth of fanciful imaginings of a religious nature, and thinks that the closer the approach to the condition of nature the greater the range of belief. He evidently assumes that the course of the sun and the other phenomena of the heavens must be infinitely more impressive and stimulative of active thought to the primitive than to the civilized man. But that is by no means the case. Both among the Indians of Brazil and among the negroes, when travellers have asked about these things, the response has been that people never thought about them; and Herbert Spencer[14] has collected an abundance of examples which show that the lower races do not manifest any interest even in the most novel phenomena. The Patagonians, for example, displayed utter indifference when they were made to look into a mirror; and Dampier reports that the Australians whom he had taken on board of his ship paid attention to nothing but what they got to eat. Burton[15] calls the East Africans "Men who can think, but who, absorbed in providing for their bodily wants, hate the trouble of thinking. His [the East African's] mind, limited to the object seen, heard, and felt, will not, and apparently can not, escape from the circle of sense, nor will it occupy itself with aught but the present. Thus he is cut off from the pleasures of memory, and the world of fancy is altogether unknown to him."[16]

The same force, then, that impels the lower animal, the instinct for preserving its existence, is also the dominant instinctive impulse of primitive man. This instinct is limited in scope to the single individual; in respect of time, to the moment at which the want is felt. In other words: *the savage thinks only of himself, and thinks only of the present.* What lies beyond that is as good as closed to his mental vision. When, therefore, many observers reproach him with a boundless egoism, hardness of heart towards his fellows, greed, thievishness, inertness, carelessness with regard to the future, and forgetfulness, it means that sympathy, memory, and reasoning power are still entirely undeveloped. Nevertheless it will be wise for us to make these very characteristics our starting-point, in order to comprehend the relation of primitive man to the external world.

In the first place, as concerns the egoism of the savage and his *hardness of heart* towards his nearest relations, this is a natural consequence of the restless nomadic life in which each individual

---

[14] *Principles of Sociology,* vol. I, §§ 45-6.

[15] *The Lake Regions of Central Africa* (New York, 1860), p. 489.

[16] Comp. the similar opinion of the missionary Cranz, *Historie von Gronland* (Frankfurt, 1780), p. 163, and Lubbock, *Origin of Civilization* (4th ed.), pp. 516-7.

cares only for himself. It shows itself most prominently in the extraordinarily widespread custom of *infanticide,* which extremely few primitive peoples are entirely free from.[17] The children impede the horde on the march and in the search for food. Therein lies the chief reason for their removal. Once become a custom, infanticide lives on in later stages of civilization; indisputable traces of it have been found not merely among the primitive peoples of Asia, Africa, America, Australia, and Polynesia, but even among the Arabs, the Romans, and the Greeks.

To infanticide is universally ascribed the exceptionally slow increase of the uncivilized races. But this is also dependent upon their short lives, and long lactation periods, during which, as is well known, conception rarely occurs, and this it is which forms the chief cause of their protracted tarrying at the same stage of civilization. That the natural bond between parents and children is nowhere very firm is seen also in the extremely common custom of adoption.[18] It is even said, for example, that in the "families" of the Mincopies the children of other parents are in the majority. It is significant that between their own and their adopted children they make, as a rule, not the slightest difference. Adoption may have arisen from the substitution of child-exposure for infanticide. If the natural mother was not in a position to take the new-born child along with her, perhaps another woman who was childless could, and thus the life of the child was saved.

Recent ethnographers have been at great pains to prove that the strength of maternal love is a feature common to all stages of civilization. It is, indeed, a matter of regret to us that we find wanting in our own species a feeling that exhibits itself in such a pleasing way among many families of lower animals. But there have been too many observations showing that among the lower races the mere care for one's own existence outweighs all other mental emotions, in fact that beside it nothing else is of the least importance. All observers are amazed and even indignant at the indifference with which children, when once they can shift for themselves, separate from their blood-relations.[19]Yet we have here only the reverse side

---

[17]Comp. Lippert, II, pp. 201 ff.; Ratzel, *Völkerkunde,* I, pp. 108, 154, 252. 277, 306, 338. 425.

[18]Comp. Lubbock, *Origin of Civilisation,* pp. 95-6.

[19]Comp. the striking example in Ratzel, *Volkerkunde,* I. p. 677, of a boy of Tierra del Fuego who, when taken on board a European ship, did not show the slightest grief over the separation, while his parents were delighted to get a

of that hardness of heart which "enables husbands to refuse food to their wives, and fathers, to deny it to their hungering children, when they themselves would but feast upon it."

This same trait of unbounded selfishness is manifest in the regardlessness with which many primitive peoples leave behind them on the march, or expose in solitary places, the *sick* and the *aged* who might be an impediment to the vigorous.[20] This trait has often been interpreted as a sign of superstition, as due to the fear of evil powers to whom the illnesses are ascribed. And in fact in the case of tribes that have become settled and whose means of subsistence would admit of the care of the sick, appearances favour such an explanation. But at the same time it is forgotten that customs, once firmly rooted, perpetuate themselves with great persistence, even when the causes that gave rise to them have long since passed away.

From exposure to intentional killing is only a short step. Indeed we find even among peoples on a higher plane of civilization that old age is deplored as a state of extreme joylessness. Barbarism had no affection between relatives to alleviate this condition, but it had it in its power to shorten it; and so, along with exposure, we find the burying, or the killing, or even the devouring of the aged and sick, as numberless examples from Herodotus down to modern times attest. Indeed primitive man was able to look upon the solemn performance of this horrible act as a behest of piety.[21]

When we see how this unbroken nomadic life forced man to devote his whole activity to the securing of food, and forbade the concurrent development of those feelings which we regard as the most natural, and how it even succeeded in giving the appearance of religious duty to what we consider the most abominable crime, we begin to conceive how loose must have been the personal bond that held together those little roving groups of human beings. Sexual intercourse could not grow to be such a bond; for what we call love was entirely wanting in it.[22] Domestic life, the conception of property

few necklaces and some biscuits in return for him. The selling of children and women into slavery does not occur in Africa alone. Martius, as above, p 123. Comp. Post, *Afr. Jurisprudenz,* I, p. 94.

[20]Lippert, as above, pp. 229 ff., has treated the subject so exhaustively that I may refrain from citing examples. Comp also Fritsch, pp 116, 334, 351; Waitz, as above, II, p 401.

[21]Comp. the examples cited by Lippert, p, 232, and Martius, as above, p 126. Also Ehrenreich, *Beiträge z. Völkerkunde Brasil,* pp. 69-70; Waitz, as above, I, p. 189 — *Introd to Anthropol* (trans), p. 161.

[22]The many writers who write nowadays about the family pay altogether too

and labour in common were as good as non-existent. These could originate only when the circle of wants advanced beyond the mere food requirement. But this took a much longer time than the majority are willing to admit. The needs of primitive peoples with regard to clothing and house-shelter are most markedly of an altogether secondary nature.

Turning now to the no less common characteristic of *improvidence,* we must certainly at first glance be struck with astonishment. One would think that hunger, which often brings such great torture to the savage, would of itself have been sufficient to induce him to store up for future use the food that at times he possesses in superabundance. But the observations that have been made all indicate that he never thinks of that. "They are not accustomed," says Heckewelder[23] of the North American Indians, "to laying in stores of provisions except some Indian corn, dry beans, and a few other articles. Hence they are sometimes reduced to great straits, and are not seldom in absolute want of the necessaries of life, especially in the time of war." And of the South American tribes another observer reports:[24] "It is contrary to their nature to be in possession of food-supplies for longer than one day at most." With many negro tribes it is looked upon as improper to store up food for future need, which belief, it is true, they base upon the superstition that the fragments left over may attract spirits.[25]

Where these peoples, through the short-sighted greed of gain of Europeans, are placed in possession of modern weapons, they usually work incredible havoc with the game in their hunting-grounds. The extermination of the boundless buffalo herds of North America is well known. "The greatest quantities of meat were left lying unused in the thickets," only for the natives in winter-time, when deep snow prevented hunting, to fall a prey to awful hunger, in which even the bark of trees and the roots of grass were not despised. And to-day the natives of Africa, in districts where they carry on a profitable trade with Europeans, are ruthlessly destroying the sources of their incomes, the elephant and the caoutchouc-tree.

---

little attention to this point, to which prominence has justly been given by Lubbock, as above, pp. 72 ff. In the same way they overlooked the connection between the family and the economy of the home [Comp p. 10 above.—ED]

[23]Heckewelder, *Indian Nations,* etc New edition (Phil, 1881), pp. 198, 212 (Memoirs of Hist Soc of Penn., vol 12)

[24]Appun, *Unter den Tropen,* p. 365

[25]Lippert, as above, I, pp. 39-40.

Even among the more advanced tribes and individuals this characteristic does not fail. "When the carriers received fresh rations," relates P. Pogge,[26] "I am certain that they lived better for the first few days than I did. The best goats and fowl were devoured. If I gave them rations for a fortnight, the rule was to consume them in riotous living during the first three or four days, only afterwards either to steal from the supply-trains, to beg from me, or to go hungry." In Wadai everything that remains over from the sultan's table is buried,[27] and at the sacrificial feasts of the Indians the guests were obliged to eat up their meat and bread clean. "Overloading of the stomach and vomiting are not unusual on such occasions."[28]

Closely connected with this waste of supplies is the use that primitive man makes of his *time*. It is entirely erroneous, though customary, to imagine that primitive people are particularly expert in measuring time by the position of the sun. They do not measure time at all, and accordingly do not make divisions in it. No primitive people observe fixed meal-times, according to which civilized man regulates his time for work.[29] Even such a relatively advanced tribe as the Bedouins has no conception of time. They eat when they are hungry. Livingstone in one place calls Africa "the blissful region where time is absolutely of no account and where men may sit down and rest themselves when they are tired."[30] "Even the most trivial work, though it is urgently necessary, is postponed by the negro to as late a date as possible. The native dreams away the day in laziness and idleness, although he knows quite well that for the night he needs his draught of water and his log of wood; nevertheless until sundown he will certainly not disturb himself, and only then, or perhaps not before darkness, will he finally procure himself the necessaries."[31]

In these words we have touched upon the reproach of inertia to which primitive man is universally subject.[32] What has here appeared to observers as *laziness* is again lack of forethought, living

---

[26] As above, p. 14; comp. p 6. Also Wissmann, Wolf, etc., *Im Innern Afrikas,* p. 29.

[27] Nachtigal, *Sahara u. Sudan,* III, p. 230.

[28] Heckewelder, as above, p. 213. [Dr. Bücher, quoting from the German translation, has evidently mistaken the meaning of the passage cited. The vomiting and fasting referred to by Heckewelder are preparatory to the ceremonies, the vomiting being self-induced.—ED.]

[29] Comp. W. Wundt, *Ethics,* I (London, 1897), pp 171-2.

[30] *Expedit to the Zambesi* (New York, 1866), p. 104.

[31] W. Junker's *Travels in Africa*; comp. Eng trans., II, p. 168.

[32] For details see my work *Arbeit u. Rhythmus* (2d ed., Leipzig, 1899).

for the moment. Why should the savage exert himself when once his wants are satisfied, particularly when he is no longer hungry? This does not imply that he is inactive. With his wretched facilities the individual often performs on the whole as much work as the individual civilized man; but he does not perform it regularly, nor in ordered succession, but by fits and starts, when necessity forces him to it, or a feeling of exaltation takes possession of him, and even then not as a serious duty of life, but rather in a playful fashion.

In general, primitive man follows only the prompting of the moment; his conduct is purely impulsive, mere reflex action, so to speak. The nearer his wants and their satisfaction lie together, the better he feels. Primitive man is a child; he thinks not of the future, nor of the past; he forgets easily, each new impression blots out its predecessor. All the sufferings of life, which he has to experience so often, can scarcely cloud for a moment his naturally cheerful temperament. "Of the New Caledonians, Fijians, Tahitians, and New Zealanders we read that they are always laughing and joking. Throughout Africa the negro has the same trait, and of other races, in other lands, the descriptions of various travellers are: 'full of fun and merriment,' 'full of life and spirits,' 'merry and talkative,' 'skylarking in all ways,' 'boisterous gaiety,' 'laughing immoderately at trifles.'"[33]

It is significant, as has often been remarked, that natives of Africa lose their cheerfulness when they have been for some time in the service of Europeans, and become sullen and morose. The explanation of Fritsch is that servants of this kind gradually acquire from their masters the habit of troubling themselves about things to come, and that their temperament cannot endure engrossment in such cares.[34]

Such a hand-to-mouth existence cannot be burdened with *conceptions of value*, which always presupposes an act of judgment, an estimation of the future. It is well known how in America and Africa the natives often sold their land to foreign colonists for a gaudy trifle, a few glass beads of no value according to our economic standards; and even to-day the negro, though he stands no longer at the lowest stage, is in many instances ready to give away any

---

[33]Spencer, as above, § 34. Considerable material also in his *Descriptive Sociology* in the chapter on "Moral Sentiments."

[34]Reference may also be made to the not infrequent examples of savages who had been brought up under civilized conditions voluntarily returning to their tribes and to the complete savagery of their people Comp Peschel, as above, pp. 152-3; Fritsch, as above, p. 423; K. E. Jung in Petermanns Mitth, XXIV (1878), p. 67.

piece of his property, no matter how important it may be for his existence, if he is offered some glittering bauble that happens to catch his eye.[35] On the other hand his covetousness knows no bounds, and it is a constant complaint of travellers that amid all the hospitality shown them they are simply plundered, because every village chieftain desires to be presented with everything he sees.[36] Here, again, is that naive egoism in its complete regardlessness of self and others, that unbounded covetousness which has nothing in common with the love of gain of economic man. The impression of the moment is ever the sole controlling force; what is further removed is not thought of. Primitive man is incapable, it would seem, of entertaining two thoughts at the same time and of weighing the one against the other; he is always possessed by one alone and follows it with startling consistency.

The collection of experiences, the transmission of knowledge, is therefore exceedingly difficult, and therein lies the chief reason why such peoples can remain at the same stage for thousands of years without showing any appreciable advance. The acquisition of the first elements of civilization is often conceived as an easy matter; it is imagined that every invention, every advance in house-construction, in the art of clothing, in the use of tools, that an individual makes, must pass over as an imperishable treasure into the common possession of the tribe and there continue to fructify. The invention of pottery, the taming of domestic animals, the smelting of iron ore have even been made the beginnings of entirely new epochs of civilization.

Yet how imperfectly does such a conception appreciate the conditions under which primitive man lives! We may indeed assume that he possesses a peculiar fondness for the stone axe which with endless exertion he has formed in the course perhaps of a whole year, and that it seems to him like a part of his own being;[37] but it is a mistake to think that the precious possession will now pass to children and children's children, and thus constitute the basis for further advance. However certain it is that in connection with such things the first notions of "mine and thine" are developed, yet many

---

[35]Comp. Fritsch, as above, pp 305-6.

[36]Says Burton, as above, p 499: "In trading with [the African] . . . all display of wealth must be avoided A man who would purchase the smallest article avoids showing anything beyond its equivalent."

[37]Comp. *Arbeit u. Rhythmus* (2d ed.), p. 16.

are the observations indicating that these conceptions do not go beyond the individual, and that they perish with him. The possession passes into the grave with the possessor, whose personal equipment it formed in life. That is a custom which is met with in all parts of the earth, and of which many peoples have preserved traces even down into civilized times.[38]

In the first place it is prevalent among all American peoples to such an extent that the survivors are often left in extreme need. The aborigines of California, who are among the lowest people of their race, place along with the dead all the weapons and utensils which he had made use of in life. "It is a curious paraphernalia," says an observer, "that follows the Wintum into the grave: knives, forks, vinegar-jars, empty whiskey-bottles, preserve-jars, bows, arrows, etc.; and if the dead has been an industrious housewife, a few baskets of acorns are scattered over as well." "At the grave of the Tehuelche" (Patagonia), runs another account, "all his horses, dogs, and other animals are killed, and his poncho, his ornaments, his bolas and implements of every kind are brought together into a heap and burned." And of a third and still lower tribe, the Bororo in Brazil, a recent very reliable observer says:[39] "A great loss befalls a family when one of its members dies. For everything that the dead man used is burned, thrown into the river, or packed in with the corpse in order that the departed spirit may have no occasion whatever to return. The cabin is then completely gutted. But the surviving members of the family receive fresh presents; bows and arrows are made for them, and when a jaguar is killed, the skin is given to the brother of the last deceased woman or to the uncle of the last deceased man."

Among the Bagobos in southern Mindanao (one of the Philippines) the dead man is buried in his best clothes, and with a slave, who is killed for the purpose. "The cooking-utensils that the deceased used during his lifetime are filled with rice and placed, along with his betel-sacks, upon the grave; his other things are left in the house untouched. On penalty of death no one may henceforth enter

---

[38]Comp. in general, Andree, *Eihnogr. Parallelen u.* Vergleiche (Stuttgart, 1878), pp. 26-7; Schurtz, *Grundriss emer Entsteh. Gesch. d. Geldes* (Weimar, 1898), pp. 56 ff; Pauckow, Ztschr. d. Ges. f. Erdkunde zu Berlin, XXXI, pp. 172-3.

[39]K. von den Steinen, *Unter den Naturvolkem Brasiliens* (2d ed.), p. 389. Comp. also Ehrenreich, *Beiträge zur Volkerkunde Brasihens,* pp 30, 66; Heckewelder, as above, pp. 270-1, 274-5.

either the house or the burial-place; and it is equally forbidden to cut from the trees surrounding the house. The house itself is allowed to go to ruin."[40]

In Australia and Africa the custom is very common for all the stores of the deceased to be eaten up by the assembly of the mourners; in other parts the utensils are destroyed, while the food is thrown away. Many negro tribes bury the dead in the hut in which he lived, and leave the dwelling, now deserted by the survivors, to decay; others destroy the hut.[41] If a chieftain dies, the whole village migrates; and this is true even of the principal towns of the more important kingdoms, such as those of the Muata-Yamwo and the Kasembe. In the Lunda kingdom the old royal Kipanga is burned down, and a new provisional one at once erected, for which the newly chosen ruler has to kindle a fresh fire by rubbing together pieces of wood, as it is not permissible to use the old fire any longer. The principal or residence town changes its location with each new ruler.[42] Among the ancient Peruvians, as well, the conception prevailed that with each new Inca the world, so to speak, began anew. The palaces of the dead Inca, with all their stores of wealth, were closed for ever; the ruler for the time being never made use of the treasures that his ancestors had amassed.

Though we see from this that the origin and preservation of the first elements of civilization among primitive peoples were attended with the greatest difficulties, and that the possibility of rising to better conditions of existence and higher modes of life could not even be conceived by them, yet it must not be forgotten that the observations that have been sifted and presented here have been taken from peoples of very varied character and different cultural stages. To raise himself of his own strength to the plane of the Tongan or Tahitian, the Australian of the continent would probably have required many thousands of years; and a similar gulf separates the Bushman

[40]Schadenberg in the Ztschr. f. Ethnol, XVII (1885), pp. 12-13. The same thing is found in Halamahera, p. 83; and among the hill tribes of India, Jellinghaus in the same review, III, pp. 372, 374.
[41]Examples may be found in M. Büchner, *Kamerun,* p. 28; Fritsch, as above, p. 535; Bastian, *Loangokuste,* I, p. 164; Livingstone, as above, p. 158. From Australia: Parkinson, *Im Bismarck-Archipel,* pp. 102-3; Ztschr. f. Ethnol., XXI, p. 23; Kubary, *Ethnogr. Beiträdge zur Kenntnis d. Karolin. Inselgruppe u. Nachbarschaft* (Berlin, 1885), pp. 70-71, note.
[42]Pogge, as above, pp. 228, 234. Livingstone in Petermanns Mitth., XXI (187s), p. 104.

from the Congo negro and Wanyamweza. But this very fact, it seems to me, speaks for the persistence of the presumptive psychic conditions under which the satisfaction of the wants of uncivilized man is accomplished; and we are undoubtedly justified in tracing back the whole circle of this class of conceptions to a condition that must have prevailed among mankind for aeons before tribes and peoples could have originated.

From all that we know of it, this condition means exactly the opposite of "economy." For economy implies always a community of men rendered possible by the possession of property; it is a taking counsel, a caring not only for the moment but also for the future, a careful division and suitable bestowal of time; economy means work, valuation of things, regulation of their use, accumulation of wealth, transmission of the achievements of civilization from generation to generation. And even among the higher primitive peoples we have found all this widely wanting; among the lower races we have hardly met with its faint beginnings. Let us strike out of the life of the Bushman or of the Veddah the use of fire, and bow and arrow, and nothing remains but a life made up of the individual search for food. Each individual has to rely entirely upon himself for his sustenance. Naked and unarmed he roams with his fellows, like certain species of wild animals, through a limited stretch of territory, and uses his feet for holding and climbing as dexterously as he uses his hands.[43] All, male and female, devour raw what they catch with their hands or dig out of the ground with their nails: smaller animals, roots, and fruits. Now they unite in little bands or larger herds; now they separate again, according to the richness of the pasturage or hunting-ground. But these unions do not develop into communities, nor do they lighten the existence of the individual.

This picture may not have many charms for him who shares the civilization of the present; but we are simply forced by the material empirically gathered together so to construct it. Nor are any of its lines imaginative. We have eliminated from the life of the lowest tribes only what admittedly belongs to civilization—the use of weapons and of fire. Though we were obliged to admit that even among the higher primitive peoples there is exceeding much that is non-economic, that at all events the conscious application of the economic principle forms with them rather the exception than the

---

[43]R. Andree, *Der Fuss als Greiforgan*, in his *Ethnogr. Parallelen u. Vergl.* (New Series), pp. 228 ff.

rule, we shall not be able in the case of the so-called "lower nomads" and their predecessors just sketched to make use of the notion of economy at all. With them we have to fix a pre-economic stage of development, that is not yet economy. As every child must have his name, we will call this the *stage of individual search for food.*

How economic activity was evolved from the individual search for food can to-day hardly be imagined. The thought may suggest itself that the turning-point must be where production with a more distant end in view takes the place of the mere seizing of the gifts of nature for immediate enjoyment, and where work, as the intelligent application of physical power, replaces the instinctive activity of the bodily organs. Very little would be gained, however, by this purely theoretical distinction. Labour among primitive peoples is something very ill-defined. The further we follow it back, the more closely it approaches in form and substance to *play.*

In all probability there are instincts similar to those that are found among the more intelligent of the lower animals, that impel man to extend his activities beyond the mere search for food, especially the instinct for imitating and for experimenting.[44] The taming of domestic animals, for example, begins not with the useful animals, but with such species as man keeps merely for amusement or the worship of gods. Industrial activity seems everywhere to start with the painting of the body, tattooing, piercing or otherwise disfiguring separate parts of the body, and gradually to advance to the production of ornaments, masks, drawing on bark, petrograms, and similar play-products. In these things there is everywhere displayed a peculiar tendency to imitate the animals which the savage meets with in his immediate surroundings, and which he looks upon as his equals. The partly prehistoric rock drawings and carvings of the Bushmen, the Indians, and the Australians represent chiefly animals and men;[45] pottery, wood-carving, and even wicker-work begin with the production of animal forms.[46] Even when the advance is made to the construction of objects of daily use (pots, stools, etc.), the animal figure is retained with remarkable regularity;[47] and lastly, in

---

[44]Comp. K. Groos, *Die Spiele d. Tiere* (Jena, 1896).

[45]Andree, *Ethnogr. Parallelen u. Vergleiche,* pp. 258-299. Ehrenreich, as above, pp. 46-7.

[46]Comp. the interesting accounts by K. v. d. Steinen, as above, pp. 231 ff., and particularly pp. 241 ff.

[47]Abundant examples are afforded by every ethnographic picture-collection The incredulous are invited to take a glance at the following works: J. Boas,

the dances of primitive peoples, the imitation of the motions and the cries of animals plays the principal part.[48] All regularly sustained activity finally takes on a rhythmic form and becomes fused with music and song in an indivisible whole.[49]

It is accordingly in play that technical skill is developed, and it turns to the useful only very gradually.[50] The order of progression hitherto accepted must therefore be just reversed; play is older than work, art older than production for use.[51]Even when among the higher primitive peoples the two elements begin to separate from each other, the dance still precedes or follows every more important work (war-, hunting-, harvest-dance), and song accompanies work.

Just as economy, the further we have traced it backwards in the development of peoples, has during our inquiry assumed more and more the form of non-economy, so work also has finally resolved itself into its opposite (Nichtarbeit). And we should probably have the same experience with all the more important phenomena of economy, if we were to continue our inquiries regarding them. One thing alone appears permanent—consumption. Wants man always had, and wants must be satisfied. But even our wants, considered from an economic point of view, exist only in very small part naturally; it is only in the matter of bodily nourishment that our consumption is a necessity of nature; all else is the product of civilization, the result of the free creative activity of the human mind. Without this activity man would always have remained a root-digging, fruit-eating animal.

Under these circumstances we must forego the attempt to fix

The Central Eskimo (Washington, 1888); Sixth Annual Report of the Bureau of Ethnology to the Secretary of the Smithsonian Institution, 1884-5; *Ethnogr. Beschrijving van de West-en Noordkust van Nederlandsch Niew Guinea,* by F. S. A. de Clercq and J. D. E. Schmeltz (Leiden, 1893); Joest, *Ethnogr. aus Guyana* (Suppl. to vol. 5 of the Intern. Archiv fur Ethnogr.); and again Von den Steinen, as above, pp. 261 ff. Comp. also Fritsch, as above, p. 73; Schwemfurth, *The Heart of Africa* (3d ed., London, 1878), I, pp 129- 130; and Grosse, *Die Anfange d. Kunst,* Chaps. VI and VII.

[48]K Grosse, as above, pp. 208-9.

[49]Reference must here again be made to my work on *Arbeit u. Rhythmus.*

[50]"On examination of the primitive tools [of the Papuans] . . . we see that there is not a single one which does not bear testimony by some little design or ornament to the good taste of its maker, not an article which does not show some trifling accessories surpassing mere utility and present in it solely for beauty's sake." — Semon, *In the Austral. Bush,* p. 400.

[51][The general ethnographic aspect of art is, of course, another and wider problem than the one involved in this conclusion with regard to "first things."—ED.]

upon some definite point at which simple search for food ceases
and economy begins. In the history of human civilization there are
no turning-points; here everything grows and decays as with the
plant; the fixed or stationary is only an abstraction which we need
in order to make visible to our dim eye the wonders of nature and
humanity. Indeed economy itself, like all else, is subject to constant
changes. When it first presents itself in history, it appears as a form
of communal life based upon material possessions, guided by definite
rules of conduct, and closely connected with the personal and moral
community of life of the family.[52] It was under this form that it was
seen by the people who first fixed its characteristics in language.
Landlord is still in Middle High German synonymous with husband
(Wirt, Ehemann), *landlady* is wife (Wirtin, Ehefrau), and the word
economy, derived from the Greek, is formed in a similar way.

We may therefore assume the existence of economy as certain
where we find co-dwelling communities that procure and utilize things
adapted to their needs according to the dictates of the economic principle. Such a condition is certainly fulfilled by the higher primitive
peoples, even though their carrying out of the economic principle
always remains incomplete. But there is nevertheless much that
still recalls the pre-economic period of individual search for food;
economy has still, so to speak, gaps in various places.

Among all peoples of a lower cultural stage the distribution of
labour between the two sexes is firmly fixed by custom, although
difference of natural aptitude seems by no means to have been the
sole determining factor. At least it cannot be maintained that in all
cases the lighter share of the work fell to the weaker sex. While in
the normal domestic economy of civilized nations we have a cross-
section, so to speak, which assigns to the man the productive work
and to the woman the superintendence of consumption, the economy
of these peoples seems to be divided in longitudinal section. Both
sexes take part in production, and frequently each has a particular
department of the consumption for itself. It is particularly significant
in this connection that upon the woman devolves, as a rule, the
procuring and preparing of the vegetable foods and for the most

[52]E. Grosse has in his recent book entitled *Die Formen d. Familie u. die
Formen d. Wirtschaft* (Leipzig, 1896) investigated the connection of family with
economic forms In doing so he has, for the economic side of the work, adhered
to the altogether external classification into nomadic, pastoral, and agricultural,
but has scarcely devoted due attention to the inner economic life, particularly
to that of the household.

part also the building of the hut, while hunting and the working up of the products of the chase fall to the man. If cattle are kept, the tending of the animals, the erection of inclosures for them, the milking, etc., are the business of the men. This division is often so sharply defined that we might almost speak of a cleavage of the family economy into a purely male and a purely female economy.

In an interesting account of the useful plants of the Brazilian Shingu tribes, *K. von den Steinen*[53] describes the outcome of the earlier development of these tribes in the following words:

"Man followed the chase, and in the mean time woman invented agriculture. Here, as throughout Brazil, the women have exclusive charge not only of the preparation of manioc in the house but also of its cultivation. They clear the ground of weeds with pointed sticks, place in position the stakes with which the manioc is planted, and fetch each day what they need, carrying it home in heavily laden wicker baskets. . . . The man is more courageous and skilful; to him belong the chase and the use of weapons. Where, then, hunting and fishing still play an important part, the woman must attend, as far as a division of labour takes place at all, to the procuring, transporting, and preparing of the food. This division has a result that is not sufficiently appreciated, namely, that the woman m her field of labour acquires special knowledge just as the man does in his. This must necessarily hold true for each lower or higher stage. The counterpart of the Indian woman cultivating her manioc with skill and intelligence is already found in the purely nomadic state. The wife of the Bororo went into the forest armed with a pointed stick to search for roots and tubers; during wanderings through the camping-ground, or whenever a company of Indians changed its locality, such hunting fell to the woman, while the man tracked the game; she climbed the tree for cocoanuts, and carried heavy loads of them laboriously home. And though the Indian woman was the slave of her husband, this relation was certainly not to her advantage in regard to the division of the fish and meat; she still had to depend upon the supply of vegetables that she could gather for herself. On the Shingu the men made ready the roast and broiled fish and meat; the women baked the beijus (manioc cakes), prepared the warm drinks, cooked the fruits, and roasted the cocoanuts. What other meaning could this division into animal cooking for the men and vegetable cooking for the women have than that each of the sexes had still kept to its original sphere?"

If we add that the men also made the weapons for the chase, and that hunting and fishing were the source whence they drew all their implements for cutting, scraping, polishing, piercing, tracing,

---

[53] *Unter d. Naturvolk. Central-Brasil.,* pp. 206 ff.

23

and carving, while the women produced the pottery for cooking,[54] we have for each sex a naturally defined sphere of production upon which all their activity is independently expended. But this is not all. The consumption is also in one chief particular distinct: there are no common meals in the family. Each individual eats apart from the rest, and it is looked upon as improper to partake of food in the presence of others.[55]

Similar characteristics of an individual economy are also found among the North American Indians, who had already arrived at a fully developed domestic economy. While they know nothing whatever of a special ownership of the soil, "there is nothing in an Indian's house or family without its particular owner. Every individual knows what belongs to him, from the horse or cow down to the dog, cat, kitten, and little chicken. Parents make presents to their children, and they in return to their parents. A father will sometimes ask his wife or one of his children for the loan of a horse to go a-hunting. For a litter of kittens or brood of chickens there are often as many different owners as there are individual animals. In purchasing a hen with her brood one frequently has to deal for it with several children."[56]

"In cases where the Indians permitted polygamy, it was customary for a special hut to be erected for each wife; among tribes dwelling in common-houses each wife had at least her special fire."[57]

"The same characteristics are presented by the economy of the Polynesians and Micronesians, except that here fishing and the raising of smaller live stock take the place of hunting. In New Pomerania the various duties are strictly divided between the men and boys on the one hand, and the women and girls on the other.[58] To the male

---

[54]As above, pp. 197 ff., 217 ff., 318.
[55]Von den Steinen, as above, p. 69, and Ehrenreich, *Beiträge z. Völkerkunde Brasil.*, p. 17: "Etiquette among the Karaya demands that each one shall eat by himself apart from the others." Eating alone is almost suggestive of the animal. The savage acts like the dog, which grows cross when his meal is disturbed. Among the natives of Borneo "the men usually feed alone, attended on by the women, and always wash their mouths out when they have finished eating. They are very particular about being called away from their meals, and it takes a great deal to make a man set about doing anything before he has concluded his repast; to such an extent is this practice observed, that it is considered wrong to attack even an enemy whilst he is eating, but the moment he has finished it is legitimate and proper to fall upon him." Hose, in Journ. of Anthropol Inst., p. 160.
[56]Heckewelder, as above, p. 158.
[57]Waitz, *Anthropologie,* III, p. 109.
[58]Parkinson, as above, pp. 113, 122.

portion of the population falls the labour of making and keeping in repair the weapons and the fishing-gear, especially the fishing-nets and the ropes necessary for them, of casting the nets in the sea and caring for them daily, of building canoes, erecting huts, and, in the wooded districts, of felling trees and clearing away the roots for the laying out of new plantations, as well as of protecting them by enclosures against wild boars."[59]

Besides having to care for their little children it devolves upon the women to prepare the food, to dig and cultivate the ground, to raise and garner the produce of the field, and to carry the heavily laden baskets to market-places miles away.

"In certain kinds of work both men and women take part. To these belong the twisting of the strong basten cordage of which the fishing-nets are woven, the plaiting of baskets with finely cut strips of rattan and padanus-leaves, the weaving of a very rough and coarse stuff called *mal,* made from the bark of the broussonetia-tree, in which the women wrap their infants to protect them from the cold."

This latter is very significant: we have here to do with arrangements for the transformation of materials, such as could not have existed in the period of individual search for food.

Separate preparation of food for men and women, and separate meals are also met with in the South Sea regions. In Fiji the men prepare such kinds of food as can be cooked out of doors by means of heated stones. "This is confined to-day to the roasting of swine's flesh; formerly the preparation of human flesh was also reserved for the men."[60] In the Palau Islands the cooking of the taro and the preparing of the sweetened foods fell to the lot of the women, the preparation of the meats to the men.[61] In most parts of Oceania "it is neither permissible for women and men to eat in common, nor for the men to eat what the women have prepared. Eating with another from the same dish seems to be avoided with almost equal scrupulousness."[62]

The economy of many negro tribes shows a like arrangement; a sharp division of the production and of many parts of the consump-

---

[59]These labours preparatory to the cultivation of the land are still often performed by the women. Parkinson, p. 118.

[60]Bassler, *Sudsee-Bilder,* pp. 226-7.

[61]M Kubary, as above, p. 173.

[62]M Ratzel, *Volkerkunde,* I, p. 240. Separate meals for men and women; comp. Stanley, *How I Found Livingstone* (New York, 1887), p. 550; Nachtigal, *Sahara u. Sudan,* I, p. 664.

tion according to sex, indeed even the extension of this distinction to the sphere of barter. As P. Pogge,[63] one of our most reliable observers, says concisely of the Congo negroes: "The woman has her own circle of duties independent of that of her husband." And in the description of the Bashilangas he observes:[64] "No member of the family troubles himself about another at mealtimes; while some eat the others come and go just as it suits them; but the women and the smaller children generally eat together." And finally he reports further regarding the Lundas: "Under ordinary conditions, when a caravan has pitched its camp in a village, the women of the place are accustomed to bring vegetables and fowl into the camp for sale, while goats, pigs, and sheep are usually sold only by the men.[65] It is similarly related by L. Wolf[66] that in the market at Ibaushi all the agricultural products and materials, mats, and pottery are sold by the women, and only goats and wine by the men. Each sex is thus possessor of its special product of labour, and disposes of it independently.[67]

---

[63] *Im Reiche d. Muata Jamwo*, p. 40.

[64] Wissmann, *Unter deutsch. Flagge quer durch Afrika*, p. 387. *Im-Reiche d. Muata Jamwo*, pp. 178, 231.

[65] *Im Reiche d. Muata Jamwo*, p. 29.

[66] Wissmann, etc., *Im Innern Afrikas*, p. 249. Comp. Livingstone, *Exped. to the Zambesi*, pp. 122; 577; Paulitschke, *Ethnographie Nordost-Afrikas*, I, p. 314.

[67] Of the family and the domestic establishment of the Wanyamwezls, who assuredly no longer stand upon a low plane, Burton gives the following picture: " Children are suckled till the end of the second year. . . . After the fourth summer the boy begins to learn archery. ... As soon as [he] can walk he tends the flocks; after the age of ten he drives the cattle to pasture, and, considering himself independent of his father, he plants a tobacco-plot and aspires to build a hut for himself. Unmarried girls live in the father's house until puberty; after that period the spinsters of the village, who usually number from seven to a dozen, assemble together and build for themselves at a distance from their homes a hut where they can receive their friends without parental interference. . . . Marriage takes place when the youth can afford to pay the price for a wife. [The price] varies, according to circumstances, from one to ten cows. The wife is so far the property of the husband that he can claim damages from the adulterer, but may not sell her except when in difficulties. . . . Polygamy is the rule with the wealthy. There is little community of interests, and apparently a lack of family affection in these tribes. The husband, when returning from the coast laden with cloth, will refuse a single shukkah to his wife; and the wife, succeeding to an inheritance, will abandon her husband to starvation. The man takes charge of the cattle, goats, sheep, and poultry; the woman has power over the grain and the vegetables; and each must grow tobacco, having little hope of borrowing from the other.

The division of the labour of production between the two sexes
in Africa varies in detail from tribe to tribe; as a rule, however,
agriculture and the preparation of all the vegetable foods are also
assigned here to the woman, and hunting, cattle-raising, tanning,
and weaving to the man.[68] This arrangement is often supported
by superstitious usages. In Uganda the milking of the cows falls
exclusively to the men; a woman is never permitted to touch the
udder of a cow.[69] In the Lunda territory, again, no man is allowed
to take part in the extraction of oil from the ground-nut, as his
presence is thought to frustrate the success of the operation.[70] As
a rule the carriers whom Europeans engage refuse to do women's
work; Livingstone[71] even reports a case of famine among the men in
a certain district because no women were there to grind the corn they
had on hand. The separation of the two sexes in the preparation and
consumption of food is often made still more rigid by regulations[72] of
a semi-religious character, forbidding the women the use of certain
kinds of meat, which are thus reserved for the men alone.[73]

Everywhere among primitive peoples the children become independent very early in youth and desert the society of their parents.
They often live then for some years in special common-houses, of
which there are others for married men. These common-houses for
the men-folk grouped according to age, and frequently also for the

---

. . . . The sexes do not eat together: even the boys would disdain to be seen
sitting at meat with their mothers. The men feed either in their cottages or,
more gen-erally, in the iwanza [public house, one being set apart for each sex]."
(As above, pp. 295-8; comp. pp. 493-4.)

[68]Comp. especially Fritsch, as above, pp. 79 ff., 183, 229, 325; Livingstone,
as above, pp. 77, 118, 311-12. An extended treatment now in H. Schurtz, *Das
afr. Gewerbe* (Leipzig, 1900), pp. 7 ff.

[69]Emin Bey, in Petermanns Mitth., XXV (1879), p. 392.

[70]Wissmann, Wolf, etc., *Im Innern Afrikas*, p. 63.

[71]As above, pp. 188, 565. Similarly among the Indians; comp. Waitz, as
above, III, p. 100.

[72]More frequent still in Polynesia. Comp. Andree, *Ethnogr. Parallelen u.
Vergleiche*, pp. 114 ff.

[73]For a peculiar further development of this economy comp. Schweinfurth,
Sahara u. Sudan, III, pp. 162, 244, 249. In some places the separation of the
spheres of activity of the two sexes extends even to their intellectual life. Among
several Caribic tribes the women and the men have different names for many
things, whence it was inferred that there existed distinct languages for men and
for women. More recently this phenomenon is supposed to have its foundation
in the difference in social position of the sexes and in the sharp division between
their two spheres of employment. Comp. Sapper, Intern. Archiv. f. Ethnogr.,
X, pp. 56 f.

unmarried women grouped in the same way, are found very widely distributed in Africa and America, and especially in Oceania. They serve as common places of meeting, work, and amusement, and as sleeping-places for the younger people, and are used also for lodging strangers. They naturally form a further obstacle to the development of a common household economy based upon the family, for each family is generally subdivided into different parts with separate dwellings. In Yap, one of the Caroline Islands, for instance, we find besides the febays, or sleeping-houses of the unmarried, a principal house for each family which the father of the family uses, and also a dwelling-house for each wife; finally, "the preparation of food in the dwelling-house is forbidden and is transferred to a *separate hut for each member of the family,* which serves as a fire-cabin or cooking-house."[74]   A similar arrangement prevails in Malekula in the New Hebrides.[75] Further than this, economic individualism can hardly be carried.

It may be asserted as a general rule for primitive peoples practising polygamy that each wife has her own hut.[76] Among the Zulus they go so far as to build a separate hut for almost every adult member of the household, — one for the husband, one for his mother, one for each of his wives and other adult members of his family. These huts all stand in a semicircle about the enclosed cattle-kraal in such a way that the man's dwelling is in the centre. Of course it is to be remembered that a hut of this kind can be constructed in a few hours.

Thus we see that everywhere, even among the more developed primitive peoples, there is still wanting much of that unified exclusiveness of domestic life with which the civilized peoples of Europe, from all we know of them, first appeared in history. Everywhere wide clefts still gape, and the individual preserves an economic independence that strikes us with its strangeness. However much it behooves us, in our consideration of this minute economic separation, to guard against overlooking the unifying forces of working and caring for each other, and carefully as we must refrain from exag-

---

[74]Kubary, *Ethnogr. Beiträge z. Kennt. d. Karol.-Archip.* (Leiden), p. 39.

[75]Journal of the Anthropol. Inst, of Gr. Br., XXIII (1894), p. 381.

[76]This is the case, to mention only a few instances, in the Antilles: Starcke, *The Primitive Family* (New York, 1889), p. 40; in Mindanao: Schadenberg, Ztschr. f. Ethnol., XVII, p. 12; among the Bakuba: Wissmann, *Im Innern Afrikas,* p. 209; among the Monbuttoos: Schweinfurth, Ztschr. f. Ethnol., V, p. 12; *The Heart of Africa,* II, pp. 17-18; Casalis, *Les Basoutos,* p. 132.

gerating the centrifugal forces here at work, it is nevertheless not to be denied that they are all traceable to one common origin — to the individual search for food practised through thousands of years by all these peoples.

In this lies the justification of the method followed in this investigation, in which we have taken together peoples of very different stock and cultural stages, and considered the economic phenomena separately.

This procedure is, in political economy as in all social sciences, entirely justified; provided that, from the prodigious mass of disconnected facts that fill ethnology like a great lumber-room, we succeed in bringing a considerable number under a common denominator and rescuing them from the mystic interpretations of curiosity-hunters and mythologizing visionaries. For political economy in particular this method offers the further and not inconsiderable advantage, that the toy mannikin in the form of a savage freely invented by the imagination of civilized man vanishes from the scene, and gives place to forms that are taken from life, although the observations from which they are drawn may leave much to be desired in point of accuracy.

Our travellers have hitherto devoted little special attention to the economy of primitive peoples. In the midst of their attention to dress, forms of worship, morals, religious beliefs, marriage customs, art, and technical skill, they have often overlooked what lay closest at hand, and in the gossipy record? of ethnographic compilations the word "economy" has no more found a place than has the word "household" in the chronicles of the numerous investigators into the constitution of the family. But just because the observations we have utilized have been made for the most part only incidentally and not by trained economists, they possess a high measure of credibility. For they have on that account generally escaped the fate of being forced into some scheme categorically arranged in accordance with the conditions of our own civilization, and for that very reason unable to do justice to the differently conditioned life of primitive peoples.

Chapter II. The Economic Life of Primitive People

THE designation *natural people* seems a particularly apt characterization of the lower races of men on their economic side. They stand in more immediate touch with nature than do we; they are more dependent upon her, are more directly susceptible to her powers, and succumb to them more easily. Civilized man lays by stores for the future; for the preservation and embellishment of his existence he possesses a wealth of implements; in the event of failure of his crops the harvests of half a world stand at his disposal through our highly perfected means of transportation; he subdues the powers of nature and impresses them into his service. Our commerce places the labour of a thousand men at the command of every individual amongst us, and in every household watchful eyes guard the careful and economical consumption of the goods destined for our bodily subsistence. Primitive man, as a rule, gathers no stores; a bad harvest or other failure of the natural sources of his sustenance strikes him with its full weight; he knows no labour-saving implements, no system in disposing of his time, no ordered consumption; limited to his meagre natural powers, threatened on all sides by hostile forces, each day he has to struggle anew for his existence, and often knows not whether the morrow will vouchsafe him the means to still his hunger. Yet he does not regard the future with anxiety, he is a child of the moment; no cares torment him; his mind is filled with a boundless naive egoism. With thoughts extending no further, he instinctively follows his impulses, and in this regard also stands closer to nature than ourselves.[77]

The former rule was to classify primitive peoples according to the manner in which they procured their sustenance into hunters, fishers, pastorals, and agriculturalists. In this it was believed that each people must traverse these four stages of economic development in its progress towards civilization. The starting-point was the tacit assumption that primitive man began with animal food and only gradually passed over, under the stress of necessity, to a vegetable diet. The procuring of vegetable food moreover was considered the more difficult inasmuch as the picture of our European system of agriculture was ever in mind with its draught-animals and artificial apparatus of implements and tools.

But this conception is erroneous, just as is the assumption from which it proceeds. Certainly all economic activity begins with the *procuring of food*, which is wholly dependent upon the local distribution of the gifts of nature. From the beginning man was primarily dependent upon vegetable nourishment, and wherever tree-fruits, berries, and roots were to be gained, he first made use of these. In case of need he turned to petty animals which could be consumed raw: shell-fish, worms, beetles, grasshoppers, ants, etc. Like the lower animal in continuous quest of food, he devoured at the moment what he found without providing for the future.

If from this stage we seek the transition to the next, a little reflection tells us that it could not have been difficult to gain the practical knowledge that a buried bulb or nut furnishes a new plant, — certainly not more difficult than taming animals or inventing fish-hooks and bow and arrow, which transition to the hunting stage required.[78] As regards technical skill many hunting and nomadic peoples stand far above so-called agricultural peoples. Of late men have come to believe that nomads should rather be considered savage agriculturalists; and as a matter of fact it is highly improbable that a tribe of

---

[77]Comp. in general R. Vierkandt, *Naturvölker u. Kulturvolker* (Leipzig, 1896), pp. 260 ff On the conception of *natural peoples* see further Panckow, Ztschr. d Ges. f. Erdkunde zu Berlin, XXXI (1896), pp. 158, 159. Anyone inclined to find fault with the indefiniteness of the definition should not overlook the fact that no single case has presented itself raising the point whether a certain people was to be regarded as primitive or not.

[78]Comp. in general E. Hahn, *Die Hausthiere u. ihre Beziehungett s. Wirthschaft d. Menschen* (Leipzig, 1896); P. R. Bos, *Jagd, Viehzucht u. Ackerbau als Kulturstufen* in Intern. Archiv f. Ethnographie, X (1897), pp. 187 ff.

hunters should first have hit upon the taming of animals before they could procure milk, eggs, and meat. Moreover, except in the extreme north, there is probably no fishing, hunting, or pastoral people that does not draw a more or less considerable portion of its sustenance from the vegetable kingdom. For this supply many of them have long been dependent upon trade with more highly developed neighboring peoples. They thus lack that economic independence which our study requires if it is to arrive at conclusions universally applicable.

Now since the instances of hunting, fishing, and nomadic tribes, which are accepted as typical, are only to be found under special geographical and climatic conditions that hardly permit of a different manner of obtaining sustenance (hunters and fishers in the farthest north, nomads in the steppes and desert places of the Old World), it may be advisable in our further consideration to leave them wholly aside and limit the field of our investigation to the intertropical districts of America, Africa, Australia, the Malay Archipelago, Melanesia, and Polynesia. This is still an enormous circuit, within which the diversity of natural conditions surrounding primitive man produces many peculiarities in his material existence. The differences between the individual tribes in this regard are, however, not so great as, for instance, between the Esquimaux and the Polynesian. At any rate, notwithstanding the great differences of the races in conditions of life and ways of living, they have still sufficient in common to occupy our attention. In addition to this we have here the oldest regions inhabited by man, which, however, in spite, or perhaps on account, of the bounties of tropical nature, also appear to be those in which their development has been most slow.

At all stages of his development the primitive man of these regions manifestly finds in vegetable diet the basis of his sustenance. This is evident from the simple fact that he has always found animal food much more difficult to obtain. This is not contradicted by the circumstance that at times we notice an eagerness for flesh break forth among many savage races which appalls us, since it does not shrink even from its own kind. The explanation in all probability is that the definite quantity of salt requisite for the normal maintenance of the human body cannot be conveyed to it through purely vegetable diet, while it is quite possible with occasional raw-flesh food to live without salt. The same desire for salt is manifested even by the purely herbivorous among our domestic animals.

The *need of nourishment* [we have seen] is the most urgent, and originally the sole, force impelling man to activity, and causing him to wander about incessantly until it is satisfied. The species of *division* of *labour* between the two sexes, which this primitive search for food gives rise to, reaches its highest form when the wife procures the vegetable, the man the animal, portion of the food. And since, as a rule, the food gained is immediately devoured, and no one takes thought for the other as long as he himself is hungry, a difference in the nourishment of the two sexes arises that has perhaps contributed in an important degree to the differentiation of their bodily development.

The division of labour of these primitive roaming hordes is continued at higher stages of development, and receives there such sharp expression that the rigidly limited spheres of activity of the man and the woman form almost a species of secondary sex-characteristics whose understanding gives us the key to the economic life of primitive peoples. In particular almost all their *production of goods* is dominated by it.

Turning now to the latter, we should note by way of preface that by far the greater part of our primitive peoples, when they came under the view of Europeans, were acquainted with, and practised, *agriculture.* This is true, for instance, of all the negro races of Africa with but few exceptions, of the Malays, the Polynesians, and Melanesians, and of the primitive races of America, save those living at the extreme north and south of that hemisphere. It is a widely prevalent error, for which our youthful reading is responsible, that makes pure hunting races out of the North American Indians. All the tribes east of the Mississippi and south of the St. Lawrence were familiar with the cultivation of food-plants before the coming of Europeans; and, in the regions lying beyond, they at least gathered the grain of the water-rice *(zizania aquatica)* and ground meal from the berries of the manzanita shrub.[79]

The agriculture of primitive peoples is, however, peculiar.[80] In the first place it knows nothing of an implement that we think indispensable, namely, the plough. Wheel and wagon and draught-animals are likewise unknown. Furthermore, cattle-raising forms no integral part of their agriculture. Fertilizing of the soil occurs at times, but it is extremely rare. More frequent are irrigation arrangements, especially for rice and taro plantations. As a rule, however,

[79]Waitz, *Anthropologie d. Naturvölker*, III, pp. 78 ff.
[80]Comp. E. Hahn, as above, pp. 388 ff.

the cultivated land must be changed when its nutritive elements are exhausted; and the change is facilitated by the absence of individual property in the soil, which belongs to the tribe or the village community as a whole. Lastly, [we may recall,] the preparing of the soil is almost exclusively woman's work. Only in the first clearing of a piece of land do the men assist.

Of late years this system of culture has been designated the *hack* or *hoe system*, a short-handled hoe being its chief implement. With some tribes the primitive digging-stick still retains its place. At the basis of its plant production lie the tropical tuberous growths: manioc, yam, taro, sweet potato, pignut, and in addition bananas, various species of gourds (*cucurbitacece*), beans, and of the grains, rice, durra, and maize. Rice has its oldest home in South China probably, the durra in Africa, and maize, as is well known, in America. There belong, finally, to this system of agriculture the tropical fruit-trees — sago-, date-, and cocoa-palms, the breadfruit-tree, and the like.

On account of the imperfect nature and limited productivity of the implements, only small stretches of land can ever be taken into cultivation under the hack system. It is closely related externally, and also in the manner in which it is carried on, to our garden culture. The fields are generally divided into beds, which are often hilled in an exemplary fashion and kept perfectly free of weeds. The whole is surrounded with a hedge to keep out wild animals; against the grain-eating birds, which are particularly dangerous to the harvests of the tropics, the Malays set up very ingeniously constructed scarecrows; in most places in Africa special watch-towers are erected in the fields from which the young girls make noises to frighten away the animals. As a rule a definite *crop rotation* is observed. in the Congo basin, for instance, when the land is newly broken up it is first planted with beans, and when these are harvested, millet is sown; interspersed with the latter the sprouts of the manioc are often set out. The manioc does not yield full returns for from one and a half to two years, and occupies the land until the roots commence to become ligneous, and virgin soil must be taken up. In New Pomerania the rotation is yam roots first, then taro, and finally bananas, sugar-cane, and the like.[81]

---

[81] Descriptions of hack agriculture in Angola, Congo district: Pogge, pp. 8, 9; Wissmann, *Unter deutsch. Flagge,* pp. 341 ff.; among the Monbuttos: Schweinfurth, *In the Heart of Africa,* II, pp. 37-39; in Mindanao: Ztschr. f. Ethnol.,

Travellers have often described the deep impression made upon them when, on coming out of the dreary primeval forest, they happened suddenly upon the well-tended fields of the natives. In the more thickly populated parts of Africa these fields often stretch for many a mile, and the assiduous care of the negro women shines in all the brighter light when we consider the insecurity of life, the constant feuds and pillagings, in which no one knows whether he will in the end be able to harvest what he has sown. Livingstone gives somewhere a graphic description of the devastations wrought by the slave-hunts; the people were lying about slain, the dwellings were demolished; in the fields, however, the grain was ripening, and there was none to harvest it. But as yet the life of these people is by no means firmly attached to the soil; seldom do their settlements remain for several generations on the same spot;[82] their houses are fugitive structures of poles and grass; their other possessions may easily be carried away on their backs or quickly replaced, and on another spot a new village in a few days can be erected in which nothing from the old is lacking save the vermin.

Hack agriculture is exactly suited to just such a life. It requires no fixed capital beyond the small hoe and, where corn is cultivated, perhaps a knife to cut the ears. The keeping of supplies is scarcely necessary, since in many quarters the climate permits several harvests in the year. Where grain is grown, however, it is customary to store it in small granaries built on posts, or in pits in the earth, or in great earthen vessels. But even where thus stored it must soon be used if it is not to be destroyed through dampness, weevils, and termites. Livingstone thinks this explains why the negroes in case of abundant harvest brew so much beer.[83]

Hack agriculture is still one of the most widely prevalent systems of husbandry. It is to be found throughout all Central Africa (i8° N. lat. to 22° S. lat.), in South and Central America, in the whole of the Australian islands, in great sections of Further India and the East Indian Archipelago. Everywhere, [as already noted], it appears to have been originally woman's work; and as such it is a great factor in advancing civilization. Obviously through hunting for roots, which

---

XVII, pp. 19 ff.; in New Guinea: Finsch, *Samoafahrten,* pp. 56 ff.; in New Pomerania: Parkinson, *Im Bismarck-Archipel,* pp. 118 ff.; in South America: Martius, *Zur Ethnogr. Amerikas,* pp. 84, 85, 489, 490.

[82]Ratzel, I, p. 85; Panckow, pp. 167 ff.

[83]Expedit. *to Zambesi,* p. 253.

she had practised from the earliest times, woman was led on to agriculture. Farinaceous bulbs and root-crops form accordingly the chief part of her plantations. In this manner she gained technical experiences which the man did not enjoy. Her labour soon yielded the most important part of the requirements of life; and therewith was laid the foundation of a permanent family organization, in which the man undertook the offices of protection and the procuring of animal food. Only where there are no large quantities of game does the man take part in the cultivation of the soil, as, for instance, among the Malays.

Let us now turn to the second source of sustenance, hunting and fishing. Through the imperfect nature of their weapons *hunting* has ever had among primitive peoples a strong resemblance to the method of the beast of prey stealing upon its victim. A larger animal can only be wounded by an arrow-shot or spear-thrust, not killed; and then it is the hunter's task to pursue the beast until it sinks down exhausted. As this species of hunt may, however, under certain circumstances, become very dangerous, the most varied ways of trapping have been invented—pits, barricades, and falling trees; or in attacking the animal directly the hunt is carried on by whole tribes or village communities.[84] Under such circumstances communal ownership of the hunting-grounds and the establishment of very detailed rules for the distribution of the booty among the participants and the owners of the ground have been early developed; but on such matters we cannot enter here.[85] The essential thing for us to note is that the part of the duties pertaining to the providing of food necessitates a certain organization of work conformable to the principle of labour in common — a circumstance that has certainly been of the greatest importance for the birth of primitive political communities.

The same is to be said of *fishing*,[86] especially where the industry is followed along the seashore with boats and large nets, which can be produced and handled only with the help of many. The New Zealanders, for instance, wove nets one thousand yards in length and it took hundreds of hands to use them. Innumerable are the modes

[84] On the hunting methods of the Kaffirs comp. Fritsch, pp. 81 ff.; of the South Americans, Martius, pp. 82, 101.

[85] Some particulars in Post, *Afr. Jurispr.,* II, pp. 162, 163; Lubbock, *Origin of Civilization,* p. 455.

[86] As to fishing comp. in general Ratzel, I, pp. 234, 396, 506, 531.

of catching fish which primitive peoples have invented; besides hook and net, arrows, spears, bow-nets, and methods of stunning the fish are resorted to. All our information on this subject indicates that fishing acquired a much more regular character among primitive peoples than hunting. On many islands of the South Sea, indeed, definite days of the week have once for all been set apart for the communal fishing; and the leaders of the fishing expeditions are also the leaders in war. Stream-fishing has been especially developed by the primitive inhabitants of South America, among whom there are tribes that have been called fishing nomads because they wander from stream to stream. The same also occurs here and there in Africa. The actual labour of fishing seems always to fall to the men; it is only in some districts of Polynesia that the women take a limited part in it.

Because of the very perishable nature of meat, hunting and fishing in tropical regions can, in the majority of cases, supplement the vegetable diet only occasionally. True, the drying and even the smoking of the fish and meat cut into strips was early learned and practised. This is the usage with the Polynesians as well as among the Malays and Americans, and even among the negroes and Australians. Yet the part of the food requirement which can be regularly met in this manner is so small that it is a rule among many tribes that only the more prominent persons may enjoy certain kinds of game. It is quite common also for the use of certain kinds of meat to be forbidden to the women. It is only small forest and coast tribes, who are able with their dried meat to carry on trade with agricultural neighbours, that find their support in hunting and fishing.

It would accordingly be quite natural to assume that primitive peoples must early have hit upon the taming and raising of animals as a source of a regular food-supply. But we can speak of *cattle-raising* as a practice among the peoples of the tropical regions only in a very restricted sense. The hen alone, of our domestic animals, is to be found everywhere; besides it there is in Africa the goat, among the Malays and Polynesians the pig, and among the Americans the turkey, the musk-duck and the guinea-pig. Cattle are found only among one section of the Malays and in one strip, more or less broad, of East Africa, which runs through almost the whole continent, from the Dukas and Baris on the Upper Nile to the Hottentots and Namaquas in the south. But most of these peoples

37

do not use them as draught-animals; many of them do not even use their milk; many East African cattle-raisers never slaughter a beast except when they have captured it from another tribe.[87] Here and there in Equatorial Africa the ox serves as a riding and pack animal; but, generally speaking, the possession of cattle is for the negro peoples merely "a representation of wealth and the object of an almost extravagant veneration,"— merely a matter of fancy.

And this in general is the character of cattle-keeping among primitive peoples. An Indian village in the interior of Brazil, [as we have remarked in our last chapter], resembles a great menagerie; even the art of dyeing the plumage of birds is known; but none of the many animals are raised because of the meat or for other economic purpose; the very eggs of the hens, which are kept in large numbers, are not eaten.[88] To the Indian the lower animals are beings closely related to man, and in which he delights; but, as is evident, this keeping of animals is much more closely allied to the hunt than to agriculture. Here we have to do with tamed, not with domestic, animals. With such a state of affairs the place of the pig in the domestic economy of the Oceanians has many cognate features; it is petted by the whole family; its young are not infrequently suckled by the women; and its flesh is eaten only on feast days and then by the more prominent people alone. The sole animal, [other than the hen], which is found among all primitive peoples is the dog; but it also is a pure luxury and is almost nowhere employed in the hunt; only a few tribes eat its flesh, and it has been claimed from observation that these are always such as are devoted to cannibalism.

On the whole, then, no importance can attach to cattle-raising in the production of the food-supplies of primitive peoples; in their husbandry it forms little more than an element of consumption.

But the needs of these peoples are not confined to sustenance. Even the lowest among them paint, or in other ways decorate, their bodies, and make bows and arrows; the more advanced erect more or less substantial houses, plait and weave all kinds of stuffs, carve implements, make burnt earthen vessels; all prepare their food with fire, and with few exceptions know how to concoct intoxicating beverages. For all this labour of different kinds is necessary which we

---

[87]Schweinfttrth, I, pp. 59. 60; Livingstone, p. 553; Pogge, p. 23; Wissmann, I*m Innern Afrikas,* pp. 25, 127.

[88]Ehrenreich, pp. 13, 14, 54; Martius, pp. 672 ff.; K. v. d. Steinen, pp. 210, 379. Similarly among the Oceanians: Ratzel, I, p. 236.

can characterize in a simple manner as the *transformation* or *working up of material*, and which in the main embraces what we designate industry. Now what system did and does such work exhibit among primitive peoples?

If we are to answer this question we must distinguish sharply the technical and the economic sides of industry.

Technique in connection with the transformation of material is primarily dependent on natural conditions, and accordingly develops among most primitive peoples only along special lines.[89] Their implements are at first simple, natural objects, such as stones, animal bones, shells, sharpened pieces of wood, destined almost solely to increase the working power of the human members. Of implements., consisting of more than one part, we may mention the hand-mill and crushing-mortar. The first is merely a stationary and a movable stone with which the grains of corn are ground in the same manner as our artisans grind paint in a mortar. The crushing-mortar is a hollowed tree-trunk with a wooden pestle. The simplest labour-saving mechanical helps, such as wedge, lever, tongs, and screw, are unknown to them. Their boats are tree-trunks hollowed out with fire, or pieces of bark sewn together; the rudders are spoonlike pieces of wood with short handles representing little more than a broadening out of the hand. The art of joining together pieces of wood or other hard material by pegs, nails, dovetailing, or glue they are ignorant of; for this purpose they use tough fibres or cords or even mere tendrils of climbing plants. Metal-working was unknown to the Australians, Melanesians, Polynesians, and the native inhabitants of America before the coming of the Europeans. On the other hand the negro peoples are universally familiar with the procuring and working up of iron, and here and there of copper as well. A more advanced technique as regards metals is found only among the Malays. But even in the iron-forging of the negroes all the technical awkwardness of these peoples can be perceived. Their smiths did not even hit upon the idea of making their own tools out of iron. Hammers and anvils are stones, and very often the tongs are only the rib of a palm-leaf.

In spite of this technical backwardness many primitive peoples with their wretched tools produce wares of such quality and artistic taste as to arouse our highest admiration. This is possible only when the particular technical processes are applied in the simplest,

---

[89]On what follows comp. *Arbeit u, Rhythmus*, pp. 10 ff.

and at the same time most comprehensive, manner. Preeminent are weaving, pottery, and wood-carving. What indeed do the tropical peoples not make out of the bast and fibrous material of their forests, of the tough grasses and rushes — from mats and clothing-stuffs of bark to water-tight baskets, dishes, and bottles? What is not made by the East Indians and Eastern Asiatics from bamboo — from the timbers of the house to water-vessels, blowing-tubes, and musical instruments? How highly developed is woodwork among the Papuans; and what patience and perseverance it demands! To weave a piece of stuff of raffia fibre in Madagascar often takes several months; and in South America the same time is required to finish a hammock. The polishing and piercing of the milk-white pieces of quartz that the Uaupes of Brazil wear about their necks is frequently the work of two generations.

This leads us directly to the *industrial organisation in the working up of material.* For such labour there are, with few exceptions, no distinctly professional craftsmen. Each household has to meet all economic requirements of its members with its own labour; and this is accomplished by means of that peculiar division of duties between the two sexes, which we have come to know [in the preceding chapter]. Not only is it that a definite part of the providing of food is assigned to either sex, but each looks after the preparing of such as is gained along with all attendant tasks. To the woman falls all that is connected with the procuring and preparing of the vegetable foods; to the man the making of weapons, and of implements for hunting, fishing, and cattle-raising, the working-up of animal bones and skins, and the building of canoes. As a rule the man also looks after the roasting of the meats and the drying of fish, while the woman must attend to the laborious grinding of the corn, which she has grown, the brewing of beer, the shaping and burning of earthen pots for cooking, and in many instances the building of the huts as well. Besides these there are many species of the transforming of material, which are allotted now to one sex, now to the other. We may mention spinning, weaving, plaiting, the preparing of palm-wine and of bark stuffs. But, on the whole, this division of duties between the male and the female members of families is sharply drawn. Indeed it is continued even in consumption, for men and women never eat together; and, where polygamy exists, a separate hut must be provided for each wife.

We cannot enter upon a more detailed discussion of this peculiarly evolved *dualism in household economy* among primitive peoples. It devolves upon us, however, to establish that the labour of the members of the household, which is of such an individualistic character, cannot suffice for all tasks of their economic life. For undertakings that surpass the strength of the single household, assistance must therefore be obtained: either the help of the neighbours is solicited or all such labours are performed at one time by the whole village community. The latter is the rule in Africa, for instance, with the breaking of stretches of forest land for cultivation, the laying of barricades and pits for trapping wild animals, and elephant-hunting; in Polynesia, with the weaving of large fishing-nets, the building of large houses, the baking of breadfruit in a common oven, and the like. Where clanship or slavery or polygamy exists, there is offered a means for multiplying the domestic working strength, and thus for accomplishing services of a higher order for which the individual's strength does not suffice.

Within the separate tribes, accordingly, the working and refining of the raw products does not lead to the development of distinct trades, in that such work is carried on with uniform independence in each separate household From the reports of travellers, who judged from appearances, the existence of artisans among various primitive peoples has indeed been asserted. Thus on certain islands of the South Sea there are said to be professional carpenters, shoemakers, net-knitters, stone-borers, and wood-carvers. On closer examination of the particular cases these observations are open to doubt; to me the case of the native metal-worker seems alone to be proved. Among the negroes of Africa, as far as I can judge, only among the semi-civilized peoples of the Soudan are there the beginnings of a special industrial class. Beyond this any traces of a specialized industry supposed to have been discovered among primitive peoples are to be thus explained: either individuals manifesting special aptitude for some manufacture came under the observation of travellers, or entire tribes excelled in a particular kind of household occupation, as we shall see directly. Trades formed only under European influence must naturally be disregarded here.

But from tribe to tribe we find great differences in this industrial working-up of materials. It may even be safely claimed that almost every tribe displays some favourite form of industrial activity, in which its members surpass the other tribes. This is due to the varied distribution of natural products. If good potter's clay

41

is to be found in the district or village of a particular tribe, the women of this tribe or village readily acquire special skill in pottery; where native iron ore is discovered, smiths will appear; while along well-wooded seacoasts boat-building will flourish. Other tribes or localities excel in the preparation of salt from vegetable ashes, in the making of palm-wine or leather or skin garments; others again in the making of calabashes, baskets, mats, and woven materials. All these forms of skill, however, are aptitudes such as every man or every woman of the particular tribe or locality knows and also practises on occasion. When these individuals are designated by travellers as smiths, salt-makers, basket-makers, weavers, etc., that is to be taken in the same sense as when we speak of ploughmen, reapers, mowers, threshers among our⌢ peasants, according to the work in which they are for the time engaged. We have here to do not with special trades claiming the individual's whole activity, but with arrangements forming essential parts of the economy of each separate family. This naturally does not preclude single individuals from surpassing in skilfulness the other members of the tribe, just as there are among our peasant women particularly adept spinners, and among the farmers horse-breeders and bee-keepers who win in prize competitions.

Travellers have often observed this *tribal or local development of industrial technique*. "The native villages," relates a Belgian observer of the Lower Congo, "are often situated in groups. Their activities are based upon recip-rocality, and they are to a certain extent the complements of one another. Each group has its more or less strongly defined specialty. One carries on fishing, another produces palm-wine; a third devotes itself to trade and is broker for the others, supplying the community with all products from outside; another has reserved to itself work in iron and copper, making weapons for war and hunting, various utensils, etc. None may, however, pass beyond the sphere of its own specialty without exposing itself to the risk of being universally proscribed." From the Loango coast Bastian tells of a great number of similar centres for special products of domestic industry. Loango excels in mats and fishing-baskets, while the carving of elephants tusks is specially followed in Chilungo. The so-called "Mafooka" hats with raised patterns are drawn chiefly from the bordering country of Kakongo and Mayumbe. In Bakunya are made potter's wares which are in great demand, in Basanza excellent swords, in Basundi especially beautiful ornamented copper rings, on the Zaire clever wood and tablet carvings, in Loango orna-mented cloths and intricately designed mats, in Mayumbe clothing of finely woven mat-work, in Kakongo embroidered hats and also burnt-clay pitchers, and among the Bayakas and Mantetjes stuffs of woven grass.

Other similar accounts might be cited, not merely from Africa,[90] but also from the South Sea Islands and even from Central and South America.[91] We shall thus hardly err in assuming that in these *tribal industries* the controlling principle in the industrial development of primitive peoples has been discovered; that by them was furnished the means whereby the satisfaction of the needs of the individual and of whole groups was extended beyond their own immediate powers of production. For it may be taken for granted that an industrial product found only among those manufacturing it, especially if it attained to some importance in the simple life of these uncivilized peoples, would soon be coveted by the surrounding tribes. But the way from the coveting of an article to its enjoyment is a longer one in an economical organization, based upon acquisition directly by the individual himself, than we are inclined to assume in our own social life, which rests upon trade.

In fact decidedly unclear conceptions are widely prevalent as to the system of *exchange* of primitive peoples. We know that through-out Central Africa, from the Portuguese possessions in the west to the German in the east, there is a *market-place* every few miles at which the neighbouring tribes meet every fourth to sixth day to make mutual exchanges. Of the Malays in Borneo we are told that each larger village possesses its weekly market. The first discoverers of the South Sea Islands give us reports of distant "trading trips" which the natives undertake from island to island in order to make mutual exchanges of their wares. In America certain products, the raw material for which is to be found only in a single locality — for example, arrow-points and stone hatchets made of certain kinds of stone — have been met with scattered throughout a great part of

---

[90] H. Schurtz has made a collection of them in his *Afr. Gewerbe*, pp. 29-65. He has pursued further, though unfortunately not far enough, the subject of tribal industry. He has found such industry so extensively in evidence that we may assume the conditions of industrial production here portrayed to exist wherever travellers do not expressly report to the contrary.

[91] Comp. K. Sapper, *Das nördl. Mittel-Amerika* (1897), pp 299 ff., and the further examples given by us.

the continent.[92] Even among the aborigines of Australia there are instances of certain natural products, such as pitcher-plant leaves and ochre colour, which are found in but one place, and yet circulate through a great part of the country. In such phenomena we have a new and interesting proof of the civilizing power of trade; and in the primeval history of Europe itself this power has everywhere been assumed as operative when industrial products have been brought to light through excavations or otherwise far from their original place of production. Our prehistoric studies have woven together a whole spider's web of suppositions and have even brought us to speak of prehistoric "industrial districts." Our ethnographic literature speaks similarly of industrial localities for the manufacture of arms and the plaiting of mats in Borneo, for pottery at several points in New Guinea, for boat-building in several coast districts of the Duke of York Archipelago, for iron-working in negro countries, etc.

In opposition to this it must be asserted positively that *trade* in the sense in which it is regarded by national economy — that is, in the sense of the systematic purchase of wares with the object of a profitable re-sale as an organized vocation—can nowhere be discovered among primitive peoples. Where we meet native traders in Africa, it is a question either of intermediary activity prompted by European and Arabian merchants, or of occurrences peculiar to the semi-civilization of the Soudan. Otherwise the only exchange known to the natives everywhere is exchange from tribe to tribe. This is due to the unequal distribution of the gifts of nature and to the varying development of industrial technique among the different tribes. As between the members of the same tribe, however, no regular exchange from one household establishment to another takes place. Nor can it arise, since that vocational division of the population is lacking which alone could give rise to an enduring interdependence of households.

One fancies the *genesis of exchange* to have been very easy because civilized man is accustomed to find all that he needs ready made at the market or store and to be able to obtain it for money. With primitive man, however, before he became acquainted with more highly developed peoples, value and price were by no means current conceptions. The first discoverers of Australia found invariably, both on the continent and on the neighbouring islands that the

---

[92]Waitz, III, p. 75; on markets in South America, III, p. 380; on others in Mexico, IV, pp. 99 ff.

aborigines had no conception of exchange.[93] The ornaments offered them had no power whatever to arouse their interest; gifts pressed upon them were found later on strewn about in the woods where they had been cast in neglect. Ehrenreich[94] and K. v. der Steinen[95] had as late as 1887 the same experience among the Indian tribes of Brazil. Yet there was from tribe to tribe a brisk trade in pots, stone hatchets, hammocks, cotton threads, necklaces of mussel-shells, and many other products. How was this possible in the absence of barter and trade?

The solution of this riddle is simple enough, and has now been confirmed by direct observation on the spot, while previously it could only be assumed. The transfer ensues by way of *presents,* and also, according to circumstances, by way of *robbery, spoils of war, tribute, fine, compensation, and winnings in gaming.* As to sustenance, almost a community of goods prevails between members of the same tribes. It is looked upon as theft if a herd of cattle is slaughtered and not shared with one's neighbour, or if one is eating and neglects to invite a passer-by. Anyone can enter a hut at will and demand food; and he is never refused. Whole communities, if a poor harvest befall, visit their neighbours and look to them for temporary support. For articles of use and implements there exists the universal custom of *loaning* which really assumes the character of a duty; and there is no private ownership of the soil. Thus within the tribe where all households produce similar commodities and, in case of need, assist each other, and where surplus stores can only be utilized for consumption, there is no occasion for direct barter from establishment to establishment. Exceptions occur when purchasing a wife and making presents to the medicine-man, the singer, the dancer, and the minstrel, who are the only persons carrying on a species of separate occupations.

From tribe to tribe there prevail rules of *hospitality,*[96] which recur with tolerable similarity among all primitive peoples. The stranger on arriving receives a present, which after a certain interval he reciprocates; and at his departure still another present is handed

---

[93] Documentary proof in Ztschr. f. Sozial- u. Wirtschaftsgesch., IV, pp. S ff. (Sartorius v. Waltershausen).

[94] *Beiträge z. Völkerkunde Brasiliens,* p. 53.

[95] *Unter d. Naturvölkern Central-Brasiliens* (2d ed.), pp. 287 ff.

[96] On this point comp. K. Haberland, *Die Gastfreundschaft auf nied. Kulturstufen:* Ausland (1878), pp. 282 ff.

him.[97] On both sides wishes may be expressed with regard to these gifts. In this way it is possible to obtain things required or desired; and success is the more assured inasmuch as neither party is absolved from the obligations of hospitality until the other declares himself satisfied with the presents.

That this custom of reciprocal gifts of hospitality permits rare products of a land or artistic creations of a tribe to circulate from people to people, and to cover just as long distances from their place of origin as today does trade, will perhaps become more apparent to us when we consider how legends and myths have in the same way been enabled to spread over half the world. It is almost inconceivable that this could have been so long overlooked when even in Homer the custom of gifts of hospitality is attested by so many examples. Telemachos brings home from Sparta as present from Menelaos a bowl of silver which the latter had himself received in Sidon as a gift of hospitality from King Phaidimos, and his father Odysseus receives from the Phaiakes garments and linen and articles of gold as well as a whole collection of tripods and basins. All this he conceals on his arrival, as is well known, in the sacred grove of the nymphs in his native rocky island of Ithaca. Think of the poet's narration as an historical occurrence, and imagine what would have happened had Odysseus been recognised by the wooers at the right moment and slain; the presents of the Phaiakes would have rested well concealed in the grotto of the nymphs down to our own times, and would have been brought to light again by a modern archaeologist. Would he not have explained the whole treasure as the storehouse of a travelling merchant of the heroic age of Hellas, especially as he could have appealed for support to the actual barter which occurs quite extensively in Homer?

Among many primitive peoples peculiar customs have been preserved which clearly illustrate the transition from presents to exchange. Among the Dieris in Central Australia, for instance, a man or a woman undertakes for a present the task of procuring as reciprocal gift an object that another desires, or of hunting for him, or of performing some other service. The one thus bound is called *yutschin,* and until the fulfilment of the obligation wears a cord about his neck. As a rule the desired object is to be procured from a dis-

---

[97]Gift-making without recompense belongs only to a higher stage of civilization: A. M. Meyer, Ztschr. f. deutsch. Kulturgesch., V, pp. 18 ff.

tance.[98] In New Zealand the natives on the Wanganui river make use of parrots, which they catch in great numbers, roast, and preserve in fat, in order to obtain dried fish from their fellow-countrymen in other parts of the island.[99] Among the Indian tribes of Central Brazil trade is still an interchange of gifts of hospitality; and the Bakairis translate the Portuguese *comprar*, to buy, by a word signifying 'to sit down,' because the guest must be seated before he receives his present. In the countries of the Soudan the constant giving of presents frequently becomes burdensome to the traveller "since it is often only a concealed begging." "The gifts of hospitality that are received in the camp," remarks Staudinger,[100] "are in accord with good custom and are often very welcome. But with every stop in a larger town things are frequently obtained from high and low which are ostensibly given as a mark of respect to the white man; in reality they arrive only because the donors expect a three- or four-fold response from the liberality of the European. Indeed I am convinced that many a poor woman has herself first purchased the hen or duck that is to be presented in order to do a profitable piece of gift business with it."

The Indians of British Guiana appear to stand at the intermediate stage between gift-making and trading. Im Thurm reports of them:[101]

"There exists among the tribes of this, as of probably every other similar district, a rough system of distribution of labour; and this serves not only its immediate purpose of supplying all the tribes with better-made articles than each could make for itself, but also brings the different tribes together and spreads among them ideas and news of general interest. . . . Each tribe has some manufacture peculiar to itself; and its members constantly visit the other tribes, often hostile, for the purpose of exchanging the products of their own labour for such as are produced only by the other tribes. These trading Indians are allowed to pass unmolested through the enemy's country. ... Of the tribes on the coast, the Warraus make far the best canoes, and supply these to the neighbouring tribes. They also make hammocks of a peculiar kind, which are not, however, much in request except among themselves. In the same way, far in the interior, the Wapianas build boats for all the tribes in that district. The

---

[98] A. W. Howitt in Journal of Anthrop. Inst., XX (1891), pp. 76 ff.

[99] Shortland, *Traditions and Superstitions of the New Zealanders* (London, 1856), pp. 214, 215.

[100] *Im Herzen d. Haussaländer* (2d ed.), pp. 216, 217. Comp. Sachau, *Reisen in Syrien u. Mesopotamien*, p. 191; v. Hügel, *Kaschmir,* pp. 406, 407.

[101] *Among the Indians of Guiana* (London, 1883), pp. 270-273.

Macusis have two special products which are in great demand amongst all the tribes. One is the ourali, used for poisoning arrows and the darts of blowpipes, the other is an abundance of cotton hammocks; for, though these are now often made by the Wapianas and True Caribs, the Macusis are the chief makers. The Arecunas grow, spin, and distribute most of the cotton which is used by the Macusis and others for hammocks and other articles. The Arecunas also supply all blowpipes; for these are made of the stems of a palm which, growing only in and beyond the Venezuelan boundary of their territory, are procured by the Arecunas, doubtless by exchange, from the Indians of the native district of that palm. The Tarumas and the Woyowais have a complete monopoly of the manufacture of the graters on which Indians of all the tribes grate their cassava. These two remote tribes are also the great breeders and trainers of hunting-dogs. . . . The True Caribs, again, are the most skilful potters; and though the Arawaks frequently, and the other Indians occasionally, make vessels for their own use, yet these are by no means as good as those which, whenever possible, they obtain from the Caribs. The Arawaks make fibre hammocks of a kind peculiar to them. . . . The Ackawoi alone, so far as I know, have no special product interchangeable for those of their neighbours. These Indians are especially dreaded and disliked by all the others; and it is possible that the want of intercourse-thus occasioned between this tribe and the others forced the Ackawoi to produce for themselves all that they required. It is further possible that to this enforced self-dependence is due the miserable condition of most of the Ackawoi.

"To interchange their manufactures the Indians make long journeys. The Wapianas visit the countries of the Tarumas and the Woyowais, carrying with them canoes, cotton hammocks, and now very frequently knives, beads, and other European goods; and, leaving their canoes and other merchandise, they walk back, carrying with them a supply of cassava-graters, and leading hunting-dogs, all which things they have received in exchange for the things which they took. The Macusis visit the Wapiana settlements to obtain graters and dogs, for which they give ourali-poison and cotton hammocks; and they again carry such of these graters and dogs as they do not themselves require, together with more of their own ourali and of their cotton hammocks, to other Indians — to the Arecunas, who give in return balls of cotton or blowpipes; or to the True Caribs, who pay in pottery."

Once originated exchange long retains the marks of its descent in the rules that are attached to it and which are taken directly from the customs connected with gifts. This is manifested, in the first place, in the custom of payment in advance which dominates trade among primitive peoples.[102] The medicine-man does not stir

---

[102] Even European merchants trading in Africa must accommodate themselves

his hand to help the sick until he has received from the sick man's relatives his fee, which in this case closely resembles the present, and has openly announced his satisfaction. No purchase is complete until buyer and seller have before witnesses declared themselves satisfied with the objects received. Among many peoples a gift precedes or follows a deal;[103] the "good measures" of our village storekeepers, and "treating" are survivals of this custom. To decline without grounds an exchange that has been offered passes among the negroes as an insult, just as the refusal of a gift among ourselves. The idea that services interchanged must be of equal value can hardly be made intelligible to primitive man. The boy who performs a bit of work expects the same pay as the man, and the one who has assisted for one hour just as much as the one who has laboured a whole day; and as the greed on both sides knows no bounds, every trading transaction is preceded by long negotiations. Similar negotiations, however, are also the rule in the discharge of gifts of hospitality if the recipient does not find the donation in keeping with his dignity.

As time passes exchange creates from tribe to tribe its own contrivances for facilitating matters. The most important of these are markets and money.

Markets are uniformly held among negroes, East Indians, and Polynesians in open places, often in the midst of the primeval forests, on the tribal borders. They form *neutral* districts within which all tribal hostilities must cease; whoever violates the market-peace exposes himself to the severest punishments. Each tribe brings to the market whatever is peculiar to it: one honey, another palm-wine, a third dried meat, still another earthenware or mats or woven stuffs.[104] The object of the interchange is to obtain products that

---

to this custom by advancing to the black intermediaries whose services they call into requisition the price of the commodities that are to be supplied. Comp. Pogge, pp. 11, 140, 141; *M. Buchner, Kamerun,* pp. 98, 99. Even the sacrifice to the deity seems to the peoples of this stage only payment in advance for an expected service: Heckewelder, *Indian Nations,* pp. 211 ff.; and comp. pp. 232, 236.

[103]Schurtz, *Entsteh. Gesch. d. Geldes,* pp. 67, 68. Landor, *In the Forbidden Land* (Tibet), I, p. 315; II, p. 78.

[104]Although many primitive peoples can be found ready to give everything for European wares that they have come to know and value, yet their regular exchange remains altogether one-sided and confined to a few articles. Many objects of daily use are not to be had from them at any price, especially objects of adornment. Comp. Finsch, Samoafahrten, pp. 108, 119, 236, 283 f., 315; Martius, cited above, pp. 89, 596; Ztschr. f. Ethnogr., XVII, pp 24, 62.

cannot be procured in one's own tribe at all, or at least cannot be produced so well and so artistically as in neighbouring tribes. This must again lead each tribe to produce in greater quantities than it requires those products which are valued among the tribes, not producing them, because in exchange for these it is easiest to obtain that which one does not possess one's self, but which others manufacture in surplus quantities. In each tribe, however, every household produces the current market commodity of exchange that enjoys this preference. Hence it follows, when it is a question of a product of house industry, such as earthenware or wares made of bark, that whole villages and tribal areas appear to travellers to be great industrial districts, although there are no specialized artisans, and although each household produces everything that it requires with the exception of the few articles made only among other tribes which they have grown accustomed to and which exchange procures for them merely as supplements to houshold production.

Such is the simple mechanism of the market among primitive peoples. Now with regard to *money.* How much has been written and imagined about the many species of money among primitive peoples,[105] and yet how simple the explanation of their origin! *The money of each tribe is that trading commodity which it does not itself produce, but which it regularly acquires from other tribes by way of exchange.* For such article naturally becomes for it the universal medium of exchange for which it surrenders its wares. It is its measure of value according to which it values its property, which could in no other way be made exchangeable. It is its wealth, for it cannot increase it at will. Fellow tribesmen soon come to employ it also in transferring values, for because of its scarcity it is equally welcome to all. Thus is explained what our travellers have frequently observed, that in each tribe, often indeed from village to village, a different money is current, and that a species of mussel-shells or pearls or cotton stuff for which everything can be purchased today, is in the locality of the following evening's camp no longer accepted by anyone. The consequence is that they must first purchase the current commodities of exchange before they can supply their own needs in

[105]R. Andree, Ethnogr. Parallelen u. Vergleiche, pp. 221 ff. O Lenz, Veber Geld bei d. Naturvolkern (Hamburg, 1895). F. Ilwof, Tausch- handel u. Geldsurrogate in alter u. neuer Zeit (Graz, 1882). H. Schurz, Beitr'dge s. Entstehungsgesch. d. Geldes: Deutsche Geogr. Blatter (Bremen), XX (1897), pp. 1-66. Intern. Archiv f. Ethnogr., VI, p. 57.

the market. In this way, also, is to be explained the further fact, which has come under observation, that exchangeable commodities naturally scarce, such as salt, cauri shells, and bars of copper, or products of rare skill, such as brass wire, iron spades, and earthen cups, are taken as money by many tribes not possessing them; and above all is to be mentioned the well-known circumstance of objects of foreign trade, such as European calicoes, guns, powder, knives, becoming general mediums of exchange.

Certain varieties of money thus secure a more extensive area of circulation. They can even make their way into the internal trade of the tribal members through employment as mediums of payment in the purchase of a bride, for compensations, taxes, and the like; certain kinds of contracts are concluded in them. But there is no instance of a primitive people, in the absence of European influence, attaining to a currency or legal medium of payment for obligations of every kind and extent. It is rather the rule that various species of money remain in concurrent circulation; and very often certain obligations can be paid only in certain kinds. Changes in the variety of money are not infrequent; but on the other hand we sometimes find that a species will long survive the trade of the tribes from which it has gone forth, and will continue to serve in the inner transactions of a tribe, playing a singular, almost demoniacal, role, although, as regards their means of sustenance, the members of the tribe have nothing to buy and sell to one another. From an old interrupted tribal trade of this nature is to be explained the employment as money of old Chinese porcelain vessels among the Bagobos in Mindanao and the Dyaks in Borneo, the shells (dewarra) of the Melanesians, and the peculiar kinds of money of the Caroline Archipelago, for which special laws and administrative contrivances are necessary in order to keep this dead possession in circulation at all.[106] Otherwise the State does not interfere as a rule in these matters; and in the large territorial formations of Africa, such as the kingdom of Muata Yamwo, for instance, there are therefore different currencies from tribe to tribe. But even where one kind of money gains a greater area of circulation, its value fluctuates widely at the various market-places; generally, however, it advances in proportion to the distance

---

[106]We cannot enter here more in detail into these matters, and would refer to the interesting descriptions of Kubary, *Ethnog. Beiträge z. Kenntnis d. Carolinen-Archipels,* pp. 1 ff., and Parkinson, pp. 79, 101 ff.

from its source.[107]

Markets and money are intimately related so far as money in its character as a medium of exchange comes under consideration. But not every individual species of money that is met with among a primitive people has necessarily arisen from market trade. In its full development money is such an involved social phenomenon that it is natural to suppose that various influences associated with its past have been united in it. Thus, for instance, the origin of cattle-money seems to be bound up with the fact that, among the peoples referred to, the domestic animals represented the wealth and the means of gathering wealth. That for the purchase of a bride and for similar ends many tribes do not receive the current money, but for such purposes prescribe certain other objects of worth, appears to point to the admissibility of the assumption that in the complete development of money, along with the main current, various subsidiary streams may have played a part.[108]

From the standpoint of the total cultural progress of mankind the most important result of this survey, however, remains, that money as the favourite exchange commodity furnished a medium that bound together men from tribe to tribe in regular peaceful trade, and prepared the way for a differentiation of-tribes in the matter of production. In the circumstance that all members of the same tribe or village preferably carried on, along with the earning of their sustenance, other work of a definite type, lay the possibility of an advance in technical knowledge and dexterity. It was an

---

[107]Thus Cecchi reports, Fiinf Jahre in Ostafrika, p. 271: "According to the higher or lower value of the salt bar in the markets of this part of East Africa one could roughly estimate the distance from the place whence this money comes, and also judge of the more or less practicable nature of the routes over which the caravans transport it. Thus in the locality of its origin, for one thaler one receives among the Taltal, according to the statements of several travellers, several hundred salt bars. In Uorallu, the northern market of Schao, lying a distance of some two hundred miles from the country of the Taltal, its value fluctuates between fifteen and twenty for the thaler. In Ancober, eighty miles from Uorailu, the value sinks back to nine and nine and a half, and in Gera, two hundred and thirty miles beyond Ancober, one receives, according to circumstances, only six, five, four, or three salt bars per thaler."

[108]Perhaps Karl Marx rightly expresses it when he tersely remarks: "The money-form attaches itself either to the most important articles of exchange from outside, and these in fact are primitive and natural forms in which the exchange-value of home products finds expression; orelse it attaches itself to the object of utility that forms, like cattle, the chief portion of indigenous alienable wealth."—*Capital* (London, 1891), p. 61.

international, or interlocal, division of labour in miniature, which only much later was succeeded by division of labour from individual to individual within the nation, or the locality. Moreover the direct importance of the market for personal intercourse at this stage must not be undervalued, especially in lands where trading outside the market is so unusual that even travellers wishing to buy something direct are regularly refused with the words "come to market." In this one is involuntarily reminded of the prominent position that the market occupied in the social and political life of the peoples of classical antiquity.

But it is always a very *one-sided development*, permitting only to individual tribes the organization of production and trade just described. In this way is to be explained that most extraordinary phenomenon that in the interior of continents where no difficulties in communication oppose the passage of certain attainments in technical skill from tribe to tribe, it has been possible for peoples of very primitive economic stamp to remain unchanged by the side of others of higher development throughout thousands of years. One of the most remarkable examples of this nature is offered in Central Africa by the pigmy race of the Batuas or Akkas, still standing at the stage of the lower nomads, which keeps strictly within the zone of the primitive forest, but on definite days appears at the market-places of the surrounding negro tribes to exchange its chief economic product, dried meat of animals killed in the hunt, for bananas, ground-nuts, maize, and the like. In fact in some parts even a more primitive form of trading has been maintained between these pigmy people and their neighbours, in that at the period when thd fruit is ripe the Batuas break into the fields of the negroes, steal bananas, tubers, and corn, and leave behind an equivalent in meat.[109]

---

[109]Casati, *Zehn Jahre in Aequatoria*, I, p. 151. Schweinfurth, *The Heart of Africa*, II, pp. 83 ff. Dr. W. Junker's *Travels in Africa*, III, pp. 85, 86. Wissmann, Wolf, etc., *Im Innern Afrikas*, pp. 256, 258 ff. A similar report is given by W. Geiger (Ceylon), *Tagebuchbldtter u. Reiseerinnerungen* (Wiesbaden, 1897), of the Veddahs: "The method by which the Veddah is able to procure his arrow-points — which he does not make himself — is interesting. He betakes himself under cover of night to the dwelling of a Singhalese smith, and places in front of it a leaf to which the desired shape is given. To this he adds a present of some kind, wild honey, the skin of an animal, or something similar. During one of the following nights he returns and expects to find the object ordered finished. If he is satisfied, he will deposit another special gift. The smiths never refuse to execute the orders at once. If they do, they may be certain at the next opportunity to be made the target for an arrow. Moreover their labour is abundantly

The fact that the Batuas are clever hunters appears here to have caused the neighbouring tribes to neglect the production of meat through hunting and cattle-raising. On the other hand it is said that the pigmies do not even make their own weapons, but procure them in trade from the Momsus and other tribes.

Of this one-sided development another and much more widespread example is offered by the *smiths*, who not merely among many tribes of Africa but sporadically in Asia and in southeastern Europe form a hereditarily distinct caste, whose members, whether regarded with bashful awe or contempt, can neither enter into a marital nor other social alliance with the rest of the people.[110] This strange phenomenon has hitherto been explained as a matter of remnants of subject tribes preserving to their conquerors the art of metal-working, which had otherwise perished, because the victorious race was ignorant of it. It is, however, also conceivable that a voluntary dispersal of such tribes took place and that the very difference of nationality, coupled with the carrying on of an esoteric art, placed them wherever they settled outside the community of the people.

In individual instances the carrying on of such a tribal industry in this exclusive manner leads to the rise of what travellers usually designate now as *industrial peoples*, because they do work for all their neighbours; now as *trading peoples*, because one meets them in all the markets of a more extensive district, and because they monopolize the trade in certain wares. We have an instance of the former, when the consumers resort to the district where a special tribal industry flourishes, in order to get the desired wares at the seat of manufacture; of the latter, when the producers bring to the tribes lacking them such wares as they produce beyond their own requirements.

As an example of the first form of this evolution, the little tribe of the Osakas may be cited, which has its home in the valley of the Ogowe to the east of the Lolo River. Lenz[111] reports concerning it: "The Osakas are divided into five or six villages, each of which contains sixty to a hu'ndred huts; compared with their numerically so important neighbours, such as the Fans and the Oshebo-Adumas, they are thus destined to play an altogether passive role in the history of those countries. In spite of this, however, the Osakas appear

---

rewarded by what the Veddah gives in return."
[110] R. Andree, pp. 153 ff.
[111] Mittheil. d. geogr. Gesell. in Wien (1878), p. 476.

to be not altogether insignificant; for among them I found many individuals belonging to the most widely different tribes, frequently from regions quite far distant. The Osakas are recognised as the best smiths, and all the surrounding tribes, — the Oshebo-Adumas, the Akelles, the Awanshis and even the Fans, — buy of them a great part of their implements for hunting and war, although the last-named tribe itself excels at this handicraft. By the Oshebo-Adumas the iron wares of the Osakas are then brought down to the Okandes and to the Apinshis and Okotas dwelling between the rapids of the Ogowe, these last tribes on their part being but little skilled in iron-work and devoting themselves exclusively to the slave-trade. From there, through the medium of the Iningas and Galloas, weapons of this kind find their way as far as the sea-coast."

"The Oshebo-Adumas generally pay for these weapons with palm-oil and ground-nuts, while the Fans, who are the most expert hunts-men of all these various tribes, give in exchange for the spears and swordlike knives dried and smoked meat, chiefly of the antelope, the wild boar, the porcupine, the field rat and the monkey. In all the Osaka villages I saw a bustling life. As must always be the case where such widely different tribes meet together, quarrelings were extremely frequent there and often assumed great proportions."

A typical example of the second form is offered by the Kiocos and the Kanjocas in the southern part of the Congo basin. Of the latter Wissmann reports:[112] "The Kanjoka country is particularly rich in iron, and there are some excellent smiths there. Salt also is produced, so that the Kanjokas, with the products of their coun-try and their iron manufacture, undertake commercial expeditions to the south as far as the Lunda country." The Kiocos dwell in the kingdom of Lund itself, dispersed among the Kalundas, but have their own chiefs who are tributary to the Muata Yamwo. The Kio-cos are partial to placing their villages in the woodland, for they are preeminently excellent hunters, gather gum from their forests, and to obtain wax carry on a species of wild-bee keeping. They are also clever smiths, and not only make good hatchets, but can also repair old flintlocks and even fit them with new mounts and stocks. They clothe themselves in animal skins; the art of making vegetable cloths is little known to them. Their women plant chiefly manioc, maize, millet, groundnuts, and beans. The products that the Kiocos obtain from the exploitation of their forests they exchange on the

---

[112] *My Second Journey through Equat Africa* (London, 1891), p. 105.

west coast for wares, chiefly powder, with which they then betake themselves into the far interior in order to buy ivory and slaves. The ivory obtained through trade they dispose of, while the slaves they procure they incorporate with their household. The Kiocos esteem slaves above all as property. They treat the slave women as they do their wives, and the men as members of the household, and part from them so very unwillingly that in the Kioco country it is quite exceptional for travellers to be offered slaves for sale. On their hunting voyages they have penetrated farthest towards the east; and there, before entering upon their journey homewards, they usually barter a part of their weapons for slaves. Then for the time being they arm themselves again with bow and arrow. They rightly enjoy the reputation of being as good hunters as they are crafty and unscrupulous traders; and in a masterful manner they understand how to overreach and dispossess the better-natured and more indolent Kalundas.[113] This picture is often repeated in the negro countries. One readily sees that it does not adapt itself to any of the usual categories of economic history. The Kiocos are no hunting people, no nomads, no agriculturalists, no industrial and trading nation; they are all these at once. They act as intermediaries for a part of the trade with the European factories on the coast. At the same time they cany on some mediary traffic of their own in which they display the peculiar aptitude of the negro for barter, but nevertheless gain most of their living directly from hunting and agriculture.

Both forms of development are met with in the two pottery islands of New Guinea, Bilibi and Chas. The manufacture is in both places in the hands of the women. The natives of the islands round about, and even of the more distant ones, come to Chas to barter their products for the earthenware; in Bilibi the men take whole boatloads to sell along the coast. Every woman makes a special mark on the pottery she produces; but whether with one European observer we are to regard this as a trade-mark seems very doubtful.[114]

In order to leave untouched no important part of the economic life of primitive peoples, let us take a rapid glance at their *commercial contrivances* and *public administration.* Both are intimately

---

[113]Pogge, pp. 45, 46, 47, and Wissmann, *Im Itmern Afrikas,* pp. 59, 62. Comp. also Schurtz, *Afr. Gew.,* p. 50.

[114]Comp. Finsch, pp. 82, 83, 281, 282; Semon, *In the Austral. Bush,* pp. 317 ff. Similar pottery districts in Africa proven by Schurtz, p. 54.

connected. For commerce is essentially a public matter; there are no private commercial arrangements whatever among these peoples. Indeed one can claim frankly that at this stage trade scarcely displays an economic character at all.

In the first place as concerns commercial *routes*, there are overland trade routes only when they have been tramped by the foot of man; the only artificial structures to facilitate land trade are primitive bridges, often consisting merely of a single tree-trunk, or ferries at river fords, for the use of which the traveller has to pay a tax to the village chief. These dues as a rule open the door to heavy extortions.[115] On the other hand the natural *waterways* are everywhere diligently used, and there is hardly a primitive people that has not been led through its situation by the sea or on a river to the use of some peculiar kind of craft. The enumeration and description of these means of transportation would fill a volume; from the dugout and skin canoe of the Indians to the artistically carved rowboats and sailboats of the South Sea Islanders, all types are represented. On the whole, however, the technique of boat-building and navigation has remained undeveloped among these peoples; none of their vessels deserve the name of ship in the proper sense. Thus their importance is everywhere restricted to *personal transportation* and *fishing*, while nowhere has the development reached a *freight transportation* of any extent.

Curiously among primitive peoples that branch of commercial communication has enjoyed the fullest develop1ment which we would naturally associate only with the highest culture, namely, the *communication of news*. It forms indeed the sole kind of trade for which primitive peoples have created permanent organizations. We refer to the courier service and the contrivances for sending verbal messages.

The despatching of *couriers* and *embassies* to neighbouring tribes in war and peace leads, even at a very low stage of culture, to the development of a complete system of symbolic signs and means of conveying intelligence.[116] Thus among the rude tribes in the interior of Australia various kinds of body-painting, of head-dress and other conventional signs serve to apprise a neighbouring tribe of the occurrence of a death, of the holding of a feast, and of a threaten-

---

[115]Comp. Pogge, pp. 64, 70, 78, 95, 97, us, 169; Wissmann, *Unter deutsch. Flagge*, pp. 343, 361, 364, 394; and *Second Journey*, p. 71.

[116]Comp. generally R. Andree, "Merkzeichen u. Knotenschrift" in his Ethnogr. Parallel., pp. 184 ff.; Waitz, IV, p. 89.

ing danger, or to summon the tribesmen together for any purpose.[117] Among the aborigines of South America ingeniously knotted cords or leather strips (*quippus*), and among the North Americans the well-known wampum perform similar offices;[118] in Africa courier-staffs with or without engraved signs are customary, and the same are found among the Malays and Polynesians. If need be, the couriers have to learn their message by heart and communicate it verbally.[119] In the negro kingdoms, where the administrative power of the ruler reaches only as far as he is able personally to intervene,[120] the couriers of the chiefs hold a very important position; for through them the sovereign chief is as if omnipresent, and new occurrences come to his knowledge with surprising rapidity. But even for the communication of intelligence among members of the same tribe — for instance, in hunting and in war—a system of symbols exists which is often very ingeniously conceived, and which, as a rule, is hidden from the uninitiated.

Not less remarkable are the *telephonic contrivances* resting upon the ingenious employment of the *drum*, the musical instrument in widest use among primitive peoples. In one sense they take the form of a developed signal system, as among the East Indians[121] and the Melanesians,[122] in another there is a real speaking of words by which detailed conversations can be carried on at great distances. The latter is very common in Africa.[123] As a rule only the chiefs

[117]Details in Journ. of Anthropol. Inst, XX, pp. 71 ff.

[118]Martius, pp. 98, 99, 694; Waitz, III, pp. 138 ff. On knot writing in West Africa: Bastian, Die Exp. n. d. Loango-Kiiste, I, p. 181.

[119]Livingstone, p. 285. Comp. also the apt description by Casalis, *Les Bassoutos*, pp. 234, 235: "Ces messagers sont generalement doues d'une memoire prodigieuse, et l'on peut s'attendre a ce qu'ils trans- mettent textuellement les depeches orales, dont ils se chargent."

[120]This applies also to the political conditions of semi-civilization. G. Rohlfs, Land u. Volk in Afrika, p. 163: "The Abyssinian is accustomed to obey only when his master is near. Once out of reach of his voice little does he trouble himself about orders. This is the case in all half-civilized countries. To this Turkey, Morocco, Egypt, and Borooo bear witness."

[121]Martius, p. 65. For a remarkable telephonic contrivance of the Catuquinaru Indians, see Archiv f. Post u. Telegraphie (1899), pp. 87, 88.

[122]Parkinson, p. 127, comp. pp. 72, 121; Finsch, p. 68. Likewise in Africa: Schweinfurth, I, pp. 64, 290, 291.

[123]Described in greater detail by M. Buchner, *Kamerun*, pp. 37, 38; Wissmann, *Im Innern Afrikas*, pp. 4, 228, 232; Betz in *Mittheil. aus d. deutsch Schutzgebieten*, XI (1898), pp. 1-86; Wissmann, Unter deutsch. Flagge, p. 215; Stanley, *Through the Dark Continent*, II, pp. 264, 279; Livingstone, p. 93. For a signal-whistling language in Timor, see Jacobsen, *Reise in d. Inselwelt d.*

and their relations are acquainted with this drum language; and the possession of the instrument used for this purpose is a mark of rank, like the crown and sceptre in civilized countries. Less extended is the employment of fire-signs for summoning the tribe or communicating news.[124]

There is no public economy, in our sense of the word. True, where their power is to some extent established, the chiefs receive all kinds of dues in the form of shares, traditionally fixed, in the products of the chase and of husbandry, fees for the use of bridges, ferries, market-place. In more extensive kingdoms the subordinate chieftains are bound to send tribute.[125] But all this is more or less manifestly clothed in the form of gift, for which the chief has to bestow a return present even if this consist only in the entertainment that he bestows upon the bearer. Even with the market-fees, which are payable by the sellers to the owner of the market-place, in the Congo district a a return service is rendered in that the chief performs a dance in front, and to the delight, of those using the market. Of special interest to us are the presents that travellers en *route* have to pay to the village chiefs whose territories they traverse, since from such payments our *customs duty* has sprung. Not less important is it to notice that in the larger kingdoms the tribute of the subject tribes consists of those products which are peculiar to each tribe, and which are usually marketed by it. In the Lunda country, for instance, some districts bring ivory or skins, others salt or copper; from the northern parts come plaited goods of straw, and from the subordinate chiefs nearer the coast at times even powder and European cotton stuffs.[126] Not infrequently has this led such sovereign chiefs to carry on a trade in these products, which accumulate in large quantities in their hands, or to claim a monopoly in them. The saying that makes the kings the greatest merchants thus gains a deeper significance.

In general the financial prerogatives of the chiefs are limited only by their natural strength; and the wealth of the subject is without the protection that the civilized State assures to it by law. The

---

Banda-Meers, p. 262.

[124]Comp., for example, Petermanns Mittheil., XXI (1875), p. 381.

[125]Details in Post, *Afr. Jurisprudenz*, I, pp. 261 ff.

[126]Pogge, pp. 226, 227. Comp. Wissmann, *Im Innern Afrikas*, pp. 171,172, 202,249,267,286,289,308; *Unter deutsch. Flagge*, pp. 95, 332, 339. The same is true of the Marutse country north of the Zambesi: E. Holub, *Sieben Jahre in Sudafrika*, II, pp. 173, 187, 253, 254, 257, 268, 271.

expeditions sent out by the negro kings to collect the tribute and taxes degenerate only too often into robber raids. The claim of the kings to fines frequently reduces the administration of justice to an institution for extortion, and the system of gifts, which prevails in all relationships of a public character, too rapidly passes into a veritable system of bribery.

This must naturally react injuriously upon private industry. In the condition of constant feud in which the smaller tribes live with their neighbours under the arbitrary rule which in the interior usually accompanies the formation of larger states, most primitive peoples stand in peril of life and property. Through long habit this danger becomes endurable, yet economic advancement must assuredly be retarded by it. The obligation to make presents ever and everywhere, the custom of regarding food almost as free goods, leave but insufficient room for self-interest. An English writer makes the remark — from the standpoint of European life certainly not inaccurate — that this sharing-up, rendered necessary by custom, encourages the people in gluttony, since only that is safe which they have succeeded in stuffing into their bellies; it also prevents rational provision for the future, because it is difficult to keep on hand supplies of any kind.[127] Assuredly with some reason have the begging proclivities and the "tendency to steal," which is said to animate many primitive peoples in dealing with Europeans, been associated with the custom of gifts and the insufficient distinction of "mine and thine."[128] The immoderate use of alcoholic drinks is likewise a consequence of their slight forethought for their own welfare. If, however, the attempt is made to appreciate all these things apart from the conditions of culture in which they arise, one readily recognises that they lie "beyond the bounds of good and evil," and that what appears from the standpoint of the modern Englishman as vice has concealed within it the beautiful virtues of disinterestedness, benevolence, and generosity.

For many who today pose as the bearers of civilization to their black and brown fellow men primitive man is the quintessence of all economic vices: lazy, disorderly, careless, prodigal, untrustworthy, avaricious, thievish, heartless, and self-indulgent. It is true that primitive man lives only for the present, that he shuns all regular work, that he has not the conception of duty, nor of a vocation as a

---

[127]Tindall, in Fritsch, p. 351; comp. p. 362. Waitz, II, p. 402; III, p. 80.
[128]Comp. Waitz, III, pp. 163 ff.

moral function in life. But it is not less true that with his wretched implements he accomplishes an amount of work that must excite our admiration, whether we contemplate with our own eyes the neat fruit-fields of the women or view in our museums the weapons and implements of the men, the products of infinite toil. Above all, his manner of working assures to primitive man a measure of enjoyment in life and a perpetual cheerfulness which the European, worried with work and oppressed with care, must envy him.

If since their acquaintance with European civilization so many primitive peoples have retrograded and some even become extinct, the cause lies, according to the view of those best acquainted with the matter, chiefly in the disturbing influence which our industrial methods and technique have exerted upon them. We carried into their childlike existence the nervous unrest of our commercial life, the hurried hunt for gain, our destructive pleasures, our religious wrangles and animosities. Our perfected implements relieved them suddenly of an immense burden of labour. What they had accomplished with their stone hatchets in months they performed with the iron one in a few hours; and a few muskets replaced in effectiveness hundreds of bows and arrows. Therewith fell away the beneficent tension in which the old method of work had continuously kept the body and mind of primitive man, particularly as the character of his needs remained at the same low level. Under these conditions has he gone to ruin, just as the plant that thrives in the shade withers away when exposed to the glare of the noon-day sun.

Chapter III. The Rise of National Economy

EVERYONE knows that the modern man's way of satisfying his numerous wants is subject to continual change. Many arrangements and contrivances that we find necessary were unknown to our grandparents; and our grandchildren will find inadequate much that perhaps only a short time ago aroused our admiration.

All those arrangements, contrivances, and processes called forth to satisfy a people's wants constitute national economy. National economy falls again into numerous individual economies united together by trade and dependent upon one another in many ways; for each undertakes certain duties for all the others, and leaves certain duties to each of them.

As the outcome of such a development, national economy is a product of all past civilization; it is just as subject to change as every separate economy, whether private or public, and whether directly ministering to the wants of a larger or a smaller number of people. Furthermore, every phenomenon of national economy is a phenomenon in the evolution of civilization. In scientifically defining it and in explaining the laws of its development we must always bear in mind that its essential features and its dynamic laws are not absolute in character; or, in other words, that they do not hold good for all periods and states of civilization.

The first task, then, which national economy presents to science is to determine and explain the facts. But it must not be content with a merely dynamic treatment of economic processes; it must also seek to deduce their origin. A full understanding of any given group of facts in the history of a civilized people requires that we know how the facts arose. We shall, therefore, not escape the task of investigating the phases of development through which the economic activity of civilized peoples passed before it assumed the form of the national economy of today, and the modifications undergone by each separate economic phenomenon during the process. The material for this second part of the task can be drawn only from the economic history of the civilized peoples of Europe; for these alone present a line of development which historical investigation has adequately disclosed, and which has not been deflected in its course by violent disturbances from without; though, to be sure, this upward development has not always been without interruption or recoil.

The first question for the political economist who seeks to understand the economic life of a people at a time long since past is this: Is this economy national economy; and are its phenomena substantially similar to those of our modern commercial world, or are the two essentially different? An answer to this question can be had only if we do not disdain investigating the economic phenomena of the past by the same methods of analysis and deduction from intellectually isolated cases which have given such splendid results to the masters of the old "abstract" political economy when applied to the economic life of the present.

The modern "historical" school can hardly escape the reproach that, instead of penetrating into the life of earlier economic periods by investigations of this character, they have almost unwittingly applied to past times the current classifications of modern national economy; or that they have kneaded away so long at conceptions of commercial life that these perforce appear applicable to all economic periods. In so doing they have without doubt greatly obstructed the path to a scientific mastery of those historical phenomena. The material for economic history, which has been brought to light in such great quantities, has for this reason largely remained an unprofitable treasure still awaiting scientific utilization.

Nowhere is this more plainly evident than in the manner in which they characterize the differences between the present economic methods of civilized nations and the economic life of past epochs, or of peoples low in the scale of civilization. This they do by setting up so-called *stages of development*, with generic designations made to embrace the whole course of economic evolution.

The institution of such "economic stages" is from the point of method indispensable. It is indeed only in this way that economic theory can turn to account the results of the investigations of economic history. But these stages of development are not to be confounded with the time-periods of the historian. The historian must not forget to relate in any period everything that occurred in it, while for his stages the theorist need notice only the normal, simply ignoring the accidental. In treating of the gradual transformation, frequently extending over centuries, which all economic phenomena and institutions undergo, his only object can be to comprehend the whole development in its chief phases, while the so-called transition-periods, in which all phenomena are in a state of flux, must, for the time, be disregarded. By this means alone is it possible to discover the fundamental features, or, let us say it boldly, the laws of development.

All early attempts of this class suffer from the defect of not reaching the essentials, and touching only the surface.

The best known series of stages is that originated by *Frederick List*, based upon the chief direction taken by production. It distinguishes five successive periods which the peoples of the temperate zone are supposed to have passed through before they attained their present economic condition, namely: (i) the period of nomadic life; (2) the period of pastoral life; (3) the period of agriculture; (4) the period of combined agriculture and manufacture; and (5) the period of agriculture, manufacture, and commerce.

Another series evolved by *Bruno Hildebrand*, which makes the condition of exchange the distinguishing characteristic, comes somewhat closer to the root of the matter. It assumes three stages of development: period of barter; period of money; and period of credit.

Both, however, take for granted that as far back as history reaches, with the sole exception of the "primitive state," there has existed a national economy based upon exchange of goods, though at different periods the forms of production and exchange have varied. They have no doubt whatever that the fundamental features of economic life have always been essentially similar. Their sole aim is to show that the various public regulations of trade in former times found their justification in the changing character of production or exchange, and that likewise in the present different conditions demand different regulations.

The most recent coherent presentations of economic theory that have proceeded from the members of the historical school remain content with this conception, although in reality it stands upon a scarcely higher plane than the favourite historical creations of abstract English economics[129]. This we will endeavour briefly to prove.

The condition of society upon which *Adam Smith* and *Ricardo* founded the earlier theory is that of a commercial organization based upon division of labour; or let us rather say simply, of national economy in the real sense of the term. It is that condition in which each individual does not produce the goods that he needs, but those which in his opinion others need, in order to obtain by way of trade the manifold things that he himself requires; or, in a word, the condition in which the cooperation of many or of all is necessary in order to provide for the individual. English political economy is thus in its essence a *theory of exchange*. The phenomena and laws of the division of labour, of capital, of price, of wages, of rent, and of profits on capital, form its chief field of investigation. The whole theory of production and especially of consumption receives very inadequate treatment. All attention is centred upon the circulation of goods, in which term their distribution is included.

That there may once have existed a condition of society in which exchange was unknown does not occur to them; where their system makes such a view necessary they have recourse to the Robinson Crusoe fiction so much ridiculed by later writers. Usually, however, they deduce the most involved processes of exchange directly from the primitive state[130]. Adam Smith supposes that man is born with a natural instinct for trade, and considers the division of labour itself as but a result of it.[131] Ricardo in several places treats the hunter and the fisher of primitive times as if they were two capitalistic entrepreneurs. He represents them as paying wages and making profits; he discusses the rise and fall of the cost, and the price, of their products. *Thünen*, to mention also a prominent German of this school, in constructing his isolated State starts with the assumption of a commercial organization. Even the most distant region, which

---

[129] [Regarding the omission from special mention of Schmoller's territorial series: village, town, territory, and State, we may refer to Professor Schmoller's review of the first German edition and Professor Bücher's reply in Jhb. f. Gesetzgeb., etc., XVII and XVIII (1893- 94). See also Schmoller, *Grundrisz d. Volkswirtschaftslehre*, I (Leipzig, 1900).—ED.]

[130] The same is true also of the Physiocrats. Comp. Turgot, *Réflexions*, §§2ff.

[131] Book I, Chap. 2.

has not yet reached the agricultural stage, prosecutes its labours with the single end of selling its products in the metropolitan city.

How widely such theoretical constructions vary from the actual economic conditions of primitive peoples must long ago have been patent to historical and ethnographical investigators had not they themselves been in the grasp of modern commercial ideas which they transferred to the past. A thorough-going study, which will sufficiently embrace the conditions of life in the past, and not measure its phenomena by the standards of the present, must lead to this conclusion: *National economy is the product of a development extending over thousands of years, and is not older than the modern State; for long epochs before it emerged man lived and laboured without any system of trade or under forms of exchange of products and services that cannot be designated national economy.*

If we are to gain a survey of this whole development, it can only be from a standpoint that affords a direct view of the essential phenomena of national economy, and at the same time discloses the organizing element of the earlier economic periods. This standpoint is none other than the relation which exists between the production and the consumption of goods; or, to be more exact, the length of the route, which the goods traverse in passing irom producer to consumer. From this point of view we are able to divide the whole course ef economic development, at least for the peoples of central and western Europe, where it may be historically traced with sufficient accuracy, into three stages:

(1) The *stage of independent domestic economy* (production solely for one's own needs, absence of exchange), at which the goods are consumed where they are produced.

(2) The *stage of town economy* (custom production, the stage of direct exchange), at which the goods pass directly from the producer to the consumer.

(3) The *stage of national economy* (wholesale production, the stage of the circulation of goods), at which the goods must ordinarily pass through many hands before they reach the consumer.

We will endeavour to define these three economic stages more precisely by seeking a true conception of the typical features of each without allowing ourselves to be misled by the casual appearance of transitional forms or particular phenomena which, as relics of earlier or precursors of later conditions, project into any period, and whose existence may perhaps be historically proved. In this way alone shall we be able to understand clearly the fundamental distinctions between the three periods and the phenomena peculiar to each.

The *stage of independent domestic economy*, as has already been pointed out, is characterized by restriction of the whole course of economic activity from production to consumption to the exclusive circle of the household (the family, the clan). The character and extent of the production of every household are prescribed by the wants of its members as consumers. Every product passes through the whole process of its manufacture, from the procuring of the raw material to its final elaboration in the same domestic establishment, and reaches the consumer without any intermediary. Production and consumption are here inseparably interdependent: they form a single Uninterrupted and indistinguishable process; and it is as impossible to differentiate them as to separate acquisitive smd domestic activity from each other. The earnings of each communal group are one with the product of their labour, and this, again, one with the goods going to satisfy their wants, that is, with their consumption.

Exchange was originally entirely unknown. Primitive man, far from possessing a natural instinct for trading, shows on the contrary an *aversion* to it. Exchange (*tauschen*) and deceive (*taüschen*) are in the older tongue one and the same word.[132] There is no universally recognised measure of *value*. Hence everyone must fear being duped in the bartering. Moreover, the product of labour is, as it were, a part of the person producing it. The man who transfers it to another alienates a part of his being and subjects himself to the evil powers. Far down into the Middle Ages exchange is protectecf by publicity, completion before witnesses, and the use of symbolic forms.

An autonomous economy of this kind is in the first place dependent upon the *land* under its control. Whether the chief as hunter or fisher appropriates the gifts voluntarily offered by nature, whether he wanders as a nomad with his herds, whether he cultivates the soil as well, or even supports himself by agriculture alone, his daily labour and care will be shaped in every case by the bit of land that he has brought under cultivation. The greater his advancein intelligence and technical skill, and the more methodical and varied the satisfaction of his wants, so much the greater does this dependence become, until finally the soil brings into subjection the man who is

---

[132][Comp. also the early signification of our words *barter, truck,* etc. *New Oxford Diet.*—ED.]

born to rule over it. This has been designated *villenage*.[133] We may here confine ourselves to proving that at this stage the man who has direct possession of the soil can alone maintain economic independence. He who is not in this position can eke out his existence only by becoming the servant of the landowner, and, as such, bound to the soil.

In the independent domestic economy the members of the household have not merely to gather from the soil its products, but they must also by their labour produce all the necessary tools and implements, and, finally, work up and transform the new products and make them fit for use. All this leads to a diversity of employments, and, because of the primitive nature of the tools, demands a varied dexterity and intelligence of which modern civilized man can scarcely form a proper conception.[134] The extent of the tasks falling to the various members of this autonomous household community can be lessened only by division of labour and cooperation among themselves according to age and sex, or according to the strength and natural aptitudes of the individual. It is to this circumstance that we must ascribe that sharp division of domestic production according to sex, which we find universal among primitive peoples. On the other hand, owing to the unproductiveness of early methods of work the simultaneous cooperation of many individuals was in numerous instances necessary to the accomplishment of certain economic ends. Labour in Common still plays, therefore, at this stage, a more important role than division of labour.

To neither, however, would the family have been able to give much scope had it been organized like our modern family, that is, limited to father and mother with children and possibly servants. It

---

[133] *Verdinglichung.*

[134] We must turn to descriptions of early peasant life in remote parts of Europe in order to gain a conception of such conditions. Comp. one example in H. F. Tiebe, *Lief u. Esthlands Ehrenrettung* (Halle, 1804), p. 100. Similar instances are met with still among the Coreans. Thus we read in M. A. Pogio, *Korea* (Vienna and Leipzig, 1895), p. 222: "Throughout Corea the real necessaries of life have been produced within the household from time immemorial. The wife and daughters spin not only hemp but silk. For the latter a silk-bee is usual in many houses. The head of the family must be ready for all tasks, and on occasion play the painter, stone-mason, or joiner. The production of spirits, vegetable fats, and colours, and the manufacture of straw mats, hats, baskets, wooden shoes, and field implements belongs to domestic work. In a word, every one labours for himself and his own requirements. Thanks to these conditions the Corean is a Jack of all trades who undertakes work only for the things that are indispensable, and accordingly never becomes skilled in any special department.

would also have had very little stability or capacity for development if each individual in the family had been free to lead the independent existence of the present day.

Significant is it then that when the present civilized nations of Europe appear on the horizon of history, the tribal constitution prevails among them.[135] The tribes (families, gentes, clans, house communities) are moderately large groups consisting of several generations of blood-relations, which, at first organized according to maternal and later according to paternal succession, have common ownership of the soil, maintain a common household, and constitute a union for mutual protection. Every tribe is thus composed of several smaller groups of relatives, each of which is formed of a man and wife with their children. Anyone living outside this tribe is an outlaw; he has no legal or economic existence, no help in time of need, no avenger if he is slain, no funeral escort when he passes to his last rest.[136]

All the peoples in question, when they took up fixed abodes, were acquainted with the use of the plough. Their settlement came about usually by the establishment of large common dwelling-houses, farms, and villages by the members of a tribe. Once in secure possession of the land the sense of community soon weakened. Smaller patriarchal households with a limited number of members, such as are represented at the present day by the *zadrugas* of the south Slavs, and by the great family of the Russians, Caucasians, and Hindoos, separated from the larger unit. But for centuries the village house-communities continued to own the soil in common, and jointly tilled it probably for some time longer, while each household enjoyed the products apart.

In large family groups of this kind, community and division of

---

[135]Comp. on this point Fustel de Coulanges, *La cité antique* (Paris, 1864); Émile de Laveleye, *De la Propriété* (4th edition, Paris, 1891); E. Grosse, *Die Formen d. Familie u. d. Formen d. Wirthschaft* (Leipzig, 1896), especially Chap. VIII.

[136]Comp. M. Buchner, *Kamerun,* p. 188: "it is a fundamental point in the legal conceptions of the negroes, that not the man himself but the community, the family, the whole body of relatives is the individual before the law. Within the community rights and duties are transferable to an almost unlimited extent. A debtor, a criminal, can be punished in the members of his community, and the liability of the community for the crime of one born a member of it does not lapse even with emigration or separation from it. Even the death penalty can be executed upon one other than the guilty." The same thing is found among the South Sea Islanders. See Parkinson, *Im Bismarck-Archipel,* pp. 80-1.

labour may be carried out to a considerable extent. Men and women, mothers and children, fathers and grandfathers—to each group is allotted its particular part in production and domestic work, and wherever special individual skill displays itself, it finds scope and also a limit, in working for its own tribe. The feelings of brotherhood, of filial obedience, of respect for age, of loyalty and deference reach their most beautiful development in such a community. Just as the tribe pays a debt or weregild for the individual or avenges a wrong done him, so on the other hand does the individual devote his whole life to the tribe and on its behalf subdue every impulse to independent action.

And even when the strength of these feelings declines, the modern separate family with its independent organization does not immediately spring into existence. For its appearance would inevitably have resulted in a diminished capacity for work, an abandonment of the autonomous life of the household, and perhaps a relapse into barbarism. Two ways there were of avoiding this.

One was as follows: for such tasks as surpassed the powers of the now diminished family, the original large tribal unions were continued as local organizations. These formed partial communities on the basis of common property and common usufruct of the same; but, when occasion demanded, they could also undertake duties which, if left to the care of each individual household, would have demanded an unprofitable expenditure of energy, as, for example, guarding the fields and tending cattle. There were also tasks which, though not of equal concern to each separate household of the local group, were nevertheless too difficult for the individual. A house or a ship was to be built, a forest clearing made; a stream diverted, hunting or fishing engaged in at a distance; or perhaps the season of the year made some unusual work necessary for this or that house. In all such cases bidden- labour assisted;[137] that is, among neighbours there sprang up, on invitation of the head of the family, temporary labour communities which disappeared again on the completion of their work. Many institutions of this kind underwent subsequent transformation, others perpetuated themselves. We would recall the labour communities of the Slavic tribes, the *artel* of the Russians, the *tscheta* or *družina* of the Bulgarians, the *moba* of the Serbs, the voluntary assistance rendered by our peasants to each other in house-raising, sheep-shearing, flax-pulling, etc.

---

[137]Comp. *Arbeit u. Rhythmus* (2d ed.), pp. 198 ff. [and Ch. VII, below.—ED.]

Whatever the extent of such contrivances, the part they can play
in the supplying of needs is comparatively un-important,. and just as
little prejudices the economic autonomy of the individual household
as the home production subsisting among our agrarian landlords today affects the supremacy of commerce. These temporary labour
communities, moreover, are not business enterprises, but only expedients for satisfying immediate wants. Assistance is rendered now
to one, now to another of the participants; or the product of the
joint labour is distributed to the separate families for their consumption. A definite case of bargain and sale will be sought for in vain,
even where, as in the village community of India, we have a number
of professional labourers performing communal functions similar to
those of our village shepherds. They work for all and are in return
maintained by all.

The *second* method of avoiding the disadvantages arising from
the dissolution of the tribal communities consisted in the artificial
extension, or numerical maintenance of the family circle. This was
done by the adoption and incorporation of foreign (non-consanguinous)
elements. Thus arose *slavery* and *serfdom*.

We may leave undecided the question whether the enslavement
and setting to work of a captured enemy were more the cause or the
result of the dissolution of the early tribal community. It is certain
that a means was thereby found of maintaining intact the independent household economy with its accustomed division of labour, and
at the same time of making progress towards an increase in the number and variety of wants. For now the more numerous the slaves or
villeins belonging to the household, the more completely could its
labour be united or divided. In agriculture larger areas could be cultivated. Particular technical employments, such as' grinding corn,
baking, spinning, weaving, making implements, or tending cattle,
could be assigned to particular slaves for their whole life; they could
be specially trained for this service. The more prominent the family,
the more wealthy the lord, or the more extensive his husbandry, all
the more possible was it to develop in variety and extent the technical skill employed in the procuring and working up of materials.

The economic life of the Greeks, the Carthaginians, and the Romans was of this character.[138] *Rodbertus*, who noticed this a gen-

---

[138]For students of political economy it need scarcely be observed that in what
follows the object is not to furnish a compendium of the economic history of
ancient times, but, as the context shows, merely an outline of the most highly

eration ago, designates it *oikos husbandry,* because the οἶκος, the house, represents the unit of the economic system. The οἶκος is not merely the dwelling-place, but also the body of people carrying on their husbandry in common. Those belonging to them are the οἰκέ-ται, a word which, in its historic usage, it is significant to note, is confined to the household slaves upon whom the whole burden of the work of the house at that time rested. A similar meaning is attached to the Roman *familia,* the whole body of *famuli,* house-slaves, servants. The *paterfamilias* is the slave-master into whose hands flows the whole revenue of the estate; in the *patria potestas* the two conceptions of the power of the lord as husband and father and as slave-owner have been blended. A member of the household labours not for himself, but only for the *paterfamilias,* who wields the same power of life and death over all.

In the supreme power of the Roman *paterfamilias,* extending as it did equally over all members of the household, whether blood-relatives or not, the independent domestic economy was much more closely integrated and rendered capable of much greater productiv-ity than the matriarchal or even the earlier patriarchal tribe, which consisted solely of blood-relatives. The individual as a separate en-tity has entirely disappeared; the State and the law recognise only family communities, groups of persons, and thus regulate the rela-tions of family to family, not of individual to individual. As to what happens within the household they do not trouble themselves.

In the economic autonomy of the slave-owning family lies the explanation of all the social and a great part of the political history of Rome. There are no separate classes of producers, as such, no farmers, no artisans. There are only large and small proprietors, rich

---

developed domestic economy as it presents itself in the system of slave labour among the ancients. In my work on the insurrections of the unfree labourers between 143 and 129 B.C. (*Die Aufstande d. unfreien Arbeiter, 143-129 v. Chr.,* Fr.-a.-M., 1874), I have shown that before the rise of slave-work on a large scale the economic life of antiquity furnished considerable scope for free labour, the formation of separate trades, and the exchange of goods. What progress had been made in the development of an independent industry, I have set forth in the article "Industry" (Gewerbe) in the Handworterbuch der Staatsw., Ill, pp. 926-7, 929- 931; and in my articles on the Edict of Diocletian on tax prices (*Ztschr. f. d. ges. Staatsw.,* 1894, pp. 200-1) I have endeavoured to fix the position filled by trade in the system of independent domestic economy at the time of the empire in Rome. Reference may also be made, for an outline picture of the times, to the interesting address of M. Weber on *Die sosialen Griinde d. Untergangs d. antiken Cultur,* Die Wahrheit, VI, No. 3.

and poor. If the rich man wrests from the poor possession of the soil, he makes him a proletarian. The landless freeman is practically incapable of making a living. For there is no business capital to provide wages for the purchase of labour; there is no industry outside the exclusive circle of the household. The *artificers* of the early records are not freemen engaged in industry, but artisan slaves who receive from the hands of the agricultural and pastoral slaves the corn, wool, or wood which are to be transformed into bread, clothing, or implements. "Do not imagine that he buys anything," we read in Petronius of the rich *novus homo*, "everything is produced at his own house."[139] Hence that colossal development of *latifundia*, and, concentrated in the hands of individual proprietors, those endless companies of slaves amongst whom the subdivision of labour was so multiplex that their productions and services were capable of satisfying the most pampered taste.

The Dutchman, T. Popma, who in the seventeenth century wrote an able book on the occupations of the Roman slaves, enumerates one hundred and forty-six different designations for the functions of these slave labourers of the wealthy Roman households.[140] This number might today be considerably increased from inscriptions. One must go minutely into the details of this refined subdivision of labour in order to understand the extent and productive power of those gigantic household establishments that placed at the free disposal of the owner goods and services such as today can be supplied only by the numerous business establishments of a metropolitan city in conjunction with the institutions of municipality and State. At the same time this extensive property in human beings afforded a means for the amassing of fortunes equalled only by tfie gigantic

---

[139]Sat. 38: "Nec est quod putes ilium quicquam emere; omnia domi nascuntur." E. Meyer translates that, "everything is grown on his own land"! Now the satirist specifies wool, wax (?), pepper, sheep, honey, mushrooms, mules, and cushions with covers of purple or scarlet. Do all of these things grow from the soil? Compare also Petronius, ch. 48, 52, and 53: "nam et comcedos emeram," etc. That this is all greatly exaggerated it is unnecessary to remind anyone who has really read Petronius. Ch. 50 speaks of the purchase of Corinthian jars; ch. 70 of knives made of Noric iron bought in Rome; ch. 76 of the shops of Trimalchio, who himself gives as his motto the words *bene etno, bene vendo*. But for a satirtist to venture such an exaggeration as Petronius in ch. 38 would have been impossible if Roman economic life had been similar to that of today. A modern satirist in a similar case would have made his boaster give the values of his horses, wines, cigars, his stocks, etc.

[140]Titi Popmse Phrysii de operis servorum liber. Editio novissima. Amstelodami 1672.

possessions of modern millionaires.

The whole body of slaves in the house of a wealthy Roman was divided into two main groups, the *familia rustica* and the *familia urbana*. The *familia rustica* engages in the work of production. On every large country estate there are a manager and an assistant manager with a staff of overseers and taskmasters who in turn have under them a considerable company of field-labourers and vine-dressers, shepherds and tenders of cattle, kitchen and house servants, women spinners, male and female weavers, fullers, tailors, carpenters, joiners, smiths, workers in metal and in the occupations connected with agriculture. On the larger estates each group of labourers is again divided into bands of ten each (*decuriœ*) in charge of a leader or driver (*decurio, monitor*).[141]

The *familia urbana* is divided into the administrative staff, and the staff for the service of master and mistress within and without the house. First comes the superintendent of the revenue with his treasurer, bookkeepers, supervisors of rents, buyers, etc. If the proprietor takes over public leases or engages in the shipping trade, he keeps for that purpose a special staff of slave officials and labourers. Attached to the internal service of the house are house-administrator, porters, attendants in rooms and halls, guardians of the furniture, the plate, and the robes; the commissariat is in charge of the steward, the cellar-master, and the superintendent of supplies; the kitchen, swarms with a great company of cooks, stokers, bakers of bread, cakes, and pastry; special table-setters, carvers, tasters, and butlers serve at the table, while a company of beautiful boys, dancing-girls, dwarfs and jesters amuse the guests. To the personal service of the proprietor are assigned a master of ceremonies for introducing visitors, various valets, bath attendants, anointers, rubbers, surgeons, physicians for almost every part of the body, barbers, readers, private secretaries, etc. For service in the household a savant or philosopher is kept, also architects, painters, sculptors, and musicians; in the library are copyists, parchment-polishers, and bookbinders, who under the direction of the librarian make books in the private manufactory of the house. Even slave letter-writers and stenographers must not be wanting in a wealthy house. When the master appears in public he is preceded by a large body of slaves (*anteambulones*), while others follow him (*pedisequi*); the *nomen-*

---

[141] Comp. the graphic account of work on a Roman estate during the empire, by M, Weber, Die Wahrheit, VI, pp. 65, 66.

clator tells him the name of those whom he meets and who are to be greeted; special *distributores* and *tesserarii* scatter bribes among the people and instruct them how to vote. These are the *camelots* of ancient Rome; and, what gives .them special value, they are the property of the distinguished aspirant employing them. This system for exerting political influence is supplemented by the institution of plays, chariot-races, fights with wild beasts, and gladiatorial games, for which troops of slaves are specially trained. If the lord goes to a province as governor or sojourns on one of his country estates, slave couriers and letter-carriers maintain daily communication with the capital. And how shall we begin to tell of the slave retinue of the mistress, on which Bottiger has written a whole book (*Sabina*), and of the endlessly specialized service for the care and education of the children! It was an incredible squandering of human energy that here took place. Lastly, by means of this many armed organism of independent domestic economy, maintained as it was by a colossal system of breeding and training, the personal power of the slave owner was increased a thousandfold, and this circumstance did much to render it possible for a handful of aristocrats to gain control over half the world.[142]

The work of the State itself is not carried on otherwise. Both in Athens and Rome all subordinate officials and servants are slaves. Slaves build the roads and aqueducts whose construction fell to the State, work in quarries and mines, and clean the sewers; slaves are the policemen, executioners and gaolers, the criers in public assemblies, the distributors of the public doles of corn, the attendants of the colleges of priests in the temples and at sacrifices, the State treasurers, secretaries, the messengers of the magistrates; a retinue of public slaves accompanies every provincial officer or general to the scene of his duties. The means for their support came chiefly from the public domains, the tributes of the provinces (in Athens,

---

[142]Naturally this highly developed slave system is only to be found among the most wealthy class; but with similar conditions it recurs everywhere. Ellis, for example, says in his *History of Madagascar*, I, p. 194: "When a family has numerous slaves, some attend to cattle, others are employed in cultivating exculent roots, others collect fuel; and of the females, some are employed in spinning, weaving and making nets, washing and other domestic occupations" Even in the country of the Muata Yamwo, where, with the exception of smiths, there appear to have been no special craftsmen, the ruler had in his household his own musicians, fetich-doctors, smiths, hairdressers, and female cooks. Pogge, *Im Reiche d. Muata Jamwo*, pp.231, 187.

of the allies), of which Cicero says that they are *quasi prœdia populi Romani*; and finally, from contributions resembling fees.

Similar fundamental features are presented by the economic life of the Latin and Germanic peoples in the early Middle Ages. Here, too, necessary economic progress leads to a further development of the autonomous household economy, which found expression in those large husbandries worked with serfs and villeins upon the extensive landed possessions of the kings, the nobility, and the Church. In its details this m*anorial system* has many points m common with the agricultural system of the later Roman Empire as developed by colonization. It has, also, considerable similarity with the centralized plantation system described above from the closing years of the Roman Republic. This rise of husbandry on a large scale with its subdivision of labour differs, however, in one important particular from the Roman. In Rome large estates engulf the small, and replace the arm of the peasant by that of the slave, who is later on transformed into the colonist. The economic advance involved in the extensive οἶκος husbandry had to be purchased by the proletarizing of the free peasant. In the manorial system of the Middle Ages the free owner of a small estate becomes, it is true, a vassal. But he is not ejected from possession; he preserves a certain personal and economic independence, and, at the same time, shares in the fuller supply of goods which husbandry on a large scale provides under the system of independent domestic economy.

How did this come about?

In ancient Italy the small cultivator was ruined through his inability to support certain public burdens, especially military service, and because the pressure of war and famine drove him into the lamentable servitude of the debtor. In the Germanic and Latin countries of the Middle Ages he placed his homestead for like reasons under the control of the large landed proprietor from whom he received protection and assistance in time of need.

We can best understand the mediaeval manor by picturing to ourselves the economic life of a whole village as a unit with the manorhouse its central point.[143] Under this system the small landowner

---

[143]Though there were numerous villages whose inhabitants owed service to various proprietors, and many manors that included peasant holdings from various villages, yet the case here supposed must be regarded as the normal one. At the same time we must not forget that most of the original evidence relating to these matters that we possess refers to the scattered possessions of the monasteries for which the manors formed the focal points, while for the estates of the great, and

supervises in person, the large landowner through an overseer. The
demesne land lying immediately about the manor-house is cultivated
by serfs permanently attached to it, who there find food and lodging,
and are employed in agricultural and industrial production, household duties, and the personal service of the lord, under a many-sided
division of labour. The demesne land is intermixed with the holdings of a larger or smaller number of unfree peasants, each of whom
tills his hide of land independently, while all share with the lord the
use of pasture, wood, and water. At the same time, however, every
peasant-holding binds its occupant to perform certain services and
to furnish certain dues in natural products to the estate. These services consist of labour reckoned at first according to requirement,
later according to time, whether given in the fields at seed-time or
harvest, on the pasture-land, in the vineyard, garden or forest, or in
the manorial workshops or the women's building where the daughters of the serfs are spinning, weaving, sewing, baking, brewing beer,
etc. On the days devoted to manorial service the unfree labourers
receive their meals at the manor-house just as do the manor-folk
themselves. They are further bound to keep in repair the enclosures about the manor-house and its fields, to keep watch over the
house, and to undertake the carrying of messages and the transport
of goods. The dues in kind to be paid to the estate are partly agricultural products, such as grain of all kinds, wool, flax, honey, wax,
wine, cattle, hogs, fowl, or eggs; partly wood cut in the forests of
the mark and made ready for use, such as firewood, timber, vine-
stakes, torchwood, shingles, staves and hoops; partly the products
of industry, such as woollen and linen cloth, stockings, shoes, bread,
beer, casks, plates, dishes, goblets, iron, pots and knives. This pre-

still more so for those of the smaller temporal proprietors in ancient times, we
have scarcely any material at all. For these, however, our supposed case is to be
regarded as normal in so far as the villages arose through a colony grouping itself
about a single estate. For the purposes of our sketch we may also leave out of
view the many distinctions in the legal position of those owing rent and service
dues, especially the distinction between those belonging to the manor and those
belonging to the mark. The latter, by virtue of the lord's supreme proprietorship
over the common land, were also included in the economic system of the manor.
Finally, I do not fail to appreciate the difference between the constitution of
the villas of Charles the Great and the later administrative organization of the
large landowners, though I am of the opinion that the latter has only superficial
points of contact with the economic life of the individual farm. For all further
details I must refer the reader to Maurer, *Gesch. d.* Fronhofe; Inama-Sternegg,
Die Ausbildung d. grossen Grund kerrschaften in Deutschland; and Lamprecht,
Deutsches Wirtschaftsleben im M. A., especially I, pp. 719 ff.

supposes alike among the serfs and those bound by feudal service a certain specialization of industry, that would of necessity hereditarily attach to the hides of land in question and prove advantageous not merely to the lord's estate, but also to the occupants of the hides in supplying commodities. Intermediate between service and rent are duties of various kinds, such as hauling manure from the peasant's farm to the fields of the lord, keeping cattle over winter, providing entertainment for the guests of the manor. On the other hand the lord renders economic assistance to the peasant by keeping breeding-stock, by establishing ferries, mills, and ovens for general use, by securing protection from violence and injustice to all, and by giving succour from his stores, in accordance with his pledge, when crops failed or other need arose.

We have here a small economic organism quite sufficient unto itself, which avoids the rigid concentration of the Roman slave estates and employs slaves only to the extent necessary for the private husbandry of the landlord conceived in its strictest sense.[144] For this reason it is able to secure to the general body of manorial labourers separate agricultural establishments for their own domestic needs, and therewith a certain personal independence. This is an instance of small partial private estates within the economy of the independent household similar to that which occurs, though of course on a much smaller scale, within the zadruga of the South Slavs when conjugal couples establish separate households.[145] When the manorial group coincides in membership with the people of a mark, the members are in a certain sense, owing to the regulations forbidding the alienation of land or mark servitudes to non-residents, economically shut off from their neighbours. Internal unity is realized by means of separate weights and measures, which, however, serve not for safeguarding trade, but for measuring the dues in kind coming to the lord.

For we must always bear in mind that the economic relation of the lord to those attached to his land, however much it may be regarded from the general point of view of mutual service, is entirely removed from the class of economic relations that arise from a sys-

---

[144] According to Lamprecht, I, p. 782, the field labour-services of the serfs were applied to the cultivation of the individual stretches of manorial land (*Beunden*) or balks [unploughed strips] i,n the common land, while the manorial serfs were employed only for the cultivation of the demesne.
[145] Comp. Laveleye, as above, p. 468.

tem of exchange. Here there are no prices, no wages for labour, no land or house rent, no profits on capital, and accordingly neither entrepreneurs nor wage-workers. We have in this case peculiar economic processes and phenomena to which historical political economy must not do violence, after such frequent complaints of harsh treatment in the past at the hands of jurisprudence.

The surpluses of the manorial husbandry are the property of the lord. They consist entirely of goods for consumption which cannot be long stored up or turned into capital. On the estates of the king they are devoted as a rule to supplying the needs of the royal household, and the king, travelling with his retinue from castle to castle, claims them in person; while the large landed proprietors among the religious corporations and the higher nobility have them forwarded by a well-organized transport of their villeins to their chief seats, where as a rule they are likewise consumed.

Thus in this economic system we have many of the phenomena of commerce, such as weights and measures, the carriage of persons, news, and goods, hostelries, and the transference of goods and services. In all, however, there is lacking the characteristic feature of economic exchange, namely, the direct connection of each single service with its reciprocal service, and the freedom of action on the part of the individual units carrying on trade with one another.

But it matters not to what extent independent household economy may be developed through the introduction of slave or villein labour, it will never succeed even in its highest development, to say nothing of its less perfect forms, in adapting itself sufficiently to the needs of human society for all time. Here we have continuously unfilled gaps in supply, there surpluses which are not consumed on the estates producing them, or fixed instruments of production and skilled labour which cannot be fully utilized.

Out of this state of things arise fresh commercial phenomena of a particular kind. The landlord, whose harvest has failed, borrows corn and straw from his neighbour until the next harvest, when he returns an equal quantity. The man reduced to distress through fire or the loss of his cattle is assisted by the others on the tacit understanding that he will show the like favour in the like event. If anyone has a particularly expert slave, he lends him to a neighbour, just as he would a horse, a vessel, or a ladder; in this case the slave is fed by the neighbour. The owner of a wine-press, a maltkiln, or an oven allows his poorer fellow villager the temporary use of it, in return for which the latter, on occasion, makes a rake, helps at sheep-shearing, or runs some errand. It is a mutual rendering of assistance; and no one will think of classifying such occurrences under the head of exchange.[146]

Finally, however, real exchange does appear. The transition-stage is formed of such processes as the following: the owner of slaves lends his neighbour a slave weaver or carpenter, and receives in return a quantity of wine or wood of which his neighbour has a surplus. Or the slave shoemaker or tailor, whose labour cannot be fully turned to account, is settled upon a holding, on the condition that he work each year a certain number of days at the manor. At times when he has no labour dues to pay and little to do on his own land, he gives his fellow villeins in their peasant houses the benefit of his skill, receiving from them his keep, and in addition a quantity of bread or bacon for his family. Formerly he was merely the servant of the manor; now he is successively the servant of all, but of each only for a short time.[147] At an early stage barter in kind, aiming at a mutual levelling of wants and surpluses, is also met with, as corn for wine, a horse for grain, a piece of linen cloth for a quantity of salt. This trading process expands owing to the limited occurrence of many natural products and to the localization of the production of goods for which there is a large demand; and if the various household establishments are small, and the adjoining districts markedly dissimilar in natural endowments, it may attain quite a development.[148] Certain articles of this trade become, as has often been described, general mediums of exchange, such as skins, woollen goods, mats, cattle, articles of adornment, and finally the precious metals. Money comes into existence, markets and peddling trade arise; the beginnings of buying and selling on credit appear.

But all this affects only the surface of the independent household economy;, and, though the literature on the early history of trade

---

[146] On the social duty of lending among primitive peoples, comp. Kubary, *Ethnogr. Beiträge z. Kenntnis d. Karolinen-Archipels*, p. 163.

[147] On the corresponding conditions in Greece and Rome, comp. my accounts in the Handwort. d. Staatswiss. (2d ed.), IV, pp. 369-71.

[148] To this circumstance is to be ascribed the relatively highly developed weekly market trade of ancient Greece and of the negro countries of today; in Oceania the small size of the islands and the unequal development among their inhabitants of both household work and agriculture even calls forth in places an active maritime trade. Similarly is the oftcited maritime commerce of the ancient Greeks to be regarded.

and of markets has hitherto been far from familiarizing us with a proper estimate of these things, yet it cannot be too strongly emphasized that neither among the peoples of ancient times nor in the early Middle Ages were the articles of daily use the subject of regular exchange. Rare natural products, and locally manufactured goods of a high specific value form the few articles of commerce. If these become objects of general demand, as amber, metal implements, ceramic products, spices and ointments in ancient times, or wine, salt, dried fish, and woollen wares in the Middle Ages, then undertakings must arise aiming at the production of a surplus of these articles. This means that the other husbandries will produce beyond their own immediate requirements the trade equivalents of those articles as do the northern peoples their skins and *vadhmâl*, and the modern Africans their wares of bark and cotton, their kola nuts and their bars of salt. Where the population concentrates in towns there may even come into being an active market trade in the necessaries of life, as is seen in classic antiquity, and in many negro countries of today. In fact even the carrying on of industry and trade as a vocation is to a certain extent possible.

Still this does not affect the inner structure of economic life. The labour of each separate household continues to receive its impulse and direction from the wants of its own members; it must itself produce what it can for the satisfaction of these wants. Its only regulator is utility. "That landlord is a worthless fellow," says the elder Pliny, "who buys what his own husbandry can furnish him"; and this principle held good for many centuries after.

One must not be led away from a proper conception of this economic stage by the apparently extensive use of money in early historic times. Money is not merely a medium of exchange, it is also a measure of value, a medium for making payments and for storing up wealth. Payments must also constantly be made apart from trade, such as fines, tribute money, fees, taxes, indemnities, gifts of honour or hospitality; and these are originally paid in products of one's own estate, as grain, dried meat, cloth, salt, cattle, and slaves, which pass directly into the household of the recipient. Accordingly all earlier forms of money, and for a long time the precious metals themselves, circulate in a form in which they can be used by the particular household either for the immediate satisfaction of its wants or for the acquisition by trade of other articles of consumption. Those of special stability of value are preeminently serviceable

81

in the formation of a treasure. This is especially true of the precious metals, which in time of prosperity assumed the form of rude
articles of adornment, and as quickly lost it in time of adversity.
Finally, it is manifest that the office of a measure of value can be
performed by metal money even when sales are actually made in
terms of other commodities, as is shown by the use in ancient Egypt
of *uten*, a piece of wound copper wire according to which prices were
fixed, while payment was made in the greatest variety of needful articles.[149] This is also shown by numerous mediaeval records in which,
far beyond the epoch here under review, prices are fixed partly in
money and partly in horses, dogs, wine, grain, etc., or the purchaser
is left at liberty to make a money payment "in what he can" {*in quo
potuerit*).[150]

Lamprecht, discussing economic life in France in the eleventh
century, affirms that purchases were made only in cases of want;[151]
the same holds m the main for sales as well. Exchange is an element
foreign to independent household economy, and its entrance was re-
sisted as long and as stubbornly as possible. Purchase always means
purchase with immediate payment, and it is attended with solemn
and cumbrous formalities. The earliest municipal law of Rome pre-
scribes that the purchase must take place before five adult Roman
citizens as witnesses. The rough copper that measures the price is
weighed out to the seller by a trained weigh-master (*libripens*), while
the purchaser makes a solemn declaration as he takes possession of
the purchased article. Contrasting with this the formal minuteness
of early German trade laws, we are easily convinced that in the
economic period which witnessed the creation of this rigid legal for-
malism buying and selling, and the renting of land or house, could
not be everyday affairs. Exchange value accordingly exercised no
deep or decisive influence on the internal economy of the separate
household. The latter knew only production for its own requirements; or, when such production fell short, the practice of making

---

[149]Erman, *Aegypten u.ägypt. Leben im Altertum*, pp. 179, 657.
[150]Under similar circumstances the same is true today. "Throughout West,
Central, and East Africa quite definite and often quite complex standards for
the exchange of goods have been formed, just as among ourselves, but with this
difference, that coined money is generally wanting. This, however, by no means
prevents the existence of a system of intermediate values, though it be but as
notions and names."—Buchner, *Kamerun*, p. 93.
[151]*Französ. Wirtschaftsleben*, p. 132. Comp. further his *Deutsches
Wirtschaftsleben im M. A.*, II, pp. 374 ff.

gifts with the expectation of receiving others in return, of borrowing needful articles and implements, and, if need be, of plundering. The development of hospitality, the legitimizing of begging, the union of nomadic life and early sea trade with robbery, the extraordinary prevalence of raids on field and cattle among primitive agricultural peoples, are accordingly the usual concomitants of the independent household economy.

From what has been said it will be clear that under this method of satisfying needs the fundamental economic phenomena must be dissimilar to those of modern national economy. Wants, labour, production, means of production, product, stores for use, value in use, consumption— these few notions exhaust the circle of economic phenomena in the regular course of things. As there is no *social* division of labour, there are consequently no professional classes, no industrial establishments, no capital in the sense of a store of goods devoted to acquisitive purposes. Our classification of capital into business and trade capital, loan and consumption capital, is entirely excluded. If, conformably to widely accepted usage, the expression capital is restricted to means of production, then it must in any case be limited to tools and implements, the so called fixed capital. What modern theorists usually designate circulating capital is in the independent household economy merely a store of consumption goods in process of preparation, unfinished or half-finished products. In the regular course of affairs, moreover, there are no sale goods, no price, no circulation of commodities, no distribution of income, and, therefore, no labour wages, no earnings of management, and no interest as particular varieties of income.[152] Rent alone begins to differentiate itself from the return from the soil, still appearing, however, only in combination with other elements of income.

Perhaps, indeed, it is improper at this stage to speak of income at all. What we call income is normally the fruit of commerce; in

---

[152]For most of the conceptions here mentioned there are no expressions in Greek or Latin. They must be expressed by circumlocutions or by very general terms. This is true, in teh first instance, of the conception *income* itself. The Latin *reditus* denotes the returns from the land. Tacitus makes use of a similar liberty when (*Ann.*,IV, 6, 3) he designates the revenues of the state as *fructus publici*. Compare with this the numerous and finely distinguished expressions for the conception *wealth*. Merces means not only wages, but also land-rent, house-rent, interest, price. So also the Greek μισθός For the expressions vocation, occupation, undertaking, industry, neither of the classic languages has corresponding terms.

independent domestic economy it is the sum of the consumption goods produced, the gross return. This return, however, is all the more inseparable from general wealth the more the subjection of the husbandry to the hazard of the elements compels the accumulation of a store of goods. Income and wealth form indistinguishable parts of a whole, one part of which is ever moving upward towards availability for use, another part downward to consumption, while a third is stored up in chest and box, in cellar or storehouse, as a kind of assurance fund.

To the last belongs money. In so far as it is used in trade it is for the recipient as a rule not a provisional but a final equivalent. It plays its chief part not as an intermediary of exchange, but as a store of value and as a means of measuring and transferring values. Loans from one economic unit to another do indeed take place; but as a rule they bear no interest, and are made only for purposes of consumption. Productive credit is incompatible with this economic system. Where money-lending on interest intrudes itself it appears unnatural, and, as we know from Greek and Roman history, is ultimately ruinous to the debtor. The canonical prohibition of usury thus had its origin not in moral or theological inclination, but in economic necessity.

Where a direct state tax arose, it was regularly a tax on wealth, generally a species of land-tax. Such was the Athenian εἰσΦορά, the Roman *tributum civium*, and the scot or the bede of the Middle Ages. Along with these demand was made upon the wealth of the individual for direct services to the State or community, such as the furnishing of ships, the institution of festivals and entertainments (liturgies). The idea of taxing income, however natural and selfevident it may appear to us, would have been simply inconceivable to our ancestors.

By a process extending over centuries this independent household economy is transformed into the *system of direct exchange*; in the place of production solely for domestic use steps custom production. We have designated this Stage *town economy*, because it reached its typical development in the towns of the Germanic and Latin countries during the Middle Ages. Still it must not be forgotten that even in ancient times beginnings of such a development are perceptible, and that at a later date they also appeared in the more advanced Slavic countries, albeit in considerably divergent form. The transition to this economic stage is seen at the stage of domestic economy itself in the loss by the separate household, founded upon the cultivation of the soil, of a part of its independence through inability longer to satisfy all its needs with its own labour, and through the necessity of permanent and regular reinforcement from the products of other estates. Yet there do not spring up at once establishments independent of the soil, whose members would derive their income entirely from the working up of industrial commodities for others, or the professional performance of services, or the conducting of exchange. On the contrary, each proprietor still seeks, as far as possible, to gain his livelihood from the land; if his wants go beyond this, he calls into requisition any special manual skill he may possess, or any particular productive advantage of his district, whether in field, forest, or water, in order to produce a surplus of some particular article. One will produce grain, another wine, a third salt, a fourth fish, a fifth linen or some other product of domestic industry. In this manner separate establishments come into existence specially developed in some one direction, and dependent upon a regular, reciprocal barter of their surplus products. This exchange does not at first demand an organized system of trade. But it does require more flexible commercial methods than were offered by the early laws. These are furnished by *markets* which still arise, in the main, under the household system.

A market is the coming together of a large number of buyers and sellers in a definite place and at a definite time. Whether this occur in connection with religious feasts and other popular gatherings, or whether it owes its origin to the favourable commercial situation of a locality, it is always an opportunity for producer and consumer to meet with their mutual trade requirements; and such in its general features it has remained down to the present day. Markets and fixed trade are mutually exclusive. Where a merchant class exists, no markets are needed; where there are markets, merchants are superfluous. Only in cases where a country must import articles for which there is a demand and which it does not itself produce can there be developed at the early stage of household economy a distinct though not very numerous class, uniting under their control the purchase, transport, and sale of these goods, and utilizing for this last purpose the trade opportunities presented by the markets.

What changes, then, were wrought in this condition of things by the mediaeval town, and in what does the economic system which we have designated as exclusive town economy consist?

85

The mediaeval town is, above all things a *burg*, that is, a place fortified with walls and moats which serves as a refuge and shelter for the inhabitants of the unprotected places round about. Every town thus presupposes the existence of a defensive union which forms the rural settlements lying within a greater or narrower radius into a sort of military community with definite rights and duties. It devolves upon all the places belonging to this community to cooperate in maintaining inlact the town fortifications by furnishing workmen and horses, and in time of war in defending them with their arms. In return they have the right, whenever occasion arises, to shelter themselves, their wives and children, their cattle and movables, within its walls. This right is called the *right of burgess*, and he who enjoys it is a burgher (*burgensis*).

Originally the permanent inhabitants of the town differ in nowise, not even in their occupations, from those living in the rural hamlets. Like the latter they follow farming and cattle raising; they use wood, water, and pasture in common; their dwellings, as may still be seen in the structural arrangement of many old cities, are farmhouses with barns and stables and large yards between. But their communal life is not exhausted in the regulation of common pasturage and other agricultural interests. They are, so to speak, a permanent garrison stationed in the burg, and perform in rotation the daily watch service on tower and at gate. Whoever wishes to settle permanently in the town must therefore not only be possessed of land, or a house at least; he must also be provided with weapons and armour.

The sentinel service and the extensive area of the town rendered necessary by the law of burgess demanded a great number of men; and soon the town limits no longer sufficed for their maintenance. Then it was that the one sided development of the household establishments, already described, lent its influence, and the town became the seat of the industries and of the markets as well. In the latter the country peasant continued to dispose of his surplus supplies, obtaining from the townsman that which he himself could no longer provide and which the latter now exclusively or almost exclusively produced, namely, industrial products.

The burgess rights underwent a consequent extension. All who enjoyed them were exempt from market dues and town tolls. The right of free purchase and sale in the town market is thus in its origin an emanation from the rights of burgess. In this way the military defensive union became a territorial economic community based upon mutual and direct exchange of agricultural and industrial products by the respective producers and consumers.

All market traders on their way to and from a market enjoyed—doubtless also in the period previous to the rise of towns—a particularly active royal protection, which was further extended to the market itself and to the whole market-town. The effects of this market peace were to secure the market tradesmen during the time of their sojourn in the town against legal prosecution for debts previously incurred, and to visit injuries inflicted upon their property or person with doubly severe punishment as being extraordinary breaches of the peace. The market tradesmen are commonly known as *Kaufleute, mercatores, negotiatores, emptores.*[153]

---

[153]Recent literature relating to the origin of the constitution of German towns has overlooked the very wide significance of the word *Kaufmann* and imagined that the innumerable towns existing within the German Empire towards the close of the Middle Ages, from Cologne and Augsburg down to Medebach and Radolfzell, were inhabited by merchants in the modern sense of the term, that is, by a specialized class of professional tradesmen, who are as a rule still represented as wholesale merchants. All economic history revolts against such a conception. What did these people deal in, and in what did they make payment for their wares? Besides, the very terms used are opposed to it. The most prominent characteristic of the professional merchant in his relation to the public is not his custom of buying, but of selling. Yet the chapman (Kaufmann) of the Middle Ages is named from the word for buying—kaufen. In the State records of Otto III. for Dortmund from 990 to 1000 A.D. the *emptores Trotmannia*, whose municipal laws, like those of Cologne and Mainz, are said to serve as a model for other cities, are spoken of in the same connection as *mercatores* or *negotiatores* in other records. If the abbot of Reichenau in the year 1075 can with a stroke of the pen transform the peasants of Allensbach and their descendants into merchants (*ut ipsi et eorurn posteri sint mercatores*), no possible ingenuity of interpretation can explain this if we have in mind professional tradesmen. That in point of fact merchant meant any man who sold wares in the market, no matter whether he himself had produced them or bought the greater part of them, is evident, for example, from an unprinted declaration of the Council of Frankfurt in 1420 regarding the toll called Marktrecht (in Book No. 3 of the Municipal Archives, Fol. 80). There we find at the beginning that this toll is to be paid by "every merchant who stands on the street with his merchandise, whatsoever it be." Then follow, specified in detail, the individual "merchants" or the "merchandise" affected by this toll. From the lengthy list the following instances may be given: dealers in old clothes, pastry books, food-vendors, ropemakers, hazelnut sellers, egg and cheese sellers with their carts, poultry vendors who carry about their baskets on their backs, strangers having in their possession more than a malter of cheese, cobblers, money-changers, bakers who use the market-stalls, strangers with bread-carts, geese, wagons of vitch (fodder), straw, hay, cabbages, all vendors of linen, flax, hemp, yarn, who sell their wares upon the street. Here we have a confused medley of small tradesmen of the town, artisans and peasants. That buyers as well as sellers on the market were

Inasmuch as the town inhabitants were themselves peculiarly dependent upon the market for their buying and selling, the specific name of market people or merchants was more and more applied to them as the importance of the market as their source of supply increased. Proportionately with this change, however, the region from which this market drew its supplies and to which it sold extended farther into the country. No longer did it coincide with the domain of burgess rights, whose importance for the rural population must of itself have diminished with the increasing security of the whole country against external attack. On the other hand, with the growth of the industries the whole town, and not merely the space originally set apart for the exclusive purpose, became the market; market-peace became town peace, and for the maintenance of the latter the town was separated from the general state administration as a special judicial district. "City air makes free" became a principle. Thus arose a social and legal gulf between burgher and peasant which the thirteenth and fourteenth centuries vainly sought to bridge over by an extramural and intramural citizenship. The name burgher was finally restricted to the members of the community settled within the town limits; and the times lent to this title a legal and moral significance in which the state idea of the ancient Greeks appeared to have returned to life.

We cannot here occupy ourselves further either with the development of the municipal constitution and its self administration based upon corporative gradations, or with the political power which the towns of Germany, France, and Italy obtained in the later Middle Ages. We have to do only with the matured economic organization of which these towns formed the central points.

If we take a map of the old German Empire and mark upon it the places that, up to the close of the Middle Ages, had received grants of municipal rights—there were probably some three thousand of them—we see the country dotted with towns at an average distance of four to five hours' journey in the south and west, and in the north and east of seven to eight. All were not of equal importance; but the majority of them in their time were, or at least endeavoured to be, the economic centres for their territory, leading just as independent an existence as the manor before them. In order to form a conception

---

designated as *Kaufleute* (merchants) is evident from numerous records; in fact, passages might be cited in which, when the merchant is spoken of, it is the buyer that seems to be chiefly meant.

of the size of these districts, let us imagine the whole country evenly
divided among the existing municipalities. In this way each town in
southwestern Germany has on the average forty to somewhat over
fifty square miles, in the central and northeastern parts between
sixty and eighty-five, and in the eastern from somewhat over one
hundred to one hundred and seventy. Let us imagine the town as
always situated in the centre of such a section of country, knd it
becomes plain that in almost every part of Germany the peasant
from the most distant rural settlement was able to reach the town
market in one day, and be home again by nightfall.[154]

The whole body of municipal market law, as formulated in early
times by the lords of the town and later by the town councillors,
is summed up in the two principles, *that, as far as at all possible,
sales must be public and at first hand, and that everything which
can be produced within the town itself shall be produced there.* For
products of local manufacture intermediary trade was forbidden to
everyone, even to the artisans; it was permitted with imported goods
only when they had already been vainly offered on the market. The
constant aim was to meet amply and at a just price the wants of
the home consumers, and to give full satisfaction to the foreign customers of local industry.

The territory from which supplies were drawn for the town market, and that to which it furnished commodities, was identical. The
inhabitants of the country brought in victuals and raw materials,
and with what they realized paid for the labour of the town craftsmen, either in the direct form of wage-work or in the indirect form
of finished products, which had been previously ordered or were selected in the open market from the artisan's stand. Burgher and
peasant thus stood in the relationship of mutual customers: what

---

[154] Although since the Middle Ages many places have lost their town franchises,
while others have gained them for the first time, yet the number of places that
today bear the name of town (Stadt) furnishes a pretty correct idea of what it
then was. There is in Baden at present one city to every 132 square kilometres
of territory [1 sq. km.=about $\frac{2}{5}$ sq. mile], in Wiirtemberg to 134, in Alsace-
Lorraine to 137, in Hesse to 118, in the kingdom of Saxony to 105, in Hesse-
Nassau to 145, in the Rhine Province to 193, in Westphalia to 196, in the province
of Saxony to 175, in Brandenburg to 291, in the kingdom of Bavaria to 328,
in Hanover to 341, in Schleswig-Holstein to 350, in Pomerania to 412, in West
Prussia to 473, and in East Prussia to 552. The fever for founding municipalities,
which racked many mediaeval rulers, called into existence a multitude of towns
that lacked vitality. Well known is the prohibition in the *Sachsenspiegel* that
"No market shall be founded within a mile of another." Weiske, III, 66, § 1.

the one produced the other always needed; and a large part of this exchange trade was performed without the mediation of money, or in such a way that money was introduced only to adjust differences in value.

Town handicraft had an exclusive right of sale on the market. The productions of other places were admitted only when the industry in question had no representatives within the town. They were usually offered for sale by the foreign producers at the annual fairs; at this one point the spheres of the various town markets overlap. But even here the most essential feature, the direct sale by producer to consumer, is also observed, though only in exceptional instances. If a trade capable of supporting a craftsman was not represented in the town, the council called in a skilled master workman from outside and .induced him to settle by exemption from taxation and other privileges. If he required considerable initial capital, the town itself came to his aid, and at its own expense built work and sale-shops and established mills, grinding-works, cloth-frames, bleaching-places, dye-houses, fulling-mills, etc.,—all with a view to satisfying the greatest possible variety of wants by home production.

Although direct dealing with the consumer of his. wares[155] tended necessarily to keep alive in the artisan a sense of personal responsibility, an effort was made to brace this moral relationship by special ordinances. Handwork is an office that must be administered for the general welfare. The master shall furnish "honest" work. So far as the personal services of the craftsman remained available to his customers, a regular rate was fixed governing the amount he could claim in wages and board while on his itinerancy. In cases where the customer furnished him with the raw material in his own home, as, for instance, tin to the pewterer, silver and gold to the goldsmith, or yarn to the weaver, provision was made that it should not be adulterated. Where, on the contrary, the artisan supplied the material there were erected in the market, about the churches, at the town gates, or in particular streets, public sale-booths which often served also as work-shops (bread stands, meat stalls, drapers' and cloth shops, furriers' booths, shoemakers' benches, etc.). It was a market rule that those vending the same wares should do their selling alongside one another in open and mutual competition and under

---

[155] Here and there this was further secured by the regulation that not even the wife of the craftsman might represent him in selling. Comp. Gramich, *Verf. u. Verw. d. St. Wurzburg vom.* XIII. *vis* XV. *Jhdt.*, pp. 38 f.

the supervision of the market wardens and overseers, and this rule was extended to craftsmen who merely worked at home on orders, in that for the most part they lived side by side on the same street. Many cities have preserved to the present day the remembrance of this condition of things in the names of their streets (such as Shoemaker, Turner, Weaver, Cooper, Butcher, Fisher Streets), many of which led directly into the old market square. In this way the greatest part of the town, or even the whole of it, bore the outward aspect of one large market. It is well known that the many prescriptions regarding the raw material to be used, the method of doing work, the length and breadth of cloths, and the direct regulation of prices must have served' for the protection of the consumer.[156]

Just as the urban craftsman enjoyed within the town and the extramural judicial district (*Bannmeile*) the exclusive right of selling the products of his handicraft, so the urban consumer possessed for the same area the exclusive right to purchase imported commodities. This right can be exercised, to be sure, only when the imported goods actually come to market and stand on sale for the proper length of time. To effect this a law of staple is introduced; foreselling in the country places or before the town gates is forbidden; selling to middlemen, artisans, and strangers is permitted only after the consumers are supplied, and then usually with the limitation that the latter, if they so wish, may have a share; and lastly, the withdrawing of goods once brought to market was forbidden, or permitted only after they had remained three days unsold.[157]

But against the *foreign seller* there always prevails a deep-rooted mistrust. To this is due the existence of that peculiar system of exchange through official intermediaries, measurers, and weighers. Today the State controls weights and measures by official standards and public inspections, and leaves the terms to the buyers and sellers themselves. In the Middle Ages the technical means for constructing exact measures and ensuring their accuracy were wanting. Common field-stones—and at the Frankfurt fairs as late as the fifteenth century even wooden blocks—were usefd as weights. In order, however, to determine accurately the amount of goods exchanged, the handling of the measures was withdrawn from the parties themselves

---

[156]For the sake of brevity we refer for all details in this connection to Stieda in the Jhb. f. N.-Ök. u. Statistik, XXVII, pp. 91 ff.

[157]These ordinances were most carefully wrought out for the corn trade. See Schmoller, Jhb. f. Gesetzg. Verw. u. Volksw., XX, pp. 708 ff.

and entrusted to special officers, whose presence was made obliga-
tory at every sale made by an outsider. It was the duty of these
intermediaries to bring buyer and seller together, to assist in fixing
the price, to test the goods for possible defects, to select for the purchaser the quantity he had bought, and to see to its proper delivery.
The intermediary was forbidden to trade for himself; he was not
even allowed at the departure of the foreign tradesman, whom he
generally lodged, to purchase remnants of goods remaining unsold.

This system of direct exchange is found, though with many local
peculiarities, carried out to the most minute details in all mediaeval towns. This means that the actual circumstances in which its
principles were developed render it inevitable. How far it was really
practicable can only be decided when we are able to determine what
proportions *trade* assumed under it

It is beyond question that a *retail trade* had taken root in the
towns. To it belonged all who "sell pennyworths for the poor man."
To understand this, we must bear in mind that all well-to-do towns-
people were accustomed to purchase their supplies directly from foreign merchants at the weekly and yearly markets. The poor man
was unable to make provision for any length of time; he lived, as he
does today, "from hand to mouth." For him the retail tradesman,
accordingly, undertook the keeping of stores for daily sale.

We can distinguish three groups of such small tradesmen, namely,
grocers, peddlers, and cloth-dealers. In the earlier half of the period
of town economy the last were the most important, as in many
towns there was no local wool-weaving done. With its development
their activity was limited to the handling of the finer kinds of Dutch
cloths, silks, and cottons, or else they made room for the weavers in
their shops.

The *wholesale* trade was exclusively itinerant and market or fair
trade; and down to the close of the Middle Ages the majority of
the towns probably saw no merchants settled within their walls who
carried on wholesale trade from permanent headquarters. Only commodities not produced within the more or less extensive district from
which a town drew its supplies were the subject of wholesale trade.
We know of but five kinds: (1) spices and southern fruits, (2) dried
and salted fish, which were then a staple food of the people, (3) furs,
(4) fine cloths, (5) for the North German towns, wine. In certain
parts of Germany salt would also have to be included. In most cases,
however, the town council ordered it in large quantities directly from

the places of production, stored it in, the municipal salt warehouses, and after a monopolistic advance of its price gave it out to be disposed of by peddler and saltman, who paid a fee for the privilege. Usually the foreign wholesale dealers[158] were permitted to sell their wares only in large lots or in minimum quantities—in the case of spices, for example, not under 12½ pounds. The local retailers and peddlers then carried on the sale in detail. This also holds good for many large producers, as, for instance, hammersmiths, who might sell to founders the iron they had failed to persuade smiths and private individuals to buy.

Though the limits of the territory from which the market of a mediaeval town drew its supplies and to which its sales were made cannot be determined with precision, seeing that they varied for different wares, yet from the economic point of view they formed none the less an independent region. Each town with its surrounding country constituted an autonomous economic unit within which its whole course of economic life was on an independent footing. This independence is based upon special currency, and special weights and measures for each locality. The relation between town and country is as a matter of fact a compulsory relation such as that between the head and the limbs of the body, and it displays strong tendencies to assume the forms of legalized compulsion. The extramural jurisdiction of the town, the prohibitions of export and import already met with, the differential tolls, and the direct acquisition of territory on the part of the large towns plainly point in that direction.

Many as are the objections which may be urged against deducing the constitution of the town from that of the manor, the economic system of the town can be properly understood and explained only as a continuation of the manorial system. What existed in the latter in mere germs and beginnings grew into finished organisms and systems of organisms; factors that under the independent household economy were found grouped in primitive shapelessness, have now been differentiated by subdivision and made independent. The

---

[158]In Jhh. f. Nat.-Ök. u. Stat., 3 F., XX (1900), pp. 1 ff., G. v. Below attempts to prove that in the Middle Ages there existed no class of wholesale merchants, and that the characteristic feature of those times was for wholesale and retail trade to be carried on by the same person. He therefore takes exception to our use of the term wholesale merchant. I cannot, however, see why when these persons appeared as wholesalers they should not receive the name, particularly as there is no evidence to show that wholesale merchants were ever met with who were not at the same time retail traders.

forced division of labour of the manor has broadened into a free
division of production between peasants and burghers, displaying
morever among the latter a varied multiplicity of separate trades.
The manorial workman carrying on domestic labour has become
the wage earning craftsman, who in time comes to possess his own
business capital in addition to his tools. The vital thread connecting manorial and cottier economy has at length been severed; the
separate household establishments have gained an independent existence; trade between them is no longer conducted on the basis of
a general return, but on the basis of a specific payment for services
given and received. To be sure they have not yet fully emancipated
themselves from the soil, even in the town; production is still dependent in large measure upon the domestic husbandry; but there
have been formed the distinct *vocations* of agriculturalist, artisan,
and tradesman which have given a specific direction to the activities
and lives of those following them. Society has become differentiated;
classes now exist; and these were unknown before.

The whole circle of economic life has gained in fulness and variety
in comparison with the independent domestic economy; the membership of the separate household establishments has become smaller;
the individuals are interdependent; they undertake certain functions
for each other; exchange value is already forcing its way as a determining factor into their inner life. But the producing community
still coincides with the consuming community; the handicraftsman's
assistants drawn from outside, and even the tradesmen, are members
of their employer's household, subject to his disciplinary control. He
is their "master," they are his "servants."

And still, as ever, by far the greater proportion of commodities does not pass beyond the lintels of the place of production. A
small part finds its way by the process of exchange into other establishments, but the way travelled is a very short one, namely, from
producer to consumer. There is no *circulation of goods*. The sole
exceptions are the articles of foreign trade few in number, and of
the petty retail trade. They alone became wares. They alone must
frequently take on the form of money before reaching their domestic
destination. But here we deal with an exception to the system of direct exchange, not with a constituent element of the whole economic
order.

Though at this early point there is a social division of labour,
and also an interrelationship of trades, there are as yet neither fixed

industrial undertakings nor the necessary industrial capital. At most we are justified in speaking of trade capital. Handicraft undertakes work, but it Is no business undertaking. In the forms of itinerant handicraft and home work it almost totally lacks capital. It means wage labour embodied in the material of another. Even where the craftsman works with his own tools the product does not increase in value from the constant incorporation of fresh increments of capital, but from the fact that labour is being invested in it.

The amount of loan and consumption capital is also exceedingly small. It may even be doubted whether in mediaeval trade credit operations can be spoken of at all. Early exchange is based upon ready payment; nothing is given except where a tendered equivalent can be directly received. Almost the entire credit system is clothed in the forms of purchase. This was the case with the hereditary peasant holding and with the giving of town building sites in return for a ground rent, in which instances the land was looked upon as the purchase-price for the right to levy rent.[159] So it was also under the earlier law where the land placed at the disposal of the money-lender passes as a temporary equivalent into the keeping of the "creditor" and becomes his property if the debtor fails to repay the loan. Economically considered, this commercial act differs in no way from selling in order to buy again; and it is admitted that it is now scarcely possible to discover a legal distinction between the two. A similar character is borne by the most common of urban credit transactions, the purchase of rents or stocks,[160] as the name itself indicates. The price is the capital loaned; the commodity exchanged is the right to draw a yearly rent, which the borrower on the security of a house transfers in such a manner that the owner for the time being receives the rent. The rent is of the nature of a charge upon the soil, and is for a long time incapable of release; the party responsible answers for it with the house or land upon which it is fixed, but not with his other assets. It is thus a charge only upon the real property that carries it, whose rentability it proportionately diminishes. The person entitled to the rent has absolutely resigned the purchase price paid; the document conferring the right to draw the rent can be transferred without formality, just as a bill payable to bearer. Every personal relationship is thus eliminated from the whole transaction,

---

[159] Compare in connection with this whole section the luminous explanation by A. Heusler, *Institutionen d. deutsch. Privatrechts*, II, pp. 128 ff.

[160] *Rentenkauf* and *Gultkauf*.

which lacks that element of trust peculiar to credit. The right of redemption bears the same character; it is the sale of the rent under reservation of the privilege of re-purchase.

As in dealings in real property, so also with movables, the credit transaction is but a variation of ready payment. The security, as Heusler says, is a provisional transfer on the part of the debtor of an equivalent that is still redeemable (forfeitable security), not a covering of the debt, which may eventually be claimed by the creditor and realized upon by being converted into money (saleable security). The pawnbroking business of the Jews[161] is in fact similar to our modern sale with right of redemption, and the "goods credit" extended today by craftsmen and shopkeepers, takes in the Middle Ages the form of purchase on security. If at the same time we consider that when personal credit was given in those times the debtor almost always had to agree to submit to the creditor's right of security; that in most instances he could get money only by furnishing the best security under pledges to the lender and similar burdensome conditions; that the creditor in addition reserved the right, in case of default, to obtain the money from Jews at the debtor's expense; and that the fellow citizens or heirs of the foreign debtor could be distrained upon for the amount of his debt,—we see plainly that in the town economy of the Middle Ages a credit system in the modern sense cannot be spoken of.[162]

There are two things in connection with this that must appear especially strange to a student of modern political economy, namely, the frequency with which immaterial things (relationships) become economic commodities and subjects of exchange, and their treatment under commercial law as real property. These show clearly how primitive exchange sought to enlarge the sphere denied it under the existing conditions of production by awkwardly transforming, into negotiable property, almost everything it could lay hold upon, and thus extending infinitely the domain of private law. What an

---

[161]Comp. my *Bevölkerung von Frankfurt*, I, pp. 573 if.

[162]A striking resemblance to the mediaeval credit system is offered by the Greek system and its legal forms. Here likewise purchase and loan are largely synonymous terms, and the language has not arrived at the stage of distinguishing sharply the notions of buying, pledging, renting, and subjecting to conditions. The Greek mortgage laws coincide in all important points with the early German. Comp. K. F. Hermann, *Lehrbueh der griech. PrivataUertümer mit Einschluss der Rechtsaltertumer*, §§67 and 68. The old Roman *fiducia* and its later form as *pignus* may be mentioned for purpose of comparison.

endless variety of things in mediaeval times were lent, bestowed, sold, and pawned! —the sovereign power over territories and towns; county and bailiff's rights; jurisdiction over hundreds and cantons; church dignities and patronages; suburban monopoly rights; ferry and road privileges; prerogatives of mintage and toll, of hunting and fishing; wood-cutting rights, tithes, statute labour, ground rents, and revenues; in fact charges of every kind falling upon the land. Economically considered, all these rights and "relationships" share with land the peculiarity that they cannot be removed from the place where they are enjoyed, and that they cannot be multiplied at will.

Income and wealth are at this stage not yet clearly distinguished from each other. When in Basel in the year 1451 the "new pound-toll" was introduced it was prescribed that it should be paid: (1) from the selling price of wares, (2) from the capital invested in the purchase of rents, and (3) from the amount of rents received.[163] On every pound four pfennigs were to be paid, no matter whether the commodity had changed hands as purchase-money, as capital, or as interest. In the first instance we have to do, according to our terminology, with gross revenue, in the second with property, in the third with net income; and yet all three cases are treated alike. Similar examples might be adduced from the tax regulations of other cities.[164]

Two of our modern classes of income, however, now come more clearly into view, namely, ground-rent and wages. The latter bears, to be sure, a peculiar character; it is handicraft wage, compensation for the use of the craftsman's labour on behalf of the consumer, and not, as today, the price paid to the wage worker by the entrepreneur. Still this price already exists in germ in the slight money wage that the artisan gives to his journeyman in addition to free maintenance, thus enabling the latter to supply independently a limited propor-tion of his wants. Earnings of management appear only in the sphere of trade, and thus, like it, are the exception; moreover through con-nection with transportation they are more coloured by elements of labour wage thau are the earnings from trade today. As a rule in-terest takes on the form of ground rent; and the same is true of the

---

[163]Comp. Schönberg, *Finazuverhältnisse d. Stadt Basel im XIV. und XV. Jhdt.*, p. 267.

[164]For details see my paper on two mediaeval tax-regulations, *Kleinere Beitrdge s. Geschich. von Dozenten d. Leipziger Hochschule. Festschrift a. dritt. Historikertage* (Leipzig, 1894), pp. 123 ff.

many kinds of revenues arising from the juridical relationships that enter into trade. As credit operations usually take the form of purchase, they almost always mean for the creditor the actual transfer of a portion of his property, in order that he may receive a yearly income or a continuous usufruct. This is a rule, for example, of enfeoffment; with mortgaged property, according to the early law, it involved the transfer of the natural yield of the land, and with rent purchases, of the ground rent or rent. On this basis arose the earliest type of personal insurance and at the same time the chief form of public credit: the negotiating of annuities.

Public economy is still mainly of a private character: revenues from domains, sovereign prerogatives, tithes, statute labour, services, ground rents, and fees preponderate in the State, market revenues and imports on consumption in the towns. The general property tax continues to be the only direct tax, and mingled with it here and there are elements of an income tax. It is indeed levied more frequently than in the preceding period, but still it is not regular.

In Germany the economic supremacy of the towns over the surrounding country blossomed only in a few places into political sovereignty. In Italy a parallel development led to the formation of a tyranny of the cities; in France the beginnings of autonomy on the part of free municipal communities were early suppressed by the kings with the aid of the feudal nobility. The reason is that in Germany, as in France, everything that lay without the town wall was overlaid with a mass of feudal institutions. True the great landed proprietors had long since given up the personal management of their manorial estates,—which became for the owner, just as the town land and house property for the patrician families, nothing more than a source of income. But their original economic power had now become political, the landed proprietors were now territorial princes, and in the course of this transformation there had arisen a new and widely ramified class of small titled proprietors whose interests, purely agrarian in character, were closely linked to those of the princes. Hence that keen struggle in Germany between burgher and noble which fills the closing centuries of the Middle Ages, and in which the towns maintain the political autonomy they had for the most part acquired from their lords by purchase and unredeemed pledges, though they fail to wrest the peasant class from the feudal powers.

It can thus be said that the economic development of the towns in Germany and France remained incomplete; and that they did not accomplish what the most vigorous types of the period of autonomous household economy had actually achieved, namely, the transmuting of their economic power into political independence. This was perhaps fortunate for us. In Italy the wealth of the cities expropriated in all directions the possessions of the peasant, and down to the present has continued to exploit him as a wretched metayer. In Germany the nobility were, indeed, able to make of him a feudatory; but the conception of nationality, which first came to life in the territorial sovereignties, served to prevent his proletarization.

The final development of *national economy* is in its essence a fruit of the political centralization that begins at the close of the Middle Ages with the rise of territorial state organizations, and now finds its completion in the creation of the unified national State. Economic unification of forces goes hand in hand with the bowing of private political interests to the higher dims of the nation as a whole.

In Germany it is the more powerful territorial princes, as opposed to the rural nobles and the towns, who seek to realize the modern national idea, often certainly under great difficulties, especially when their territories were widely scattered. From the second half of the fifteenth century we have many indications of a closer economic union, such as the creation of a territorial currency in place of the numerous town currencies, the issue of territorial regulations regarding trade, markets, industry, forestry, mining, hunting, and fishing, the gradual formation of a system of sovereign prerogatives and concessions, the promulgation of territorial laws, conducive to greater legal unity, and the emergence of an ordered public economy.

But for centuries longer agricultural interests predominate in Germany, and as against them the exertions of the imperial power in the direction of a national economic policy lamentably failed. On the other hand the Western European states,—Spain, Portugal, England, France, and the Netherlands,—from the sixteenth century on appear externally as economic units, developing a vigorous colonial policy in order to turn to account the rich resources of their newly acquired possessions over sea.

In all these lands, though with varying degrees of severity, appears the struggle with the independent powers of the Middle Ages,—the greater nobility, the towns, the provinces, the religious and secular corporations. The immediate question, to be sure, was the annihilation of the independent territorial circles which blocked the way to political unification. But deep down beneath the movement leading to the development of princely absolutism, slumbers the universal idea that the greater tasks confronting modern civilization demanded an organized union of whole peoples, a grand living community of interests; and this could arise only upon the basis of common economic action. Each portion of the country, each section of the population, must in the service of the whole take over those duties that its natural endowments best fitted it to perform. A comprehensive partitioning of functions was necessary, a division into callings embracing the whole population; and this division itself presupposed a highly developed commerce and an active interchange of goods amongst the population. If the sole aim of all economic effort was in ancient times to make the house autonomous in the satisfaction of its wants, and in later mediaeval times to supply the needs of the town, there now comes into being an exceedingly complex and ingenious system for meeting the wants of the entire nation.

The carrying out of this system is from the sixteenth to the eighteenth century the economic effort of all the advanced European states. The measures employed to attain this object are modelled in almost every detail upon the economic policy of the mediaeval towns.[165] They are generally summed up under the name of the mercantile system. This latter has long been regarded as a theoretical edifice culminating in the principle that the wealth of a country consists in the amount of coin within its borders. Today, in all probability, this conception is universally abandoned. Mercantilism is no dead dogma, but the active practice of all leading statesmen from Charles V. to Frederick the Great. It found its typical development in the economic policy of Colbert. He sought the removal or reduction of the internal customs and tolls the introduction of a unified customs system on the national borders; the assuring to the country of a supply of the necessary raw materials and means of sustenance by hindrances to export, And the institution of the forest regalia. He fostered industry on a large scale by the establishment of new industrial branches with state support and technical supervision, by the exclusion of foreign competition through prohibitive tariffs, and by the building of roads, canals, and harbours. With the same end in view he strove to unify the system of weights and measures, and to regulate commercial law and the commercial news-service. The

---

[165]For the German states this development is excellently portrayed by Schmoller in the Jhb. f. Gesetzgeb. Verw. u. Volksw. VIII (1884), pp. 22 ff.

cultivation of the technical arts, fine arts, and science in special state institutions; the systematizing of state and communal expenditure, the removal of inequalities in taxation, also served his one purpose—to create an *independent national economy* which should satisfy all the needs of the citizens of France by national labour, and by an active internal trade bring all the natural resources of the country and all the separate forces of the people into the service of the whole. In considering the special encouragement given by "Colbertism" to foreign commerce, the marine, and colonial trade, it has all too often been overlooked that these measures also strengthened the inner resources of the country, and that the theory of the balance of trade became a necessity at a time when the transition from the still predominant household production to the system of universal exchange indispensably postulated the increase of the monetary medium of circulation.

Along with the state measures we must not fail to take account of the social forces working in the same direction. These naturally had their starting point in the towns Here, by a gradual process of transformation, loaning at interest had been evolved from the purchase of rents; and thus in the course of the sixteenth century a true credit system arose. In this we may see the influence of wholesale trade, which first discovered the secret of making money with money. Through the liberation of capital invested in rents the wealth of the rich townsmen acquired a greatly increased mobility and accumulative power. Loan capital now took its place at the side of trade capital, hitherto the only kind of capital; and the two supplemented and supported each other in their further development.

The immediate result was a notable expansion of trade. Certain towns began to rear their heads above the uniform mass of mediaeval market and handicraft towns as centres of statfe administration or as emporiums of trade. In Germany, which through the decline of the Hansa and the changfe in the highways of the world's trade, had lost most of its importance as an intermediary of trade with the North, the change manifests itself to some extent in the growing importance of the great fairs, and in the decadence of the local markets. The Frankfurt fair reached its zenith in the sixteenth century, that of Leipzig considerably later. But soon trade capital is no longer content with the importation and handling of foreign products; it becomes, for native industry and the surplus products of the peasant's domestic labour, commission capital. Wholesale production with division of labour in manufactories and factories comes into life, and with it the wage-earning class. In place of the mediaeval exchange bank there is developed first the bank of deposit and circulation, then the modern credit bank. The transport of goods, which earlier was an integral part of trade, now becomes independent. The state posts, newspapers, and the national marine arise, and the insurance system is developed. On all sides are new organizations whose purpose is to satisfy wide-spread economic wants; a national industry, a national market, national commercial institutions,—everywhere the capitalistic principle of business enterprise in trade.

Everybody knows how the absolutist State furthered this movement, and how not infrequently in the effort to accelerate it it gave an artificial existence to what would not flourish of its own strength. Nevertheless, though limited in manifold ways by state legislation, the old economic organization of the towns with its guild and monopoly privileges and the sharp separation of town and country, persisted on until about the end of the eighteenth century, heedless of the new economic life springing up roundabout and of the variety of new commercial forms which it had nurtured. When the Physiocrats and Adam Smith made these latter for the first time the subject of scientific observation, they entirely overlooked the obvious fact that they were not dealing with a spontaneous product of mere social activity, but with a fruit of the paternal government of the State. The barriers whose removal they demanded were either the fossilized survivals of earlier economic epochs, such as charges upon the soil, guilds, local coercive rights, restrictions on freedom of migration; or they were devices of mercantilism for assisting production, such as monopolies and privileges, which might cease to operate after having fulfilled their purpose.

As far as the development of national economy is concerned, the liberalism of the last hundred years has only continued what absolutism began. Expressed in this way, the assertion may easily seem paradoxical. For liberalism, outwardly considered, has only demolished; it has over thrown the antiquated forms upon which household and town economy were founded, and constructed nothing new. It has destroyed the special position and special privileges of individual territorial districts and individual social groups, and in their stead established free competition and equality before the law. But though it has thus decomposed into its elements the heritage of the past, it has at the same time cleared the way for new economic combinations of a truly national character, and made it possible for every energy, according to the technical development of the time, to enter into the service of the whole at the point where it is of the greatest usefulness.

If liberalism has made the progress of national economy absolutely contingent upon social freedom of action, and thus taken an attitude in many respects hostile to the State, it has nevertheless failed to prevent the modern State, as such, from pursuing the path chosen by it as early as the sixteenth century, and leading to an ever closer Union of all sections of the people and of the national territory for the accomplishment of the steadily expanding tasks of civilization. All the great statesmen of the last three centuries, from Cromwell and Colbert to Cavour and Bismarck, have worked towards this end. The French Revolution has been no less centralizing in its effects than the political upheavals of recent decades. In the latest phase of this evolution the *principle of nationality* has become a principle of mighty unifying power. The small separate States of earlier times were no longer equal to the comprehensive economic tasks of the present. They had either to disappear in one large national State, as in Italy, or surrender considerable portions of their independence, especially in economic legislation, to a federal State, as did the individual States in the German Empire, and the cantons in Switzerland.

We err, if we imagine ourselves justified in concluding from the extent to which international trade has been facilitated during the epoch of liberalism that the period of national economy is on the decline and is giving place to the period of world economy. The very latest political development of the States of Europe has resulted in a return to the ideas of mercantilism and, to a certain extent, of the old town economy. The revival of protective duties, the retention of national currency and of national labour legislation, the public ownership of the machinery of transportation already achieved or still aimed at, the national control of workman's insurance and of the banking system, the growing activity of the State in economic matters generally,—all this indicates that we have passed the absolutist and liberalist periods and entered upon a third period of national economy. Socially this period bears a peculiar aspect. It is no longer merely a question of meeting national wants as independently and completely as possible by national production, but a question of the just distribution of goods, of the direct action of the

State in the economic interests of the whole, and for the purpose of securing to all its subjects according to their economic services a share in the benefits of civilization. The requisite measures can be carried out only on a grand scale; they demand an intimate union of all individual forces, such as a great national State alone can furnish.

With this we might fittingly close. For to present here the multitude of new phenomena springing up under the touch of national as opposed to household and town economy one would need to reproduce almost the whole contents of a text-book on political economy. It will nevertheless contribute to a better understanding of the subject if, by a comparison of some of the leading phenomena we concisely review the fundamental features of the whole in the three stages of its development.

The most prominent of these features is, that in the course of history mankind sets before itself ever higher economic aims and finds the means of attaining these in a division of the burden of labour, which constantly extends until finally it embraces the whole people and requires the services of all for all. This *coöperation* is based, in the case of household economy, upon blood-relationship, of town economy upon contiguity, and of national economy upon nationality. It is the road traversed by mankind in passing from, clanship to society, which, as far as we can see, ends in an ever tightening social organization. On this road the means for satisfying the wants of the individual continually grow in fulness and variety, and at the same time in dependence and complexity. The life and labour of every individual becomes more and more entwined with the life and labour of many others.

At the stage of household economy every commodity is consumed in the place of its origin; at the stage of town economy it passes immediately from the producer to the consumer; at the stage of national economy, both in its production and thereafter, it passes through various hands —it circulates. In the course of the whole evolution the distance between production and consumption increases. At the first stage all commodities are consumption goods; at the second part of them become articles of exchange; at the third most of -them are wares.

The individual household at the first stage is a *producing and consuming community in one*; at the stage of town economy this state of things continues in so far as the journeyman craftsman and the peasant workman make part of the household of the person employing them; in national economy community in production and community in consumption become distinct. The former is a business undertaking from whose returns as a rule several independent households are supported.

When outside *labour* is necessary, it is at the first stage in a permanent relation of subjection to the producer (as slaves and serfs), at the second in one of service, and at the third the relationship is contractual. Under the independent household system the consumer is either himself a labourer, or the owner of the labourer; in town economy he makes a direct purchase of the workman's labour (wage-work), or of the product of his labour (handicraft); in national economy he ceases to stand in any relation to the labourer, and purchases his goods from the entrepreneur or merchant, by whom the labourer is paid.

As for *money*, it is in independent domestic economy either entirely absent, or an article of direct use and a means for storing up wealth. In town economy it is essentially a medium of exchange; in national economy it becomes a means of circulation and of profit-making as well. The three categories, payment in kind, money payment, and payment based upon credit, correspond with the various rôles played by money, though they do not exhaust them.

Capital scarcely exists at the first stage; we meet only with consumption goods. At the second stage implements of labour may be classed under the usual head of business capital, but this is by no means generally true of the raw materials. Acquisitive capital proper exists only in the form of trade capital. At the third, acquisitive capital represents the means whereby goods are raised from one stage of division of labour to the next and impelled through the whole process of circulation.[166] Here everything becomes capital. From this point of view we might describe the independent household economy as lacking capital, town economy as hostile to capital, and national economy as capitalistic.

Income and wealth under the household system compose an undivided and indivisible whole; though the beginnings of ground rent are already perceptible. In town economy interest also usually appears as ground rent; business profits are confined almost entirely to trade; the chief form of labour wage is the wage paid to the craftsman by the consumer. But even yet most commodities do not pass from their place of production into other establishments. Pure in-

---

[166]Com p. also Chaps. IV and VIII.

105

come can be realized only by one who definitely surrenders a portion of his wealth in the purchase of rents. At the stage of national economy the four branches of income are definitely separated. Almost the whole return from production is liquidated through trade. Under wealth, rent and acquisitive capital are distinct from stores for consumption, which are kept at the lowest imaginable limit, since commerce frees individuals from the keeping of supplies. On the other hand the unused surpluses of income, which at the first and second stages necessarily remained over from the wealth available for consumption, are now either directly added to business capital or transformed by means of saving and other banks into interest-bearing loans,—that is, they are, in any case, converted into capital.

At the stage of household economy the division of labour is confined to the household establishment; at the stage of town economy it consists either in the formation of, and division into, trades within the town, or in a partition of production between town and country; while the prominent features of the stage of national economy are increasing division of production, subdivision of work within the various establishments, and displacement of labour from one business to another.[167]

Industry as an independent occupation is not found at the first stage, the whole transformation of raw material being merely housework. In the town economy we indeed find labourers pursuing some special industrial occupation, but entrepreneurs are lacking; industry is either wage-work or handicraft, and he who wishes to ply it must first master it. In national economy industry carried on in factories and under the commission system is preponderant; and this presupposes extensive capital and an entrepreneur with mercantile skill. Technical mastery of the process of production by the entrepreneur is not indispensable.[168]

In similar fashion a change occurs in the forms under which *trade* is pursued. Corresponding to the household system is itinerant trade, to town economy market trade, and to national economy trade with permanent establishment. If at the first two stages trade is merely supplementary to an otherwise autonomous system of production, it becomes in national economy a necessary link between production and consumption. It draws away from transportation, which now attains an independent position and organization.

---

[167]For further details see Chap. VIII.
[168]Comp. Chap IV.

Commercial services were, to be sure, not lacking in the ancient slave and the mediaeval manorial systems; they devolved upon special slaves or serfs. In the Middle Ages we find town messengers who were originally in the exclusive service of the municipal authorities, but later added the carriage of private correspondence. At the threshold of modern times stands the postal service, at first restricted to state purposes, by-and-bye extended to the public. In our century follow the railway, telegraph, telephone, and steamship lines—with which the State interferes in the interest of economy—and along with them the most varied private undertakings for facilitating communication.[169] At all the stages, however, certain commercial services have been organized by the sovereign administration, in the initial instance always for its own special requirements.

Credit is at the first stage purely consumption credit; and can be obtained only by the person pledging himself and all his property. At the second stage, in the matter of personal credit, servitude for debt is softened to imprisonment for debt. Along with consumption credit appears a type of credit on the return from immovables which is met in garb of a purchase, and must be considered as the normal form of credit under town economy. Business or productive credit, the distinctive form of credit in modern times, is first developed in trade, whence it spreads to every sphere of industrial life. State credit appears in the States of antiquity naturally as a forced loan; in the mediaeval towns as the sale of annuities and redeemable claims; in the modern States as the disposing of perpetual rents or of redeemable interest-bearing bonds.

In the domain of *public services* similar stages may also be pointed out. Legal protection is at first a matter for the clan, later for the feudal lord; in the Middle Ages the towns form districts of separate jurisdiction; at present the enforcement of law and police protection are functions of the State. The same is the case with education. At the first stage *education* devolves upon the family, as it does today still in Iceland. The Roman *pædagogus* is a slave. In the Middle Ages it is autonomous household establishments, namely, the monasteries, that organize .the educational system; later arise the municipal and cathedral schools; peculiar to modern times are the concentration and supervision of instruction in state institutions. This development is even more apparent in the *arrangements for defence*. Among many peoples still at the stage of economic isola-

---

[169]For the analogous development in the newspaper press see Chap. VI.

tion each separate house is fortified (for example, the palisades of the Malays and Polynesians), and in early mediaeval times the manor is protected by wall and moat. At the second economic stage each city is a fortress; at the third a few fortifications along the borders secure the whole State. It is sufficiently significant that Louvois, the creator of the first system of border fortification, was a contemporary of Colbert, the founder of modern French national economy.

These parallels might be multiplied. As in moving into a new building one's first care is to introduce order for the time being, so with regard to the subject-matter of this chapter no fair-minded person will expect that everything lias been exhaustively treated and every detail assigned its proper place. The writer clearly perceives how inadequately the various phenomena of the two earlier stages of industrial evolution have as yet been worked over, and how very seriously their economic significance still demands accurate ascertainment. But for the present it may suffice if we have made clear the regularity of development both generally and in detail.

Only one thing further would we particularly emphasize. Household economy, town economy, national economy—these phrases do not denote a series whose terms are mutually exclusive. One kind of economic life has always been the *predominant*, and in the eyes of contemporaries the normal, one. Many elements of town economy, and even of independent domestic economy, still project into the present. Even today a very considerable part of the national production does not pass into general circulation, but is consumed in the households where it is produced; another portion, again, circulates no farther than from one establishment to another.

Hence it would almost appear as if those people were in error who regard the task of political economy to be the explanation of the nature and coherence of commercial phenomena, and those right who confine themselves to a description of economic forms and their historical transformations.

Yet that would be a fatal error, involving the surrender of the scientific labours of over a century, as well as a complete misconception of our economic present. Today not a sack of wheat is produced even on the most remote farm, that is not directly linked to the industrial life of the nation as a whole. Even if it be consumed in the house of the producer, nevertheless a large portion of the means of its production (the plough, the scythe, the threshing-machine, the artificial fertilizers, the draught animals, etc.) is obtained through trade; and the consumption of one's own products takes place only when from market conditions it seems economically advisable. Thus the sack of wheat is knit by a strong cord to the great intricate web of national commerce. And so are we all in our every economic thought and deed.

It is therefore a matter of great satisfaction that, after a period of diligent collection of material, the economic problems of modern commerce have in recent times been zealously taken up again, and that an attempt is being made to correct and develop the old system in the same way in which it arose, with the aid, however, of a much larger store of facts. For the only method of investigation which will enable us to approach the complex causes of commercial phenomena is that of abstract isolation, and logical deduction. The sole inductive process that can likewise be considered, namely, the statistical, is not sufficiently exact and penetrating for most of the problems that have to be handled here, and can be employed only to supplement or control.

For the economic periods of the past the task will not be different. Here, to be sure, it will be even more necessary first to collect the facts and present them according to form and function; next we must gain a proper conception of the nature of the phenomena; and then we may logically dissect them and investigate their casual connection. We will thus have to advance by the same method that "classical political economy" has applied to the industry of the present. For some phases of the economic life of the ancient οἶκος this has already been done in a masterful manner by Rodbertus; for the economic life of the Middle Ages such a task has yet scarcely been essayed. The attempt can succeed only with investigators fully able to grasp the actual assumptions of past economic periods and our ancestors' ways of thinking on economic matters; it can but fail if the half understood, half arbitrarily reconstructed economic conditions of the past continue to be reflected in terms of the modern theory of exchange.

Only in this way, in our opinion, can investigations in economic history and the theory of contemporary economics be mutually helpful; only thus can we gain a clearer insight into the regularity both of economic development and of economic phenomena.

Chapter IV. A Historical Survey of Industrial Systems.

I
N economic and social matters most people have very definite opinions on what *should be*, often much more definite than on what is. What in their view should be is by no means, an ideal state of affairs, an imaginative creation that has never been realized. Very frequently indeed it is a conception drawn from the conditions that prevailed in times more or less remote, which long custom has led us to consider normal.

Such is the case, if we mistake not, with many of our contemporaries regarding what we call *handicraft* and the so-called handicraft problem. One has become accustomed to look upon handicraft as the normal form of industry, after it has dominated five centuries or more of the life of the burgher class of Germany. The proverb says "Handicraft stands on golden ground"; and observation teaches us that this ground is, according to present day valuation, no longer golden. We ask ourselves how that happy condition can be restored, how handicraft can be "resuscitated."

But what right has one to regard handicraft as the normal form of industry and thus as it were to strive after an ideal whose realization belongs to the past?

The earlier political economists represent handicraft as the original form of industrial production. "In a tribe of hunters or shepherds," says Adam Smith,[170] "a particular person makes bows and arrows with more readiness and dexterity than any other. He fre-

---

[170]Bk. I, ch. 2.

quently exchanges them for cattle or venison with his companions; and he finds at last that he can in this manner get more cattle and venison than if he himself went to the field to catch them." Finally, "the making of bows and arrows grows to be his chief business and he becomes a sort of armourer." If we follow this historical progress a couple of stages further, the original handicraftsman will after a time probably take an apprentice, and when the latter has learned his trade, a second, while,the first becomes his journeyman.

Seek as we may, we find nothing added by subsequent development. When we speak of a craftsman today we have in mind a business undertaker on a small scale, who has passed by regular stages of transition from apprentice to journeyman and from journeyman to master workman, who produces with his own hand and his own capital for a locally limited circle of customers, and into whose hands flows undiminished the whole product of his labour. Everything that one can demand of an industrial system founded on justice seems realized in the life of the typical craftsman—gradual social progress, independence, an income corresponding to services rendered. And those forms of industry that vary from this primal type, namely, house industry and factory production, may readily appear abnormal; and the social stratification of those employed, and the accompanying unequal distribution of income out of harmony with the idea of economic justice.

Even later economists are rarely free from this popular conception. In contrasting the three industrial systems that they recognise, handicraft, house industry, and factory production, they almost unwittingly draw from the fundamental institutions of handicraft the criterion for judging the others. Until quite recently house industry was for many of them merely a degenerate handicraft or a transitional form, and the factory a necessary evil of the age of machinery. This narrowness of view was prejudicial to the scientific understanding of even modern industrial methods, open as these are to direct observation.

An historically constructive view, such as we will here present, must from the start shake off the idea that any particular form in any department of economic activity can be the norm for all times and peoples. Even handicraft is for it only one phenomenon in the great stream of history, with its origin, continuance, and success dependent upon certain given economic conditions. It is neither the original nor even a necessary form in the historical evolution of industrial

111

production. It is, in other words, just as little necessary that the industry of a country shall have passed through the handicraft phase before arriving at house industry or factory manufacture as that every people shall have been hunters or nomads before passing over to settled agriculture. Among us handicraft has been preceded by other industrial systems, which, indeed, even in Europe, still exist in part.

The great historical significance of these primitive industrial forms in the evolution of economic conditions has hitherto been almost wholly ignored, although they shaped for thousands of years the economic life of the nations and left lasting marks upon their social organizations. Only a comparatively small portion of the history of industry, namely, that part which written laws have enabled us to know, has been at all cleared up; and this, too, much more on its formal side than as regards its inner life, its method of operation. Even the guild handicraft of the Middle Ages, to which in recent times so much persevering and penetrating labour has been devoted, has, on the side of its actual operation, enjoyed scarcely more accurate investigation. In this domain arbitrary theoretical constructions based upon the postulates and concepts of modern commercial economy still widely prevail.

Our "historical" political enonomy, it is true, has a wealth of material for the economic history of the classical and modern peoples. But it has hardly yet been duly noted that the complex nature of all social phenomena renders it just as difficult for the investigator of today to reconstruct the economic conditions of the life of the nations of antiquity and of the Middle Ages as to forecast even with the most lively and powerful imagination the ultimate consequences of the "socialist State of the future." We shall not arrive at an understanding of whole epochs of early economic history until we study the economic side of the life of primitive and uncivilized peoples of the present with the care we today devote to Englishmen and Americans. Instead of sending our young political economists on journeys of investigation to these latter, we should rather send them to the Russians, the Rumanians, or the South Slavs; we should study the characteristic features of primitive economic life and the legal conceptions of the peoples of our newly acquired colonies before such features and conceptions disappear under the influence of European trade.

It is almost a fortunate circumstance that such external influences rarely affect deeply the real life of the people, but are confined chiefly to the more privileged classes. Hence it is that in extensive regions of eastern and northern Europe, which the unheeding traveller courses through by rail, there may still be observed among the rural population primitive forms of production that modern commerce has caused to vary but slightly.

In the attempt made in the following pages to give a compact presentation of what we know of the industrial methods of such "backward" tribes and the present conclusions of industrial history, our sole aim is to present in clear outline the chief stages of development.[171] In order to have a guiding thread through the perplexing variety and wealth of forms of individual ethnographical observations, it is most necessary to separate typical and casual, to disregard subsidiary and transitional forms, and to consider a new phase of development as beginning only where changes in industrial technique call forth economic phenomena that imply a radical alteration in the organization of society. In this way we arrive at five main systems of industry. In historical succession they are:

1. Housework (Domestic Work).

2. Wage-work. 3. Handicraft.

4. Commission Work (House Industry).

5. Factory Work.

We shall first attempt to give a concise outline of the characteristic economic peculiarities of these industrial systems, merely indicating the socio-historical import of the whole development. The filling out of occasional gaps and the explanation of the transitions from one system to the other may be left to detailed investigation. In our sketch we shall, naturally, devote most time to the two industrial systems precedent to handicraft,

while for the later a brief account may suffice. We begin with housework.[172]

---

[171] The present sketch brings together in popular form only the most important features. Further discussion, and references to the most essential literature, will be found in my article under the head "Gewerbe" in the Handwört. der Staatswiss. (2d ed.), IV, pp. 360-393.

[172] It is from Norway and Sweden that the expression *Hausfleisz* (housework) has been transplanted into Germany, where during the last twenty years it has become current. In those countries it was employed for certain occupations of the members of the domestic circle, such as spinning, weaving, sewing, the making of wooden utensils, and the like. It is the application of industrial technique that, favoured by climate and settlement, has from early times become indigenous in those parts. Through it the peasant household works up for its own use the raw

Housework is industrial production in and for the house from raw materials furnished by the household itself. In its original and purest form it presupposes the absence of exchange, and the ability of each household to satisfy by its own labour the wants of its members. Each commodity passes through all the stages of production in the establishment in which it is to be consumed. Production is consequently undertaken only according to the needs of the house itself. There is still neither circulation of goods nor capital. The wealth of the house consists entirely in consumption goods in various stages of completion, such as corn, meal, bread, flax, yarn, cloth, and clothes. It also possesses auxiliary means of production, such as the hand-mill, the axe, the distaff, and the weaver's loom, but no goods with which it could procure other goods by process of exchange. All it has it owes to its own labour, and it is scarcely possible to separate the operations of the household from those of production.

In the form of housework, industry is older than agriculture. Wherever explorers of new countries have come into contact with primitive peoples, they have found many forms of industrial skill, such as the making of bow and arrow, the weaving of mats and vessels out of reeds, bast, and tough roots, a primitive pottery, tanning skins, crushing farinaceous grains on the grinding-stone, smelting iron ore, the building of houses. Today the hunting tribes of North America, the fisher tribes of the South Sea, the nomad hordes of Siberia, and the agricultural negro tribes of Africa make similar display of varied technical skill without possessing actual artisans. Even the wretched naked forest tribes of Central Brazil make their clubs and bows and arrows, build houses and bark canoes, make tools of bone and stone, weave baskets for carrying and storing, scoop out gourd dishes, spin, knit, and weave, form artistically ornamented clay vessels without a knowledge of the potter's wheel, carve ornamented digging-sticks, stools, flutes, combs, and masks, and prepare

---

material from field and wood. As this technique threatened to disappear under the influence of modern commercial conditions it was the opinion in Denmark and Norway that it should be reanimated through school instruction. Few, indeed, of the promoters of manual instruction—this new branch of instruction, whose pedagogical importance cannot be denied—have formed a clear conception of what housework really signified and in part still signifies for the Northern peoples. Here and there, especially at its inauguration, manual training was regarded as a means for establishing new house industries. But housework and house industry are two industrial systems separated historically from one another (at least among us) by two centuries.

many kinds of ornaments out of feathers, skins, etc.

In the temperate and colder countries with the advance to the use of the plough, this activity loses more and more the character of the accidental; the whole husbandry acquires a settled character; the mild period of the year must be devoted to the procuring of raw material and to outdoor work; in winter the working up of this material clusters the members of the household around the hearth. For each kind of work there is developed a definite method which is incorporated into the domestic life according to the natural and imperative demands of economy; about it custom weaves its fine golden ethical thread; it enriches and ennobles the life of men among whom, with its simpie technique and archaic forms, it is transmitted from generation to generation. As people labour only for their own requirements, the interest of the producer in the work of his hands long survives the completion of the work. His highest technical skill and his whole artistic sense are embodied in it. It is for this reason that the products of domestic work throughout Germany have become for our age of artistic industry such a rich mine of models of popular style.

The Norwegian peasant is not merely his own smith and joiner, like the Westphalian _Hofschulze_ in Immermann's "Münchhausen"; with his own hands he also builds his wooden house, makes his field-implements, wagons and sleighs, tans leather, carves from wood various kinds of house utensils, and even makes metal ones.[173] In Iceland the very peasants[174] are skilful workers in silver. In the Highlands of Scotland, up to the close of last century, every man was his own weaver, fuller, tanner, and shoemaker. In Galicia and Bukowina, in many parts of Hungary and Siebenbürgen, in Rumania, and among the southern Slav peoples there could scarcely be found, down to recent times, any other craftsman than the smith, and he was usually a gypsy. In Greece and other lands of the Balkan peninsula the only additional craftsmen were occasional wandering builders.[175] Numberless examples of a similar kind might be ad-

---

[173] Eilert Sundt, _Om Husfliden i Norge_ (Christiania, 1867). Blom, _Das Königreich Norwegen_ (Leipzig, 1843), p. 237. Forester, _Norway in 1848 and 1849_ (London, 1850), p. 113. E. Sidenbladh, _Schweden, Statist. Mitteilungen s. Wiener Weltausstellung_, 1873.

[174] [Dr. Bücher is evidently speaking of the Icelandic peasant of an earlier time.—ED.]

[175] On the Austrian populations compare _Die Hausindustrie Oesterreichs. Ein Kommentar z. hausindustriellen Abteilung auf d. allgemeinen land- u._

duced from other peoples. The wonderful adroitness and dexterity of the Russian and Swedish peasants, to cite a striking instance, has its undoubted origin in the varied technical tasks of their own households. The industrial employments of women in ancient and modern times, such as spinning, weaving, baking, etc., are too well known to call for further reference. In order to obtain an idea of the wealth of domestic in-dustrial skill that characterizes the life of less civilized peoples a detailed description would be necessary. Lack of space unfortunately forbids that here. It will suffice, however, to reproduce the following sentences from an account of household work in Bukowina:[176]

"In the narrow circle of the family, or at least within the limits of his little village, the Bukowina countryman supplies all his own necessaries. In building a house the husband, as a rule, can do the work of carpenter, roofer, etc., while the wife must attend to plastering the woven and slatted walls or stopping the chinks in the log walls with moss, pounding out of the floor, and many other related duties. From the cultivation of the plant from which cloth is spun or the raising of sheep down to the making of bed and other clothes out of linen, .wool or furs, leather, felt, or plaited straw, the Bukowina country folk produce everything, including dyes from plants of their own culture, as well as the necessary though, indeed, extremely primitive utensils. The same holds in general of the food-supply. With a rather heavy expenditure of labour the peasant cultivates his field of maize, and with his handmill grinds the kukuruz meal used by him in baking mamaliga, his chief article of food, which resembles polenta. His simple farming implements, the dishes and utensils for

forstwirtschaftlich. Ausstellung zu Wien, 1890, ed. by W. Exner; also OeSterreichische Monatsschrift für Gesellschaftswissenschaft, IV, 90 ff., VIII, 22, IX, 98 and 331; A. Riegl, _Textile Hausindustrie in Oesterreich_ in the Mitteilungen d. k. k. österreich. Museums, New Series, IV, pp. 411 ff.; Braun und Krejcsi, _Der Hausfleiss in Ungarn_ (Leipzig, 1886); Schwicker, _Statistik d. Königreichs Ungarn,_ pp. 403 ff., 411, 426ff.; J. Paget, _Ungarn u. Siebenbürgen_ (Leipzig, 1842), II, pp. 163, 173, 264, 269; Franz Joseph Prinz von Battenberg, _Die Volkswirtschaftl. Entwickelung Bulgariens_ (Leipzig, 1891); Iwantschoff, _Primitive Formen d. Gewerbebetriebs in Bulgarien_ (Leipzig, 1896). On the other lands of the Balkan peninsula see _Reports from Her Majesty's Diplomatic and Consular Agents Abroad, respecting the Condition of the Industrial Classes in Foreign Countries_ (London, 1870-72); Tarajanz, _Das Gewerbe bei d. Armeniern_ (Leipzig, 1897); Petri, _Ehstland u. d. Ehsten_ (Gotha, 1802), II, pp. 230-1.
[176]C. A. Romstorfer in Exner, _Die Hausindustrie Oesterreichs,_ pp. 159 ff. Comp. H. Wiglitzky, _Die Bukowinaer Hausindustrie u. d. Mittel u. Wege z. Hebung derselb._ (Czernowitz, 1888).

household and kitchen, he, or, if not he, some self-taught villager, is also able to make. The working of iron, alone, a substance that the native population uses in exceedingly small quantities, he generally leaves to the gypsies scattered through the country."

Yet whatever the industrial skill developed by the selfsufficing household, such a method of supply was destined to prove inadequate when the household diminished to the smaller circle of blood-relations, which we call the family. The ancient family group, it is true, was broader than our present family; but just at the time when wants are increasing in extent and variety, the tribal organization of many peoples breaks down and a more minute division of labour among the members of the household is rendered impossible. The transition to specialized production and a system of exchange would at this point have been unavoidable had it not been possible, by adopting slaves or by utilizing serf labour, to enlarge artificially the household circle. The greater the number of these unfree members of the household, the easier it is to introduce a varied-division of labour among them and to train each person for a definite industrial employment.

Thus we find among the house-slaves of the wealthy Greeks and Romans industrial workers of various kinds;[177] and in the famous instructions of Charles the Great regarding the management of his country estates we have definite rules prescribing what kinds of unfree workers shall be maintained at each villa. "Each steward," we read, "shall have in his service good workmen, such as smiths, workers in gold and silver, shoemakers, turners, carpenters, shield-makers, fishers, fowlers, soap-boilers, brewers of mead (*siceratores*), bakers, and net-makers." Copious evidence of a similar kind is available for the manors of the nobility and the monasteries. The handicraftsmen maintained by them are at their exclusive service; in some cases they are merely domestic servants receiving their board and lodging in the manor-house, in others they are settled and gain their living on their own holdings, and in return render villein services in that branch of labour in which they have special skill. In token that they are engaged to hold their skill at the service of the manor, they bear the title *officiates, officiati,* i.e., officials.

Housework, we see, has here obtained an extensive organization, which allows the lord of the manor a relatively large and varied con-

---

[177]Comp. H. Francotte, *L'Industrie dans la Grèce ancienne,* I (Brussels, 1900); Wallon, Hist, de *l'Esclavage dans l'Antiquité* (2d ed., Paris, 1879).

sumption of industrial products. But housework does not remain mere production for direct consumption. At a very early stage inequality of natural endowment causes a varied development of technical skill. One tribe produces pottery, stone implements, or arrows, and a neighbouring tribe does not. Such industrial products are then scattered among other tribes as gifts of hospitality, or as spoils of war, and later as the objects of exchange. Among the ancient Greeks wealthy slaveowners caused a considerable number of their dependent labourers, whom they did not need for their own estates, to be trained for a special industry, and then to produce for the market. In a similar fashion peasant families exchange the surplus products of their household industry more frequently than the surpluses from their agriculture or cattle-raising. As in the Old Testament it is one of the good qualities of the virtuous wife to dispose of the wares that her own hands have produced,[178] so today the negro wife in Central Africa carries to the weekly market the pots or basketware she produces in order to exchange them for salt or pearls. In like manner, in many parts of Germany the rural population have from the beginning of the Middle Ages sold their linen cloths at the town markets and fairs; and in the era of mercantilism measures were taken by the government in Silesia and West-phalia to facilitate the export of home-made linen. So also in the Baltic provinces during the Middle Ages the coarse woollen cloth, *Vadhmâl,* which is still woven by the peasant women, was one of the best known articles of trade, and actually served as money. Similarly among many African peoples domestic products made by neighbouring tribes serve as general mediums of exchange. In almost every villager's house in Japan yarn is spun and cloth woven out of cotton grown in his own fields, and of this a portion comes into exchange. In Sweden the West Goths and Smalanders wander through almost the whole country offering for sale home-woven stuffs. In Hungary, Galicia, Rumania, and the southern Slav countries, everywhere one can meet with peasants offering for sale at the weekly town markets their earthen and wooden wares, and peasant women selling, along with vegetables and eggs, aprons, embroidered ribbons, and laces which they themselves have made.

It is especially when the land owned by a family becomes divided up and no longer suffices for its maintenance, that a part of the rural population take up a special branch of housework and produce for

---

[178]F. Buhl, *Die sozial. Verhaltnisse d. Israeliten* (Leipzig, 1898), p. 34.

the market in exactly the same way as our small peasants in South Germany produce wine, hops, or tobacco. At first the necessary raw material is gained from their own land or drawn from the communal forests; later on, if need be, it is also purchased. All sorts of allied branches of production are added; and thus there develops out of housework, as in many parts of Russia, an endlessly varied system of peasant industry on a small scale.

But the evolution may take another course, and an independent professional class of industrial labourers arise, and with them our second industrial system—*wage-work*. Whereas all industrial skill has hitherto been exercised in close association with property in land and tillage, the adept house-labourer now frees himself from this association, and upon his technical skill founds for himself an existence that gradually becomes independent of property in land. But he has only his simple tools for work; he has no business capital. He therefore always exercises his skill upon raw material furnished him by the producer of the raw material, who is at the same time the consumer of the finished product.

Here again two distinct forms of this relationship are possible. In one case the wage-worker is taken temporarily into the house, receives his board and, if he does not belong to the place, his lodging as well, together with the daily wage; and leaves when the needs of his customer are satisfied. In South Germany we call this going on one's itinerancy (*auf die Stör gehen*), and may accordingly designate the whole industrial phase as that of *itinerancy* (Stör), and the labourer carrying on work in this manner as the *itinerant* (Störer). The dressmakers and seamstresses whom our women in many places are accustomed to take into the house may serve as an illustration.

On the other hand, the wage-worker may have his own place of business, and the raw material be given out to him. For working it up he receives piece-work wage. In the country the linen-weaver, the miller, and the baker working for a wage are examples. We will designate this form of work *home work*.[179] It is met with chiefly in industries that demand permanent means of production difficult to transport, such as mills, ovens, weavers' looms, forges, etc.

Both forms of wage-work are still very common in all parts of the world. Examples might be drawn from India and Japan, from Morocco and the Sudan, and from almost all European countries. The system can be traced in Babylonian temple records and in ancient

---

[179] *Heimwerk.*

Egypt; it can be followed in literature from Homer down through ancient and mediaeval times to the present day. The whole conception of the relation of the customer to the independent (personally free or unfree) artisan in early Greek and Roman law rests upon wage-work;[180] and only by it are numerous ordinances of mediaeval guild law to be explained.

In the Alpine lands it is still the predominant industrial method in the country. The Styrian writer P. K. Rosegger has, in an interesting book,[181] given a picture of his experiences as apprentice to a peripatetic tailor carrying on. his trade among the peasants. "The peasant craftsmen," he says in the preface, "such as the cobbler, the tailor, the weaver, the cooper (in other places also the saddler, the wheelwright, the carpenter, and, in general, all artisan builders), are in many Alpine districts a sort of nomad folk. Each of them has, indeed, a definite abode somewhere, either in his own little house or in the rented room of a peasant's home, where his family lives, where he has safekeeping for his possessions, and where he spends his Sundays and holidays. On Monday morning, however, he jputs his tools upon his back or in his pocket and starts out upon his rounds; that is, he goes out for work and takes up his quarters in the home of the peasant by whom he has been engaged, and there remains until he has satisfied the household needs. Then he wends his way to another farm. The handicraftsman in his temporary abode is looked upon as belonging to the family." Every peasant's house has a special room with a "handicraftsman's bed" for his quarters overnight; wherever he has been working during the week, he is invited to Sunday dinner.

We find described in almost the same words the industrial conditions of rural Sweden and many parts of Norway. In Russia and the southern Slav countries there are hundreds of thousands of wage-workers, belonging especially to the building and clothing trades, who lead a continuous migratory life and who, on account of the great distances travelled, often remain away from home half a year or more.

From the point of view of development these two forms of wage-work have different origins. Itinerant labour is based upon the ex-

---

[180]In Diocletian's edict de *pretüs rerum venalium* of the year 301 it appears as the prevailing industrial form. Comp. my articles in the *Ztschr. f. die ges. Staatswissenschaft*, vol. 50 (1894), especially pp. 673 ff.

[181]*Aus meinem Handwerkerleben* (Leipzig, 1880). Comp. also *Hansjakob, Schneeballen*, First Series (Popular Ed.), pp. 12-13, 219-224. *Wilde Kirschen*, p. 347.

clusive possession of aptitude for a special kind of work, homework upon the exclusive possession of fixed means of production. Upon this basis there now arises all sorts of *mixed forms* between house-work and wage-work.

The *itinerant* labourer is at first an experienced neighbour whose advice is sought in carrying out an important piece of work, the actual work, however, still being performed by the members of the household.[182] Even later it is long the practice for the members of the customer's family to give the necessary assistance to the crafts-man and his journeyman; and this is still met with in the country, for example, in the raising of a frame building.

In the case of *homework* the later tradesman is at first merely the owner of the business plant and technical director of the production, the customer doing the actual work. This frequently remains true in the country today with oil-presses, flax-mills, mills for husking barley and oats, and cider-mills.

In many North German towns the mediaeval maltsters and brew-ers were merely the owners of malt-kilns and brewing-houses, who for a fee gave the citizens the opportunity of malting their own barley and brewing their own beer. In the flour-mills the customer at least supplied the handler who attended to the sifting of the meal. Even today it is customary in many localities for the peasant's wife, after kneading the dough, to mould the bread-loaves in her own house; the baker simply places, his oven at her disposal, heats it and attends to the baking. In French and western Swiss towns the public washing places are managed in much the same fashion, merely providing their customers with washing-apparatus and hot water, and frequently a drying-place in addition, while the work is done by the servants or fe-male members of the customer's household. These afterwards bring the washed and dried linen to the mangle to be smoothed out, in which process the owner assists by working the handle. Payment is made by the hour. In Posen and West Prussia until recently it was the custom for the owner of a smithy merely to supply fire, tools,

---

[182]The same is true of house-building in the Caroline Islands, where the *takel-bay*, or master builder, is scarcely more than the exorciser of the evil powers that threaten the new structure. See Kubary, *Ethnogr. Beiträge*, pp. 227 ff. The case is different with wagon-building in Armenia, where the skilled neighbour, in return for a present, directs the putting together of the vehicle after the sep-arate parts have been made ready by the members of the household: Tarajanz, as above, p. 27. Similarly with house-building in Faror: Ztschr. d. Ver. f.. Volksk., III (1893), p. 163.

and iron, leaving the actual work to his customers.[183]

From the economic point of view the essential feature of the wage-work system is that there is no business capital. Neither the raw material nor the finished industrial product is for its producer ever a means of profit. The character and extent of the production are still determined in every case by the owner of the soil, who produces the raw material; he also superintends the whole process of production. The peasant grows, threshes, and cleans the rye and then turns it over to the miller to be ground, paying him in kind; the meal is given to the baker, who delivers, on receipt of a baker's wage and indemnification for the firing, a certain number of loaves made from it. From the sowing of the seed until the moment the bread is consumed the product has never been capital, but always a mere article for use in course of preparation. No earnings of management and interest charges or middleman's profits attach to the finished product, but only wages for work done.

Under certain social conditions, end where needs are very simple, this is a thoroughly economic method of production and, like housework, secures the excellence of the product and the complete adjustment of supply to demand. It avoids exchange, where this would lead only to a roundabout method of supplying the producer of the raw material with wares prepared from his own products. But it also forces the.consumer to run the risk attaching to industrial production, as only those needs that can be foreseen can find suitable and prompt satisfaction, while a sudden need must often remain unsatisfied because the wage-worker happens at the very time to be elsewhere engaged. In the case of homework there is the additional danger that a portion of the material furnished may be embezzled or changed. The system has also many disadvantages for the wage-worker. Amongst these are the inconveniences and loss of time suffered in his itinerancy from place to place; also the irregu-

---

[183] *Erlebnisse eines Geistlichen im östl. Grenzgibiet*, in the Tagl. Rundschau, Unterh. Beilage, 1879, No. 258. A point of interest here is the supplying of the iron by the owner of the business, this method of carrying on work thus forming a transition to handicraft. There are also forms in which itinerancy and homework are mingled. To this class belongs the Russian migratory tailor, who in each village where he has customers rents a room for a time and does work for wages. So also, according to Tarajanz the silversmiths in Armenia. In the latter country the owner of an oil-press has to provide his machine, the necessary workmen, and the oxen for driving it; the customer not only assists in the work himself, but he pays, and also boards, the workmen and supplies the fodder for the oxen.

larity of employment, which leads now to the overwork, now to the complete idleness, of the workman. Both forms of wage-work thus act satisfactorily only when the unoccupied hours can be turned to account in some allied branch of agriculture.

In the Middle Ages, when this could be done, wage-work greatly facilitated the emancipation of the artisan from serfdom and feudal obligations, as it requires practically no capital to start an independent business. It is a great mistake still common to look upon the class of guild handicraftsmen of the Middle Ages as a class of small capitalists. It was in essence rather an industrial labouring class, distinguished from the labourers of today by the fact that each worked not for a single employer but for a large number of consumers. The supplying of the material by the customer is common to almost all mediaeval handicrafts; in many instances, indeed, it continues for centuries, even after the customer has ceased to produce the raw material himself and must buy it, as, for example, the leather for the shoemaker and the cloth for the tailor. The furnishing of the material by the master workman is a practice that takes slow root; at first it holds only for the poorer customers, but later for the wealthy as well. Thus arises *handicraft* in the sense in which it is generally understood today; but alongside it wage-work maintains itself for a long time, even entering, in many cases, into the service of handicraft. Thus the tanner is wage-worker for the shoemaker and saddler, the miller for the baker, the wool-beater, the dyer, and the fuller wage-workers for the cloth-maker.

In the towns itinerancy is the first of the two forms of wage-work to decline. This decline is considerably hastened by the interference of the guilds.[184] The itinerancy was too suggestive of early villenage. In it the workman is, so to speak, only a special kind of day-labourer, who must temporarily become a subordinate member of another household. Consequently from the fourteenth century on we find the guild ordinances frequently prohibiting the master from working in private houses. To the same cause is to be ascribed the hatred displayed by the town craftsmen towards those of the country,

---

[184]In this connection it may not be out of place to point out that in teh industrial limitation of those entitled to the privileges of the guild, the old housework was at the same time affected. In very many of the guild ordinances we find the regulation that the non-guildsman may do hancraftsman's work, but only in so far as the needs of his household demand, not for purposes of sale. the surplus house production for the market described above (pp.160, 161) was thereby made impossible.

because the migratory labour of the latter could not well be forbidden. Eventually *itinerant* or *botcher*[185] becomes a general term of contempt for those who work without regular credentials from the guilds. In the North German towns the guild masters claimed the right of entering the houses of their customers to ferret out the itinerant artisans and call them to account,—the so-called "botcherhunt"; and the public authorities were often weak enough to wink at this breach of the domestic rights of the citizen.

But the guilds did not everywhere have such an easy task in supplanting one industrial system by another. As early as the middle of the fourteenth century the sovereign authority in the Austrian duchy takes vigorous measures against them. In the statutes of the electorate of Saxony for the year 1482 shoemakers, tailors, furriers, joiners, glaziers, and other handicraftsmen who shall refuse without sufficient reason to work in the house of their customer are made liable to a fine of three florins, a high sum for those times. In Basel a definite statute governing house tailors was enacted in 1526 for the maintenance of "ancient and honourable customs." In many German territories definite ordinances were made regulating the charges of the various kinds of wage-workers. Thus in many crafts, especially in the building trade, wage-work has persisted down to the present time.

In the majority, however, its place has been taken by the industrial system that today is customarily designated handicraft, whose nature we have indicated at the beginning of the present chapter. It might also be called *price-work*,[186] which would mark the contrast with wage-work. For the handicraftsman is distinguished from the wage-worker only by the fact that he possesses all the means of production, and sells for a definite price the finished article which is the product of his own raw material and his own incorporated labour, while the wage-worker merely receives a recompense for his labour.

All the important characteristics of handicraft may be summed up in the single expression *custom production*. It is the method of sale that distinguishes this industrial system from all later ones. The handicraftsman always works for the consumer of his product whether it be that the latter by placing separate orders affords the occasion for the work, or that the two meet at the weekly or yearly market. Ordered work and work for the market must supplement

---

[185] *Bönhase.*
[186] *Preiswerk.*

each other if "dull times" are to be avoided. As a rule the region of sale is local, namely, the town and its more immediate neighbourhood. The customer buys at first hand, the handicraftsman sells to the actual consumer. This assures a proper adjustment of supply and demand and introduces an ethical feature into the whole relationship; the producer in the presence of the consumer feels responsibility for his work.

With the rise of handicraft a wide cleft, so to speak, appears in the economic process of production. Hitherto the owner of the land, though perhaps calling in the aid of other wage-workers, had conducted this whole process; now there are two classes of economic activity, each of which embraces only a part of the process of production, one producing the raw material, the other the manufactured article. It is a principle that handicraft endeavoured to carry out wherever possible—an article should pass through all the stages of its preparation in the same workshop. In this way the needed capital is diminished and frequent additions of profit to price avoided. By the acquisition of an independent business capital the artisan class is changed from a mere wage-earning class of labourers into a capitalistic producing class; and the movable property now, dissociated from land-ownership, accumulates in its hands and becomes the basis of an independent social and political reputability which is embodied in the burgher class.

The direct relationship between the handicraftsman and the consumer of his products makes it necessary that the business remain small. Whenever any one line of handicraft threatens to become too large, new handicrafts split off from it and appropriate part of its sphere of production. This is the mediaeval division of labour,[187] which continually creates new and independent trades and which led later to that jealous delimitation of the spheres of work that caused a large portion of the energy of the guild system to be consumed in internal bickerings.

Handicraft is a phenomenon peculiar to the town.. Peoples which, like the Russians, have developed no real town life, know likewise no national handicraft. And this also explains why, with the formation of large centralized States and unified commercial territories, handicraft was doomed to decline. In the seventeenth and eighteenth centuries there was developed a new industrial system, based no longer

---

[187]For details see my work, *Die Bevölkerung von Frankfurt a. M. im XIV. und XV. Jahrhundert,* I, p. 228. Compare also Chapters III and VIII.

on the local but on the national and international market. Our ancestors have denoted this system by the two names *manufactories* and *factories*, without distinguishing between the two terms. When viewed more closely these are seen to indicate two quite distinct industrial systems. The one hitherto characterized by the misleading phrase *house industry* we prefer to call the *commission system*,[188] the other is our *factory system*. Both systems undertake the work of supplying a wide market with industrial products, and both require for this purpose a large number of labourers; they differ only in the manner in which they accomplish the work and organize the labourers.

In this respect the method of the commission system is the simplest. In the first place, it leaves the existing method of production quite undisturbed and confines itself to organizing the market. The business undertaker is a commercial entrepreneur who regularly employs a large number of labourers in their own homes, away from his place of business. These labourers are either former handicraftsmen who now produce for a single tradesman instead of for a number of consumers, or former wage-workers who now receive their raw material, not from the consumer, but from the merchant; or, finally, they are peasant families, the former products of whose domestic work are now produced as market wares and by the entrepreneur introduced into the markets of the world.

In some cases the entrepreneur, advances[189] to the small producers, who at first enjoy a fairly independent position, the purchase price of their products; in some cases he furnishes them with the raw material, and then pays piecework wage; while in others he owns even the principal machinery, such as the weaver's loom, the embroidering machine, etc. As the small producers have only the one customer they gradually sink into ever-greater dependence. The entrepreneur becomes their employer, and they are employees, even when they supply the raw material themselves.

It is scarcely necessary to describe in detail the commission system and its contingent method of work, house industry. We have plenty of examples in the mountain districts of Germany, for instance, the straw-plating and the clock and brush industries in the Black Forest, the wood-carving of Upper Bavaria, the toy manufacture in the Meiningen Oberland,the embroidery of the Voigtland,

---

[188] *Verlag.*
[189] *Verleger* comes from *Verlag,* i.e. supplying or advancing.

the lace-making of the Erzgebirge, etc. The history and present condition of these industries have been fairly well investigated in recent
times. But we can no more enter into them than into the great
variety of phases presented by this form of industry.

The essential feature is ever the transformation of the industrial product, before it reaches the consumer, into capital—that is,
into a means of acquisition for one or more intermediary merchants.
Whether the entrepreneur place the product on the general market,
or keep a town ware-room from which to sell it; whether he receive
the wares from the houseworker ready for sale, or himself subject
them to a last finishing process; whether the workman call himself
master and keep journeymen, or whether he be a tiller of the soil as
well—the house workman is always far removed from the real market of his product and from a knowledge of market conditions, and
therein lies the chief cause of his hopeless weakness.

If under the commission system capital has merely assumed control of the marketing of the products, under the _factory system_ it
grasps the whole process of production. The former system, in order to accomplish the productive task falling to it, draws loosely
together a large number of homogeneous labourers, imparts to their
production a definite direction, approximately the same for each,
and causes the product of tneir labour to flow, as it were, into a
great reservoir before distributing it in all directions. The factory
system organizes the whole process of production; it unites various kinds of workers, by mutual relations of control and subjection,
into a compact and well-disciplined body, brings them together in
a special business establishment, provides them with an extensive
and complex outfit of the machinery of production, and thereby immensely increases their productive power. The factory system is as
distinguishable from the commission system as the well-organized,
uniformly equipped regular army from the motley volunteer militia.

Just as in an army corps ready for battle, troops of varied training and accoutrement—infantry, cavalry, and artillery regiments, pi-
oneers, engineers, ammunition columns and commissariat are welded
into one, so under the factory system groups of workers of varied skill
and equipment are united together and enabled to accomplish the
most difficult tasks of production.

The secret of the factory's strength as an institution for production thus lies in the _effective utilization of labour._ In order to
accomplish this it takes a peculiar road, which at first sight appears

circuitous. It divides as far as possible all the work necessary to a process of production into its simplest elements, separates the difficult from the easy, the mechanical from the intellectual, the skilled from the rude. It thus arrives at a system of successive functions, and is enabled to employ simultaneously and successively human powers of the most varied kind—trained and untrained men, women and children, workers with the hand and head, workers possessing technical, artistic and commercial skill. The restriction of each individual to a small section of the labouring process effects a mighty increase in the volume of work turned out. A hundred workmen in a factory accomplish in a given process of production more than a hundred independent master craftsmen, although each of the latter understands the whole process, while none of the former understands more than a small portion of it. As far as the struggle between handicraft and factory is fought out on the ground of technical skill, it is an evidence how the weak overcome the strong when guided by superior intellectual power.

The machine is not the essential feature of the factory, although the *subdivision of work* just described has, by breaking up the sum of labour into simple movements, endlessly assisted and multiplied the application of machinery. From early times machines for performing tasks and for furnishing power have been employed in industry. In connection with the factory, however, their application attained its present importance only when men succeeded in securing a motive power that would work unintermittently, uniformly and ubiquitously, namely, steam; and even here its full importance is felt only in connection with the peculiar industrial form of factory manufacture.

An example will serve to illustrate what has just been said. In the year 1787 the canton of Zurich had 34,000 male and female handspinners producing cotton yarn. After the introduction of the English spinning-machines a few factories produced an equal or greater quantity of thread, and the number of their workers (chiefly women and children) fell to scarcely a third of what it had been before. What is the explanation? The machines? But was not the then-existing spinning-wheel a machine? Certainly it was; and, moreover, a very ingenious one. Machine was thus ousted by machine. Or better, what had hitherto been done by the woman hand-spinner with her wheel was now done by successive collaboration of a whole series of various kinds of workers and machines. The entire spinning process had been decomposed into its simplest elements, and perfectly new operations had arisen for which even immature powers could in part be utilized.

In the subdivision of work originate these further peculiarities of factory production—the necessity of manufacture on a large scale, the requirement of a large capital, and the economic dependence of the workman.

With regard to the two last points we easily perceive an important difference between the factory and the commission system. Its *large fixed capital* assures to factory work greater steadiness in production. Under the commission system the house-workers can at any moment be deprived of employment without the entrepreneur running any risk of losing capital; but the manufacturer must in like case go on producing, because he fears loss of interest and shrinkage in the value of his fixed capital, and because he cannot afford to lose his trained body of workmen. This is the reason why it is probable that the commission system will long maintain itself alongside factory production in those branches of industry in which the demand is liable to sudden change, and in which the articles produced are of great variety.

If, in conclusion, we were briefly to characterize these five industrial systems, we might say that housework is production for one's own needs, wage-work is custom work, handicraft is custom production, commission work is decentralized, and factory labour centralized production of wares. As no economic phenomenon stands isolated, each of these systems of industry is at the same time but a section of a great economic and social order. Housework is the transformation of materials in the autonomous household economy; wage-work belongs to the period of transition from independent household economy to town economy; the hey-day of handicraft coincides with the period when town economy reached its full development; the commission system is a connecting link between town economy and national economy (independent State economy), and the factory system is the industrial system of fully developed national economy.

It would lead us too far to explain in this chapter how each industrial system fits organically into the contemporary method of production and how it is mutually determined by a series of allied phenomena in the spheres of agriculture, personal services, trade and transportation. It can scarcely escape the observant eye that all the elements of the evolution here broadly sketched are contained in the primitive cell of society, the family; or, in economic phrase, in the conditions of production in the independent household. From this primitive social unit, teeming with life and swallowing up all individual existence, parts have continually detached themselves through differentiation and integration, and become more and more independent. Wage-work is only a sprout from the root of the tree of independent household economy; handicraft still needs its protection in order to flourish; commission work makes the marketing of products a special business, while production sinks back almost to the first stages of development. Factory manufacture, on the other hand, permeates with the entrepreneur principle the whole process of production; it is an independent economic system freed from all elements of consumption, and separated as regards commodities and locality from the household life of those engaged in it.

The position of the worker changes in a similar way. With the commencement of wage-work the industrial worker separates himself personally from the independent household economy of the landed proprietor; with the transition to handicraft he also becomes, through the elimination of business capital, materially free and independent. Through the commission system he enters into a fresh personal subjection, he falls into dependence upon the capitalistic entrepreneur; under the factory system he becomes also materially dependent upon him. By four stages of evolution he passes from manorial servitude to factory servitude.

There is a sort of parallelism in this evolution. The relation between the unfree houseworker and the ancient landowner bears a certain resemblance to the relation between the factory hand and the modern manufacturer; and the wage-worker occupies much the same position with regard to the economy of the landed proprietor that the worker engaged in house industry does to the entrepreneur giving out commission work. In the middle of this ascending and descending series stands handicraft as its foundation and corner-stone. From housework to handicraft we see the gradual emancipation of the worker from the soil and the formation of capital; from handicraft to the factory system a gradual separation of capital from work, and the subjection of the worker to capital.

At the stage of housework capital has not yet emerged; there are only consumption goods at various stages of ripeness. Everything belongs to the household—raw material, tools, the manufactured article, often the worker himself. In the case of wage-work the tools are the only capital in the hands of the worker; the raw and auxiliary materials are household stores not yet ready for consumption ; the work-place belongs, under the system of migratory labour, to the domestic establishment that is to consume the finished product, or, under the housework system, to the worker who produces the article. In the case of handicraft the tools, work-place, and raw material are capital in the possession of the worker; the latter is master of the product, though he invariably sells it to the immediate consumer. In the commission system the product also becomes capital—not the capital of the worker, however, but of quite a new figure on the scene, the commercial entrepreneur; the worker either retains all his means of production, or he loses possession successively of his goods, capital, and his implements of production. Thus all the elements of capital finally unite in the hand of the manufacturer, and serve him as a foundation for the reorganization of industrial production. In his hands even the worker's share in the product becomes a part of the business capital.

This share of the worker consists, at the stage of house-work, in a participation in the consumption of the finished products; in the case of wage-work it consists in board, together with a time or piece-work wage, which even at this point includes compensation for wear and tear of tools; in handicraft it consists in the full returns from production. Under the commission system the commercial undertaker takes away a portion of the latter as profit on his business capital; under the factory system all the elements of production which can be turned into capital become crystallizing centres for further profits on capital, while for the worker there remains only the stipulated wage.

We must not, however, imagine the historical evolution of the industrial system to have been such that each new industrial method absolutely superseded its predecessor. That would be just as far astray as, for example, to suppose that a new means of communication supplants those already existing. Railways have done away neither with conveyances on the highways, nor with transportation by means of ships, pack-animals or the human back; they have only confined each of these older methods of transportation to the field in which it can best develop its peculiar advantages: it is probable that not only absolutely but relatively more horses and men are employed in the work of transportation in our civilized countries today than there were in the year 1830.

The very same causes that have produced such an enormous increase in traffic are also at work in the sphere of industry; and in spite of the continual improvement of the mechanical means of production they demand an ever-increasing number of persons. From two quarters, however, the sphere of productive industry is constantly receiving accessions; first, from the old household economy and agriculture, from which even today parts are always separating themselves and becoming independent branches of industry; secondly, from the continual improvement[190] and increase in range of articles serving for the satisfaction of our wants.

As regards the first point, there have sprung up in the industrial world during the last generation dozens of new trades for taking over such kinds of work as used formerly to fall to the women of the household or to the servants, such as vegetable and fruit preserving, fancy baking and preparation of meats, making and mending women's and children's clothes, cleaning windows, feather beds and curtains, chemical cleaning and dyeing, painting and polishing floors, gas and water installation, etc. Under the heading "Art and Market Gardening," the latest statistics of trades in the German Empire give thirty-five, and under the heading "Stock-raising," thirty-one, independent occupations, many of which are of very recent origin.

With regard to the second point, we will mention only the bicycle industry, which within a short time has not only necessitated the erection of a great number of factories, but has already given rise to special repair-shops and separate establishments for the manufacture of rubber tires, cyclometers and bicycle spokes. A still more striking example is afforded by the application of electricity. In the industrial census of 1895 there are enumerated names of twenty-two electrical occupations thatdid not exist in 1882. The production of electrical machines, apparatus and plant in the German Empire gave employment in 1895 to 14.494 persons, with 18,449 members of their families and servants—thus furnishing a living for nearly 33,000 persons.[191] In metal-work, in the manufacture of machin-

---

[190] In reply to a criticism of this expression in the Revue d'économie politique for November, 1892 (p. 1228, note), we will not omit making it more definite by saying that we do not mean by it the improvement of the quality of already existing species of goods, but the supplanting of existing goods by others which better and more cheaply supply the demand.

[191] In a report appearing in the newspapers of August, 1900, Dr. R. Burner estimates the total capital of German firms manufacturing electrical apparatus, in round numbers, at 800 million marks (200 million dollars), and the stock of the so-called *financial corporations*, which are taken up with the laying of electric

ery, chemicals, paper, in the building industries, the clothing and cleaning industries the number of recorded occupations more than doubled itself between 1882 and 1895. It is, at the same time, to be remembered not only that specialization has made immense strides, but that in many instances subsidiary articles of production and trade which have hitherto been produced by the businesses using them are the objects of separate enterprises. In these fields industry not only meets demand but frequently outruns it, as has at all times been the case. In the patent lists we find significant expression of this effort to improve the world of commodities; and though many of the new inventions prove deficient in vitality, there always remains a considerable number whereby life is permanently enriched.

If we were able statistically to bring together the whole sum of industrial products produced yearly in Germany in such a way that we could separate the output of factories, of house industry, and of handicraft, wage-work and housework, we should without doubt find that the greater part of the factory wares embraces goods which were never produced under any of the other industrial systems, and that handicraft produces today an absolutely greater quantity than ever before. The commission and factory systems, it is true, have completely absorbed some of the lesser handicrafts and robbed many others of portions of their sphere of production. But all the great guild handicrafts that existed at the close of the 18th century, with perhaps the single exception of weaving, still exist today. Handicraft is constantly being displaced by the more perfect industrial systems, just as in mediaeval times housework and wage-work were ousted by handicraft, only now it occurs in a less violent manner, on the field of free competition. This competition of all with all, supported as it is by a perfected system of transportation and communication, often compels the transition from custom to wholesale production, even where from the technical standpoint the former might still have been possible. Many independent master workmen enter the service of the entrepreneur carrying on commission or factory work just as their predecessors a thousand years ago became manorial labourers.

Handicraft has thus been relegated economically and socially to a

---

car lines and works, at 450 million marks (112 million dollars). The electric lines, electric works and block stations in Germany are credited, in round numbers, with 1,250 million marks (312 million dollars). So that the whole electrical plant of Germany represents a capital of about two and a half milliards of marks (625 million dollars).

secondary position. But even if it will no longer flourish in the large towns, it has in compensation spread all the more in the country, and here called forth, in combination with agriculture, numerous industries upon which the eye of the philanthropist can rest with delight. Handicraft, it may be said with certainty, will no more disappear than wage-work and housework have disappeared. What it has won for society in a time of universal feudalization, namely, a robust class of people independent of landed property, whose existence is based upon personal worth and a small amount of movables, and who are a repository of popular morality and uprightness—that will and must remain a lasting possession, even though the existence of those whom these virtues will in future adorn may rest upon a different basis.

In recent times there has been raised with rare persistence a cry for the uprooting of the older industry. Handicraft, house, industry, in general all forms of work on a small scale are, we are told, a drag upon the national productive power; they are "antiquated, superseded, rude, not to say socially impeditive methods of production," which in the best interests of those who follow them must be replaced by a "rational and judicious organization and regulation of human activities on a large scale," if the actual national production is not to lag far behind what is technically possible.

This short-sighted economico-political theorizing is not new. There was once a time when every peasant shoemaker who raised his own potatoes and cabbage was looked upon as a sort of enemy to the highest possible national wealth, and when people would have liked to force him by police regulation to stick to his last, even though at the same time he ran the risk of starving. Truly, it has always been much easier to censure than to understand.

If, instead of such dogmatic pronouncements, a willingness had been shown to make an unbiassed investigation of the conditions governing those older and supposedly antiquated systems of production, the conviction would soon have arisen that in the majority of cases where they still persist they are economically and socially justifiable; and the means for the removal of the existing evils would be sought in the soil in which these industrial forms are rooted instead of such drastic remedies being applied to them. In this way we should undoubtedly preserve the good of each of these individual systems and be striving only to remove their disadvantages.

For, after all, the comforting result of every serious consideration of history is, that no single element of culture which has once entered into the life of men is lost; that even after the hour of its predominance has expired, it continues in some more modest position to cooperate in the realization of the great end in which we all believe, the helping of mankind towards more and more perfect forms of existence.

Chapter V. The Decline of the Handicrafts

THERE are in Germany two handicraft problems. One is a problem belonging to the newspapers and the legislatures, which since 1848 has repeatedly occupied the liveliest public attention. For it the question is the extent to which the particular interests of hand-workers as a class should be given legislative expression. What the answer shall be depends upon the relative strength of political parties.

The other problem relates to the vitality of hand-work as a form of industrial activity. It is the query of Hamlet's soliloquy: "To be or not to be!" The answer depends upon actual conditions. Stated more explicitly, the question would read: How far has hand-work up to the present shown itself capable of holding its own? What department of industry does it still dominate?

So long as public policy weighs, not merely wishes and votes, but also the facts of the case, it will not venture to decide the first of these questions until the second has been answered. Until lately the necessary established data have been lacking. Recently, however, the German Social Science Club has conducted a most comprehensive investigation into those branches of industry belonging to the old class of handicrafts.[192] It is therefore opportune to give a general survey of the findings. In this it is not our intention to enter

---

[192] *Investigations as to the Condition of Handwork in Germany, with special Reference to its Ability to compete with industrial Undertakings on a large Scale,* in Schriften des Vereins fur Sozialpolitik, Vols. 62-70 (Leipzig, 1894-1897). A further volume (Vol. 71) relates to Austria. Supplementing this is the inquiry into the conditions of handwork, undertaken in the summer of 1895, and edited by the Imperial Statistics Bureau (3 numbers, Berlin, 1895).

upon a discussion of the present position and future prospects of particular industrial branches,[193] but rather to present the common characteristics of the development that has taken place during the past hundred years or more. This will make it possible to appreciate in their full strength and manifold modes of operation the forces in modern national economy that act as solvents and as creative agents.

A century ago handicraft still held undisputed sway over all its mediaeval inheritance and over its sixteenth and seventeenth century conquests as well. There existed besides, it is true, a few manufactories and factories. But they had developed apart from hand-work; what they produced had never been handicraft work. Rivalry between these new forms of industry and the guild hand-work there had never been. Nor had the guilds as such been interfered with by the State; they had only been made amenable to its laws, and thus been in part stripped of their local municipal character. Their scope indeed had been extended, in that those handicrafts were subjected to the guild constitution, which, because of the limited number of their representatives, had not as yet been able to form local guilds in the various towns. Through the territorial guilds, which had been constituted for these "minor handicrafts," and through the "general guild articles" compactly summarizing uniform trade regulations for all local guilds, the requirements of modern national economy had been at least formally asserted. In practice, however, the local and craft prerogatives of sale, the town monopoly and extra-mural rights of jurisdiction[194] remained in force. Competition between the members of the same handicraft from different towns and of the different crafts of the same towns was entirely lacking; settlement in rural parts was for most crafts forbidden, and to gain independence was made a matter of extreme difficulty for all journeymen who were not masters' sons or sons-in-law.

But what was the condition of the master craftsmen in exclusive possession of these privileges?

Most of those who discuss handicraft today depict the masters "of the golden era of handicraft" as well-to-do people carrying on business "with considerable capital for those times," owning "their own

---

[193]The results of the investigations of H. Grandke along this line are presented in Schmoller's Jahrbuch fur Gesetzgeb, Verwa'.t. u. Volksw., Vol. XXI (1897), PP. 1031 ff.

[194][Comp. dm the latter Roscher, *System der Volksw.*, 5th ed., Vol. 3, § 128.—ED.]

dwellings and extensive workshops," working along with master journeymen and apprentices, personally capable, honourable, respected.
All the painters dip their brush in glowing colours, so necessary for
the portrayal of a condition of prosperity.

Whence have they this picture? We have vainly sought it in
the eighteenth or seventeenth century. Moreover, our classical poets
could not have had it before their eyes; for their "gossiping tailors
and glovers" are petty, insignificant apparitions. In the multitude
of small towns the masters were able to maintain themselves only
through their bit of farming and the lucrative brewing privilege, and
in the larger towns through the little counter kept by many of them
in connection with their workshop. Even for a town of such commercial prominence as Leipzig, the mass of administrative records from
the last two centuries do not allow the impression that the craftsmen of that place were on the average well off; and the extensive
literature on guilds that has come down from the close of the last
and the beginning of the present century, the "Patriotische Phantasien" of Justus Möser, points in many instances to very narrow
circumstances.

The barriers erected against admission to mastership, though
extensive, had not been successfully defended. Among the bakers
and butchers, whom it is customary to cite as types of prosperity,
baking and killing in rotation was the almost universal rule; that is,
there were so many masters that each baker could not bake afresh
each day, nor each butcher kill a head of cattle per week. As late
as 1817 a writer cites as a normal case from Bavaria that in a town
with ten master bakers three bakings of bread were consumed daily,
so that every week the turn fell to each twice. The butchers could
slaughter regularly only the smaller kinds of stock. In North German
towns matters appear to have been in a favourable condition if one
beef were sold every week for every five or six masters.

Almost all crafts with a guild organization had a clause in their
statutes fixing the maximum number of journeymen and apprentices which a master might keep. As a rule he was limited to two.
In the 18th century this number was rarely exceeded. Under normal
conditions, however, the great majority of trades could not attain
to this number. Assuming that all who learned the handicraft acquired master's standing, that a master lived on the average thirty
years after he attained that rank, and that ordinarily a man became independent between the twenty-eighth and thirtieth year of

his life, there could not have been at any time more than half as many journeymen and apprentices as masters. The actual proportion at the end of the century was often much smaller still. In the year 1784 there were in the duchy of Magdeburg 27,050 independent masters and only 4,285 assistants and apprentices. About the same time, in the principality of Würzburg (in Bavaria), 13,762 masters with 2,176 assistants and apprentices were returned.[195] In both territories there were for every hundred masters but 15.8 journeymen and apprentices. Thus, if we assume that the assistants were equally distributed among the masters, one journeyman or apprentice hardly fell to each sixth master. In more than five-sixths of the instances the master carried on his work single-handed. In 1780 the town of Bochum (in Westphalia) counted for every five master masons one; in the other crafts they were for every twenty-six master shoemakers three, for every twenty-one master bakers, every eight carpenters and every five master masons one; in the other crafts they were altogether lacking.

In some parts of Prussia, especially in Berlin, the conditions were indeed somewhat more favourable. But in general the idea must be abandoned that our modern industrial development began with the handicrafts in a condition of general prosperity. The best that past times could offer the craftsmen was a modest competence, security against lack of work and against over-severe competition from their fellows. They deal directly with their customers, in quiet times work up a stock and take it to market, and stand firmly together in the guild if it is a question of voting down a new application for mastership, taking action against an itinerant workman or resisting an encroachment on the part of a neighbouring craft. Towards one another, however, they are possessed with the pettiest bread-and-butter jealousy, and give a great deal of trouble to the courts and administrative officials. Such was the early handicraft.

Down to the fourth decade of last century there was no really great change. After the time of Napoleon, the old industrial policy was repeatedly moderated, but in most parts of Germany it was not abolished until the sixties. It gave place to industrial freedom. Anyone might now carry on any business anywhere and on any desired scale. The local prohibitive powers fell to the ground. Each tradesman could dispose of his products where he would, and in his own

---

[195]According to Schmoller, *Zur Gesch. d. deutsch Kleingewerbe im 19. Jhdt.*, pp. 21, 22.

locality had to tolerate all external competition. The barriers between the different branches of industry dropped away, and everyone could manufacture what was to his advantage.

All this took place with the full assent of the craftsmen themselves. The conviction that the old industrial polity had become untenable was shared in at least the more advanced parts of Germany by all. If ever an old institution was abolished with the approbation of the whole nation, it was the guild system. The sole sporadic misgiving was that apprenticeship might fall into decay, and that many would establish themselves as independent craftsmen who had not regularly learned their trade. This apprehension has proved groundless. According to the results of the inquiry made into handicraft in various districts of Germany, ninety-seven per cent, of those considered as still carrying on an independent handicraft had enjoyed a preparatory training as hand-workers. The small remainder consisted mainly of those who had received their technical training in apprentice shops and technical schools, asylums for the blind, institutions for the deaf and dumb, in prison and in barracks.

The influence of the new conditions on the number, local distribution, and extent of undertakings assumed a different form. At first it was feared that the establishment of numerous petty master workmen without capital would lead to a mass of half-developed business undertakings; but this has in nowise proved the case. On the contrary, after a brief transitional period, the undertakings in the towns have on the average during the last generation numerically diminished, while in financial strength and in the number of assistants, so far as their existence has not been in general jeopardized by causes lying outside the province of industrial legislation, the respective branches of trade have increased. At the same time hand-work has made striking advances in the country, and today is approximately as strong there as in the towns.

This equalization between town and country, however, had been foreseen and aimed at at the time by the advocates of industrial freedom. If there was the further expectation that through industrial freedom the way of the artisan would be opened to technical progress and to economic advancement, this also has not lacked fulfilment. Thousands of urban master workmen have in the last two generations become large manufacturers, or at least capitalistic entrepreneurs, and have participated fully in the technical advances of the period. Freedom of industry and enterprise has made it possible for them to broaden their sphere of production and sale, and to utilize fully their personal ability. This fact men today are only too prone to overlook.

To be sure, the number of those who have not risen in the world, but remained stationary, and of those reduced to the level of master jobbers and homeworkers, or forced to become factory employees, is much larger still. Whole branches of industry formerly carried on as hand-work are almost ruined, or at least are lost to handicraft as a particular industrial form. Others are still struggling for their existence. A great weathering and transforming process has here come into operation; in its train handicraft is yielding place to other forms of business, such as the factory and commission systems, or the hybrid forms that every period of transition begets.

The public at large is content to include all involved in these processes under the simple headings: displacement of hand-work by machinery, annihilation of handicraft by the factory! The smaller cost of production by machinery is looked upon as the sole cause.

The reduction of these expressions to their true value, and the demonstration that a large part of the changes which have taken place has its cause not in the advances of manufacturing technique but in the direction taken by *economic consumption*, and that so far as this is the case handicraft disappears even without machine-work coming into competition with it—this will remain one of the greatest services rendered by recent investigators of handwork. It will be necessary first to present a summary view of these changes in consumption, since they, so to speak, condition the whole development.

In the first place, a *local concentration of demand* has taken place. The aggregations of human beings that have been formed in great cities in the course of the last half century, furthermore the standing armies, the large state and municipal institutions, prisons, hospitals, technical schools, etc., the extensive establishments for transportation, factories, and large undertakings in the departments of trade, banking and insurance, all form centres of wholesale demand for industrial products. To these are to be added the great departmental warehouses, export businesses and cooperative societies, focussing the demand of large sections of the population at a few points. This demand they are no longer able to satisfy as customers of individual craftsmen.

There comes then as a second consideration the many instances in which modern civilization has propounded such colossal tasks for

industry that they cannot be accomplished at all with the implements and methods of handicraft, although each of them generally
requires considerable hand-work. The manufacture of a locomotive,
of a steam crane, of a rapid press, the building of a river bridge
or of a warship, the equipment of a street railway with rails and
rolling stock cannot be carried out with mere hand apparatus and
manual labour. They require immensely powerful mechanical appliances, highly trained engineers and craftsmen of exceedingly varied
qualifications.

Even where technically such tasks might still be accom-plished
with the implements of hand-work, the entrusting of them to master craftsmen is economically impossible because of the consequent
heavy loss of interest. In the Middle Ages the building of a cathedral might occupy two or three generations, indeed, several centuries.
Imagine one today wishing to take as much time for the erection of a
railway station! When in 1896 the contract for the main building of
the Saxon-Thuringian Industrial Exhibition in Leipzig was to be let,
it was first offered to the master carpenters of the city—contractors
who carry on work with considerable capital and are accustomed
to large undertakings. But all hesitated because of the shortness of
the term for building and the extent of the risk. Negotiations were
thereupon entered into with a large firm of builders in Frankfurt-on-
Main. In a few hours the contract was closed. The same evening
the telegraph was working in all directions. A week later the steam
rams were busy on the building site, and whole trains were arriving
from Galicia with the necessary timber.

In fact, one can say that today there are industrial tasks of such
magnitude that they can be performed by only a few, perhaps indeed by but one or two firms in Europe. Hence the development,
beside the earlier type of factory, which finds its strength in the
wholesale production of similar articles, of a new type whose *raison
d'être* lies in the magnitude of the task of production. This more recent kind of large industrial undertaking we might designate by the
already current expression, *manufacturing establishment*[196] At the
head stands a staff of technically trained men, with extensive mechanical appliances at command, and with the necessary hand-work
in most effective combination.

But the demand for industrial labour has been not merely locally
concentrated and condensed to meet the extensive requirements of

----

[196] *Fabrikationsanstalt.*

production; it has also become more uniform, and therefore more massive. *A tendency towards uniformity* runs through our age, eliminating the differences of habits and customs in the various strata of society. Characteristic peasant costumes have disappeared down to unimportant survivals; the furnishing of the dwelling, of the kitchen, has become, it is true, more extensive, but likewise more uniform. Even in the smallest home one finds the petroleum lamp, the coffee-mill, some enamelled cooking utensils, a pair of framed photographs. To make the desired ware accessible to the poorer classes, it must be easily and cheaply produced. If an article is lifted on the crest of a wave of fashion, the demand for it in a cheap form advances even up to the better situated grades of society, and thus the outlay for the folly of fashion is made endurable. In this way there arises a large demand for cheap goods for whose manufacture the earlier type of factory is naturally adapted. Hand-work is for such too expensive; where it remains technically possible it must be extremely specialized, and then it necessarily loses the ground of custom work from beneath its feet.

There is finally another consideration to be alluded to, which belongs to *the sphere of domestic economy.* The home is being relieved more and more of the vestigial elements of production, and is restricting itself to the regulation of consumption. If our grandparents required a sofa, they first had the joiner make the frame, then purchased the leather, the horsehair and the feathers, and had the upholsterer finish the work in the house. The procedure was similar for almost every more important piece of work. Today specialized work demanding the whole strength of each individual, frequently to exhaustion, no longer permits such a participation in production. We will and must purchase what we need *ready-made.* We desire to be quickly supplied, and preferably renounce idiosyncrasies of personal taste, rather than undertake the risk of ordering from different producers. Industry has to adapt itself accordingly.

The same evolutionary process also asserts itself in departments where the individual craftsman had been accus-tomed from time immemorial to supply *finished wares.* Here again the modern city consumer will no longer trade directly with him by ordering the single piece that he requires. He is averse to waiting; he knows that often the work does not turn out as desired, and prefers to choose and compare before he buys.

Thus the craftsman can no longer remain a custom worker even

in those departments in which technically he is fully able to cope
with the demands of production. He no longer works on individual
orders, but exclusively for stock—which formerly he did only in case
of necessity. To reach the consumer he needs the intervention of
the store. By the discontinuance of personal contact between producer and consumer, hand-work as a phase of industry disappears.
It becomes a capitalistic undertaking, and demands management in
accord with mercantile principles. All now depends upon the question whether business on a large or a small scale offers the greater
advantages. In the first case the department of work formerly represented by handicraft falls to the factory, in the latter to domestic
industry.

For even where modern demand has not yet appeared as wholesale concentrated demand, or become condensed to meet the necessi-
ties of production on a grand scale, it is universally well adapted, by
virtue of its great uniformity and its emancipation from household
labour, to localization at a few points. The perfected commercial
machinery of modern times, the low tariffs for post and telegraph,
the rapidity and regularity of freight and news transportation, the
innumerable means of advertising and of making announcements afford here their mighty assistance. Industrial freedom thus found a
well-prepared soil when it sprang into life. It but created the legal
forms that voice the character of modern economic demand. All
those circles of consumers of the craftsmen so long kept artificially
asunder could now be united through the intervention of commerce
into a large manufactory and commission *clientèle*, not necessarily
limited to national boundaries.

Concentrated demand does not permit of satisfaction by scattered production. Along with the process of concentration of demand must go a process of *concentration in the department of industrial production*. It is to this that handicraft on every side succumbs.

But this process is very complicated, and it is not altogether easy
to separate from one another the individual processes of which it is
composed. We will nevertheless essay the task, choosing the fate of
hand-work as the determining factor in the divisions made by us.
We thus arrive at the five following cases:

1. Supplanting of hand-work by similar factory production.
2. Curtailment of its department of production by factory or
commission.
3. Incorporation of hand-work with the large undertaking.

144

4. Impoverishment of hand-work by shifting of demand.

5. Reduction of hand-work by way of the warehouse to home and sweat-work.

Several of these processes often go on simultaneously. In our consideration of the subject, however, we will keep them as far as possible apart.

1. The case in which *capitalistic production* on a large scale attacks handicraft along its whole front, in order to *expel it completely from its sphere of production* is comparatively rare. From earlier times we may mention weaving, clock and gun making, and also the smaller industries of the pin-makers, button-makers, tool-smiths, card-makers, hosiers; from recent times hatmaking, shoemaking, dyeing, soap manufacture, rope-making, nail and cutlery smithing, comb-making: to a certain extent beer-brewing and coopering also belong to the list.

The process of displacement assumes now a quicker now a less rapid character, according as the handicraft in ques-tion formerly carried on manufacture for stock along with market and shop sale, or restricted itself to custom work. Thus the making of shoes for market sale paved the way for the manufacture of shoes by machinery, because it had long accustomed certain classes of the people to the purchase of ready-made footwear.

For handicraft the result of such a development varies according as the factory product, after being worn out, permits of repair or not. In the latter case handicraft disappears altogether; in the former it evolves into a *repair trade*, with or without a *sale shop*. The carrying on by a hand-worker of a shop trade with factory goods in his own line is not exactly an unfavourable metamorphosis; but only craftsmen with considerable capital can manage it. On the other hand, pure repair trade very easily loses the ground of hand-work beneath its feet, if the factory product passes completely into the control of retail merchants. For then the majority of consumers prefer to have repairs made in the shop in which they have purchased the new ware. The proprietor of the shop keeps a journeyman or sends out the mending to a petty master workman. This greatly diminishes their return, and makes them completely dependent. Moreover, repairing can also be carried on on a large scale, as with the so-called rag-dyeing, which works with considerable capital and independent collecting points. Finally, the repairing can become quite superfluous through very cheap production of new wares, as, for example,

145

with clocks and shoes; repair would cost more than a new article.

2. Much more frequently does the second group of evolutionary processes make its appearance. Here it is not a question of the complete loss of the new manufacture, but merely of the *curtailment of the department of production* falling to handicraft through factory or commission business. The causes of this process may be very diverse. While recognising the impossibility of being exhaustive, we will distinguish four of them:

(a) *Various handicrafts are fused into a single manufacturing establishment*: for example, joiners, wood-carvers, turners, upholsterers, painters, lacquerers into a furniture factory; wheelwrights, smiths, saddlers, glaziers into a carriage manufactory; basket-makers, joiners, wheelwrights, saddlers, smiths, locksmiths, lacquerers into a baby-carriage factory. We may mention further all kinds of machine-shops, locomotive and car-works, piano factories, trunk factories, billiard-table factories, and also the establishments for the production of whole factory plants—distillery, brewery, sugar-refinery, etc. As a rule the part of production withdrawn from the individual handicraft through such an *incorporation* forms but a small fragment of its previous sphere of work and of its market. If, however, such blood-lettings are frequent, as among the turners, saddlers and locksmiths, there finally remains very little, and the handicraft may die of exhaustion.

(b) Various *remunerative articles adapted to wholesale production* by factory or house industry are withdrawn from hand-work. Thus bookbinding has had to resign almost its whole extensive department of production to more than forty kinds of special trades; there remains but the individual binding for private customers. Basket-making has surrendered the fine wares to homework, baby-carriages and the like to factories, and only the coarse willow wicker-work remains to handicraft. The locksmith has even lost the article, the lock, from which he has his name; the brush-maker the manufacture of paint, tooth, and nail brushes; the cabinet-maker has been compelled to renounce the intermediate wares (Berlin furniture), and ordinary pine furniture has become a stock-in-trade of the store; confectionery is threatened, in the cities at least, with being despoiled by the factories of the manufacture of bread; the tinsmith no longer makes his vessels; in short there are likely but few handicrafts that have not similar losses to record.

(c) *The factory takes over the primary stages of production.* It

146

was precisely the first rough working of the material which demands the greatest expenditure of strength, it Was exactly this primary handling that suggested the application of machinery, while the finer and individual shaping of the product in the later stages of the process of production tempted the entrepreneur but slightly. In almost all metal and wood industries the raw material is now used only in the form of half-manufactured wares. The furriers work up skins already prepared, the smith purchases the finished horseshoe, the glazier ready-made window-frames, the brush-maker cut and bored wooden parts and prepared bristles, the contracting carpenter inlaid flooring cut as desired and doors all ready to hang.

At first such a loss is generally felt by the handicraft concerned as an alleviation rather than an injury. The process of production is shortened; the individual master can produce a greater quantity of finished articles than formerly; and if he reckons on each piece the same profit as formerly, his income can easily advance provided he retains sufficient work. A locksmith, who procures all door- mountings ready-made from the hardware shop, can readily finish several buildings in one summer, while previously, when he had first to make these wares, he perhaps completed only one. But still, in most cases, through such a cutting into the roots of hand-work, not a few of the master craftsmen become superfluous. At the same time, however, the amount of business capital required increases, since the craftsman has now to make disbursements not merely for the raw material, but also for the costs of production of the partly manufactured product, and furthermore, has to furnish the manufacturer's and trader's profits as well.

This is all the more vital, since just in the first-hand purchase of the raw material and in its proper selection the greatest profit is often made. For this reason trading houses have not infrequently taken over the preparatory stages in production even where a partial manufacture with machinery is not to be thought of. There is absolutely no doubt that the hand-worker in wood was in a better position when he could purchase his wood in the form of logs in the forest than now, when he procures it in the form of boards, laths, and veneers from lumber-dealers; and that the brush-maker worked to greater advantage when he bought the rough bristles from the butcher than now, when he must buy them arranged by the dealer in innumerable classes.

Of course this trade in partly finished goods is very convenient

147

for the craftsman; he can obtain from the dealer even the smallest quantities. But it is exactly this that has contributed not a little to the decline of the handicrafts, since the journeyman can now go into business almost without capital. Thus, for instance, in the shoe trade the manufacture of vamps at first greatly promoted business on a small scale, not because it shortened the manufacturing process for the shoemaker, but because it placed him in a position to purchase a single pair of uppfcrs at the shoefinder's where formerly he had to procure from the tanner at least a whole skin.

This cooperation of mechanical preparatory work and handicraft assumes a particularly interesting frorm where the whole productive part of the labour process drops away from hand-work. The craftsman can then continue to maintain himself only if the product needs to be *set in place* or *fitted*. But he sinks back once more almost to the state of the wage-worker. Thus the locksmith and the joiner (the latter for ready-made doors and inlaid flooring) are now but "fitters"; and the role of the horseshoer nailing on ready-made horseshoes is not very different.

On the other hand, the shortening of the process of manufacture makes the business more capitalistic and the turnover more rapid. The vital element of handicraft, however, is not the profit on capital, but the labour earnings, and these under all circumstances are being curtailed.

(d) *The appearance of new raw materials and methods of production* better adapted for manufacture on a large scale than those previously employed in hand-work, handicaps the latter for a part of this sphere of production. We may cite among other instances the appearance of the curved (Vienna) furniture, the manufacture of wire nails and its influence on nail-smithing, the wire-rope manufacture in opposition to the hempen rope, the invasion by gutta percha of the consumption sphere of leather and linen. The enamelled cooking utensil has encroached simultaneously upon the manufacture of pottery, tinsmithing and the business of the coppersmith; and the invention of linen for bookbinding in place of leather and parchment has smoothed the way for wholesale bookbinding by machinery.

Thus at the most diverse points handicraft is being assailed by the modern, more progressive, forms of manufacture. The attacks, generally delivered in a manner to disarm opposition, are not infrequently made under the fair mask of the stronger friend taking a load from its shoulders, until finally nothing remains to tempt the capitalistic appetite of the entrepreneur.

3. We come now to those cases in which handicraft loses its independence through being *appended to a large business*. Every more extensive undertaking, be it manufacturing, trading, or a general commercial establishment, requires for its own business various kinds of hand-work. As long as such tasks are few in number, they are given out to master craftsmen. But if they grow more numerous and regular, it becomes advantageous to organize a subdepartment for them within the walls of the establishment. Today every large brewery or wine-house has its own cooperage; the street-railway companies maintain work-shops for smiths, saddlers, wheelwrights and machinists; canning factories have their own tinshops; a shipyard keeps cabinet-makers and upholsterers for the internal furnishing of its passenger steamers; almost every large manufactory has a machine and repair shop. The master who enters such a large establishment as foreman of the special workshop ceases, of course, to be free from the control of others, but enjoys, on the other hand, a position that is to a certain extent independent, and, above all, secure.

By the free craftsmen, however, the loss of such strong purchasers is most bitterly felt. Indeed, the system de-scribed can lead to the starving out of whole crafts—a fate that has overtaken, for example, turning, which is being appended to all trades using its products in the partially manufactured state. But this process is too much in the interests of a good economy to make it possible to check it.

The workmen for such subdepartments of a large industrial establishment, be it further remarked, receive as a rule a training in their handicraft as long as it continues to have an independent existence. An abnormally large number of apprentices can thus be employed by it, while the journeymen have a much more extended labour market than the handicraft alone could offer. This is the explana-tion, for instance, of the occasional discovery in the lock-smith's trade of ten times as many apprentices as journey-men.

4. Handicraft is *impoverished through shifting of demand*, and entirely ruined through cessation of demand. Such shiftings have occurred at all epochs—we may recall the use of parchment and peri-wigs—but perhaps never more frequently than in our own rapidly moving times. We will give only a few instances.

The cooper prepared for the household of our grand-parents divers vessels now sought for in vain, at least in a city home: meat-barrels, tubs for sauerkraut and beans, washtubs, water-buckets, rain-barrels, even bathtubs and washing vessels. We no longer keep supplies of meat and preserved vegetables; water is furnished us by the water-works system; and the place of the small wooden vessels has been taken by those of tin, china, or crockery. A second example is offered by the turner, who formerly had to supply almost every household with a spinning-wheel or two, spools and reels. To-day the spinning-wheel has sunk to the position of an "old German" show-piece. Both industries have, of course, found fresh purchasers for those they have lost, especially coopering, through the increase of barrel-packing. But the new customers are factories that at the earliest opportunity incorporate the cooperage as a subsidiary department. The industry of the pewterer presents a third example. The pewter plates and dishes that were to be found in almost every house throughout town and country have passed out of fashion. In their place have come porcelain and stoneware, and the pewterer's trade has thus to all intents lost the very foundation of its existence. Finally, we may recall the shiftings in demand which the great revolutions in the sphere of travel have brought about, and which have fallen with especial severity on the saddler, trunk-maker and furrier.

5. In a last group of instances *handicraft comes into complete dependence on trade*; the master becomes a home-worker, since his products can now reach the consumers only through the store. The cause of this phenomenon is of a double nature: on the one hand, the high rents of city business sites, which force the master to live and pen up his workshop in a garret or a rear house where he is with difficulty found, and where at no time is he sought out by his better customers; on the other, the inclination of the public to buy only where a larger selection is to be had, and where the merchant is "accommodating," that is, sends goods for inspection, takes back if they do not suit, articles like brushes, combs, fine basket-maker's wares and leather goods, small wooden and metal articles which in larger towns are now scarcely ever purchased from the producer or outside the fancy-goods and hardware stores. Indeed, we even give our orders to the stores if we wish to have a special article made. Who today orders his visiting cards from the printer, or a smoker's table from the cabinet-maker? Anyone who has the opportunity of seeing, along the streets that he must traverse perhaps several times a day, so complete a display of everything necessary for his wants that he can in a few minutes procure any desired article, will seldom care out of love for a declining handicraft to betake himself

150

to a distant suburb and there, after a long inquiry and search, climb three or four gloomy staircases before he can deliver his order, in the execution of which the appointed time will perhaps even then be disregarded. And shall, for instance, anyone who finds in a furniture stock everything that is in any way necessary to the furnishing of a room, shall a young housewife who in a few hours can gather together in a housefurnishing establishment a complete kitchen outfit, shall these preferably seek out a half dozen handworkers from whom they can obtain what they want only after weeks of waiting?

Such may be regarded as the chief features of the process of transformation that is taking place today in handicraft. We may, in conclusion, state it as a matured conviction compelled by the results of the investigations, that *in all cases where it supplies finished goods which are not very perishable, and which can be manufactured in definite styles for average requirements, hand-work is endangered in the highest degree. This applies even where a technical superiority on the part of the large undertaking does not exist.* These are, in short, cases in which the product is suited to immediate consumption without further assistance from the producer.

In all these instances trade in its various branches, down to that of hawking, will more and more form the *universal clearing-house for industrial wares.* Handicraft must specialize as far as possible; and it can save itself from the fate of dependence upon the store only by becoming a capitalized industry on a small scale. The union of a sale shop withlhe workshop is then indispensable.

In the contrary instances, where the product of handicraft must be *placed in position* or *separately fitted,* the craftsman at least does not lose touch with the consumers. But even in such cases he can maintain himself in the large towns only if the demand is strongly centralized (as with locksmiths and generally all craftsmen connected with building in the widest sense), or again if he keeps a shop (as with tinsmithing, saddlery, or ordered tailoring), which serves as a *collecting bureau* for orders. In both cases a business without some capital lacks sufficient vitality to exist.

With this conclusion correspond the results of the "Investigations into the Conditions of the Handicrafts." Everywhere in the towns the relative number of masters has greatly diminished, the number of their assistants increased: that is, the businesses have grown. In a still higher degree must their capital have advanced. Manifestly it is the *upper stratum* of city handicraftsmen which has here maintained itself by adopting business methods suited to the requirements of the present, and which probably has prospects of holding its own for some time to come. Where an equal variety is offered, the public will always prefer the shop of the master craftsman to that of the pure tradesman, if for no other reason, because of the convenience for repairs and the greater technical knowledge of the master. The latter, moreover, through the custom coming to the workshop, remains protected from that officious idleness to which the city shopkeeper so readily falls a victim.

In the country conditions have a fairly different aspect. Those causes of repression of hand-work that result from the altered form of demand and the conditions of life in the towns prevail here only in a lesser degree. Rural demand is not yet so very concentrated; it is to a large extent of an individual nature; everyone knows the handworker and his household personally. Connections with neighbours, school comrades or family relatives likewise play a part in holding trade. Here real handicraft soil is still to be found. The craftsman cultivates in many cases a bit of land; at the harvest he will assist his neighbour in mowing and the like; he possesses a cottage of his own; in short, for his sustenance he is not exclusively dependent upon his trade. In his business wage-work and the system of credit balances[197] still largely prevail.

Most of the crafts that have any real footing in the country are in our opinion secure as far as the future can be forecasted. Of course, they cannot completely escape the revolutions in urban industry. In the country the tinsmith, as a rule, no longer makes the tinware he sells, and the smith uses horseshoes purchased ready for use. But the customs connected with consumption change here but slowly; the demand remains more individual, and there is relatively far more repair work; indeed, the agricultural machines have brought fresh work of the latter type for iron-worker, smith, tinsmith, cooper, joiner. About fifty-two per cent. of the master craftsmen in Germany today are found in the country. The country has come to equal the cities in density of hand-worker population. Certainly the number of separate shops in the country is particularly large. In Prussia the average number of persons as assistants has seemingly diminished

---

[197][For a general discussion of credit balances (*Gegenrechnung*) as a feature of public financing comp. an instructive article by the author in Ztschr. d. gesamt. Staatswiss. for 1896, pp. I ff.: *Der öffentl. Haus- kalt d. Stadt Fr. im Mittelalter.*—ED]

somewhat since 1861; the number of apprentices is relatively high. But in this there is no ground for anxiety. The relation between the number of assistants and the number of masters is much more favourable today in rural parts than it was in the cities at the beginning of this century; and the condition of the rural craftsman, according to all that has been published on the subject, though modest, is still satisfactory. In this the reports to hand from Silesia, Saxony, East Friesland, Baden, and Alsace agree. There are certainly some village-craftsmen leading very meagre lives; but such there have been in handicraft at all times.

Among those who consider handicraft the ideal form of industrial activity two means have long been extolled for restoring solid footing and strength to the tottering industrial middle class; and there are many who still believe in their efficacy.

The first is the "return to artistic work." Efforts of this kind have been diligently fostered for well-nigh twenty-five years. For their encouragement museums, technical schools, and apprentice workshops have been instituted. But experience has soon taught, and the investigations of the Social Science Club have confirmed it anew, that these efforts have borne very little fruit for the small trader. Ironwork alone has gained at a few points through the renewed employment of wrought-iron trellis-work, stair balustrades, chandeliers, and the like. Otherwise all establishments successfully carrying on artistic industry are manufacturing businesses of a large, and indeed of the largest, type. This is the case, for example, with bookbinding, art furniture, pottery.

The second means is the *extension of small power machines and the electrical transmission of power*, which shall enable the smallest master to obtain the most important labour-saving machines. Even men like Sir William Siemens and F. Reuleaux have placed the greatest hopes on the popularizing of these technical achievements. These expectations they have based upon the belief that success is simply a question of removing the technical superiority of the large undertaking, this superiority resting indeed in great part upon the employment of labour-saving machines.

In this they have curiously overlooked the fact that mechanical power is the more costly the smaller the scale on which it is employed. According to a table given by Riedel in the *Centralblatt deutscher Ingenieure* for 1891, the comparative expenses of a small motor working ten hours per day and horse-power are as follows (in cents— four pfennigs equal one cent):

Type of Motor	Horse-Power of Motor						
	1/4	1/2	1	2	3	4	6
Small steam	...	...	7(1/2)	5(1/2)	4(3/4)	4(1/4)	3(3/4)
Gas	13	9(1/4)	6	4(3/4)	4(1/4)	4(1/4)	3(3/4)
Compressed Air	10(1/4)	7(1/2)	6(1/4)	5	4(3/4)	4(1/2)	4(1/4)
Electrical	16(1/2)	13(3/4)	11(1/2)	10	9(1/4)	...	...
Petroleum	...	20	15	8(3/4)	7	6(1/4)	5(1/2)

(The price of gas is taken at 3 cents per cubic metre.)

To place two businesses on a footing of technical equality is thus not to give them industrial equality. A machine must be fully utilized and able to pay for itself if it is to cheapen producton. As it cannot take over the whole process of production, but only individual parts of it, it presupposes, if it is to remain continuously in action, an expansion of the business, the employment of a larger number of workmen, greater outlays for raw material, rent of workshop, etc. For this the small master generally lacks the capital. Did he possess it, the advantages of more favourable purchase of raw material, of greater division of work, of employment of the most capable technical and artistic workmen, and of better chances of sale would always remain with the large undertaking.[198] It is difficult to imagine how shrewd men could overlook all this. Has the tailor's, shoemaker's, or saddler's handicraft gained in vitality through the sewing-machine?

The hope of finding through these two devices a new basis for handicraft must be abandoned; in most industrial branches in the larger cities there is no longer any such footing. Only in so far as the conditions of custom work continue unaltered does there remain room for a limited number of businesses leavened with capital. In these other persons take the place of the craftsmen; small and moderately large entrepreneurs, foremen of the factory workshops and skilled factory hands, contractors and home-workers. Externally all these groups, with the exception of the last, are better situated than

---

[198] An interesting proof of what has been said is offered by the wood-turning machines in cabinet-making. None of the many larger handicraft shops in the cabinet trade of Berlin (among which are,also some well-founded businesses of moderate size, with twenty or more workmen) have adopted these machines in their work, although mechanical power of any strength is to be rented in many workshops in the city at a comparatively moderate price. It seems rather to be the case that small independent wage-paying shops have been opened which take charge of the cutting and fitting; and only the largest furniture factories and cabinet-making establishments have set up those machines in their business.

the majority of the small masters of the past. Whether they are better satisfied and happier is another question.

Here, however, we are dealing rather with the tendency of the development than with the actual conditions of today. But we must not be deceived. The decline takes place slowly and silently; great misery, such as prevailed among the hand-weavers when they fought their forlorn battle against the mechanical spinning-mule, is found, with rare exceptions, only in the clothing industries. Certain grades of city population have ever remained true to the handicraftsman, and will be faithful for some time to come. There thus remains time for the coming generation to adapt itself to the new conditions. What it needs for the transition is a better general, mercantile and technical education. The thrifty, cautious person still finds opportunity to carry on work and gain a position; he is not so destitute and at a loss as those who leave school and workshop with insufficient equipment for life. It is our conviction that the process in question cannot be arrested by legislation, though it may perhaps be retarded. But would that be a gain?

In the preceding chapter the evolution of systems of industry was compared with the development of the machinery of commerce, in which the earlier forms were, it is true, pressed back, though not destroyed, by the new. The comparison is applicable likewise to handicraft. Handicraft as a form of work is not perishing; it is only being restricted to that sphere in which it can make the most of its peculiar advantages. That sphere today is the country, the districts where it still finds the conditions of existence that gave birth to it in the Middle Ages.

In rural Germany we have at present, according to tolerably exact estimates, some six hundred and seventy thousand master craftsmen and more than a half million journeymen and apprentices, or together about one and one-fifth millions engaged in active work. Adding the members of the masters' households we have, at a low estimate, a total of over three million persons. The largest part of this numerical success has been achieved by handicraft in our own century. From the socio-political standpoint there is no ground for weeping with the masters of the small country hamlets who have lost their rural customers. Rather the contrary.

During the period of the jealous exclusiveness of the town guilds, when one could pass on the highway thousands of journeymen who could nowhere obtain admittance to mastership, the journeymen smiths had a saying which the stranger at the meeting-house had to recite to the head journeyman[199]. It ran: "A master I have not been as yet, but hope to become one in time, if not here, then elsewhere. A league from the ring, where the dogs leap and break the hedges [town limits], there it is good to be a master."

Settlement in the country, at that time the sheet-anchor of the journeyman smith, still saves many thousands of craftsmen who do not feel themselves equal to the demands of city life. For the country an important social and economic advance lies in this admixture of industrial elements among the people; and the livelihoods there resting upon the foundation of handicraft are among: the most wholesome offered by present society. Of course, they are to be measured by the natural standard of early hand-work, not by the artificial standard taken from the phantasy of economic and political romancers.

For just there lies the seat of the complaints and grievances which since the beginnings of modern development have been raised so persistently by the surviving representatives of urban craftsmen, that they have given rise to a false impression of the degree of comfort that handicraft as an industrial system can possibly afford its representatives. This standard was comparatively high in the Middle Ages, because the hand-worker's position in life was then measured by the position of those in the social grade lying next below his own, from which he himself had often come—the class of villein peasantry, the "poor people" of the country. Compared with this unspeakably oppressed class, handicraft had "golden soil," for it regularly yielded a money return and secured its members civil freedom, while the peasant was exposed to all the vicissitudes of agriculture and to the oppressions of the owners of the soil. It would be false to assume that the mediaeval craftsmen had on the average considerable capital; and it was almost the same with the smaller traders. With what lay beyond—patrician families and nobility— the craftsman did not compare himself; under the system of classes founded upon birth the individual is satisfied if he obtains what is due his class.

Our social system of today rests upon classes determined by occupation. In such a system everyone, compares himself with all others, because no legal barrier separates him from the rest. In comparison with the other classes of modern society, the position of handicraft, even where it is still capable of holding its own, appears a

---

[199]Comp. L. Stock, *Grundzüge d. Verfassung d. Gesellenwesens d. deutsch. Handwerker*, p. 82.

very modest one. All other classes would seem to have raised themselves, and the hand-worker class alone to have remained stationary. Where hand-work is struggling for its very existence, it presents a sad picture of oppression.

It is certainly not a spectacle to be viewed with composure to see that broad stratum of small independent persons who formed the heart of the early town populations disappear and yield place to a disconnected mass of dependent labourers. It is a loss to society for which we find in urban soil no present compensation.

Chapter VI. The Genesis of Journalism.

HE close connection existing in Germany between scientific investigation and university instruction, while exhibiting many unquestionably pleasing features, has this one great disadvantage, that those departments of knowledge which cannot form the basis of an academic career are inadequately investigated. This is the fate of journalism. While in France and England the history of journalism presents an extraordinarily rich and developed literature, we in Germany possess but two essays worthy of mention, one treating of the beginnings, the other, in a decidedly fragmentary manner, of the later development of the daily press.[200]

In this condition of affairs there would be little profit in determining to which of the existing departments of scientific research this neglected task really falls. A subject so complex as journalism can be treated with advantage from very different standpoints: from the standpoint of political history, of literary history, of bibliography, of law, of philology even, as writings on the slovenliness of journalistic style give proof. The subject is, without doubt, of most direct concern to the political economist. For the newspaper is primarily a commercial contrivance, forming one of the most important pillars of contemporary economic activity. But in vain do we search economic text-books, and even commercial manuals in a narrower sense, for a paragraph on the daily press. If, under these circumstances, we venture a brief and summary treatment of the beginnings of journalism, we are ourselves most fully conscious of our inability to make more

---

[200]The little book by Ludwig Salomon, *Gesch. d. deutsch. Zeitungswesens von d. erst. Anfäng. bis z. Wiederaufricht. d. Deutsch. Reiches,* I, 1900, with its incomplete treatment of the subject, cannot materially alter this opinion.

than a partial presentation, and in so far as economic method is incapable of exhausting the material in all its phases, of the possible necessity of deceiving legitimate expectations.

Our descriptions of the beginnings of journalism will vary with our conceptions of what a newspaper is. If the question, What is a newspaper? be put to ten different persons, perhaps ten different answers will be received. On the other hand, no one who is asked to name the agencies that weave the great web of intellectual and material influences and counter-influences by which modern humanity is combined into the unity of society will need much reflection to give first rank to the newspaper, along with post, railroad, and telegraph.

In fact, the newspaper forms a link in the chain of modern commercial machinery; it is one of those contrivances by which in society the exchange of intellectual and material goods is facilitated. Yet it is not an instrument of commercial intercourse in the sense of the post or the railway, both of which have to do with the transport of persons, goods, and news, but rather in the sense of the letter and circular. These make the news capable of transport, only because they are enabled by the help of writing and printing to cut it adrift, as it were, from its originator, and give it corporeal independence.

However great the difference between letter, circular, and newspaper may appear today, a little reflection shows that all three are essentially similar products, originating in the necessity of communicating news and in the employment of writing in its satisfaction. The sole difference consists in the letter being addressed to individuals, the circular to several specified persons, the newspaper to many unspecified persons. Or, in other words, while letter and circular are instruments for the private communication of news, the newspaper is an instrument for its publication.

Today we are, of course, accustomed to the regular printing of the newspaper and its periodical appearance at brief intervals. But neither of these is an essential characteristic of the newspaper as a means of news publication. On the contrary, it will become apparent directly that the primitive paper from which this mighty instrument of commercial intercourse is sprung appeared neither in printed form nor periodically, but that it closely resembled the letter from which, indeed, it can scarcely be distinguished. To be sure, repeated appearance at brief intervals is involved in the very nature of news publication. For news has value only so long as it is fresh; and to preserve for it the charm of novelty its publication must follow in the footsteps of the events. We shall, however, soon see that the periodicity of these intervals, as far as it can be noticed in the infancy of journalism, depended upon the regular recurrence of opportunities to transport the news, and was in no way connected with the essential nature of the newspaper.

The regular collection and despatch of news presupposes a widespread interest in public affairs, or an extensive area of trade exhibiting numerous commercial connections and combinations of interest, or both at once. Such interest is not realized until people are united by some more or less extensive political organization into a certain community of life-interest. The city republics of ancient times required no newspaper; all their needs of publication could be met by the herald and by inscriptions as occasion demanded. Only when Roman supremacy had embraced or subjected to its influence all the countries of the Mediterranean was there need of some means by which those members of the ruling class who had gone to the provinces as officials, tax-farmers and in other occupations, might receive the current news of the capital. It is significant that Caesar, the creator of the military monarchy and of the administrative centralization of Rome, is regarded as the founder of the first contrivance resembling a newspaper.[201] We say resembling a newspaper, for journalism as now understood did not exist among the Romans; and Momm- sen's mention of a "Roman Intelligence Sheet" [202] is but a distorted modernization. Caesar's innovations are to be compared rather with the bulletins and "laundry-lists" which the literary bureaux of our own governments supply for the use of journalists, than with our modern newspapers. Thus in his case it was not a question of founding journalism, but of influencing the newspapers already in existence.

Indeed, long before Caesar's consulate it had become customary for Romans in the provinces to keep one or more correspondents at the capital to send them written reports on the course of political

---

[201]Leclerc, *Des journaux chez les Romains* (Paris, 1838). Lieberktühn, *De diurnis Romanorum actis* (Vimar, 1840). A. Schmidt, *Das Staats- zeitungswesen d. Römer*, in Ztschr. L Geschichtsw., I, p. 303 ff. N. Zell, *Über d. Zeitungen d. alten Römer u. d. DodwelTschen Fragmente*, in his Ferienschriften, pp. 1 ff., 109 ff. Hübner, *De senatus populique Romani actis*, in Fleckeisen's Jhrb. f. Philol., Suppl. Ill, pp. 564 ff. Heinze, *De spurüs diurnorum actorum fragmentis* (Greifswald, 1860).

[202]Mommsen, *Röm. Gesch.*, Ill (4th ed.), p. 601.

movement, and on other events of the day. Such a correspondent was generally an intelligent slave or freedman intimately acquainted with affairs at the capital, who, moreover, often made a business of reporting for several. He was thus a species of primitive reporter, differing from those of today only in writing not for a newspaper, but directly for readers. On recommendation of their employers, these reporters enjoyed at times admission even to the senate discussions. Antony kept such a man, whose duty it was to report to him not merely on the senate's resolutions, but also on the speeches and votes of the senators. Cicero, when pro-consul, received through his friend, M. Cselius, the reports of a certain Chrestus, but seems not to have been particularly well satisfied with the latter's accounts of gladiatorial sports, law-court proceedings, and the various pieces of city gossip. As in this case, such correspondence never extended beyond a rude relation of facts that required supplementing through letters from party friends of the absent person. These friends, as we know from Cicero, supplied the real report on political feeling.

The innovation made by Caesar consisted in instituting the publication of a brief record of the transactions and resolutions of the senate, and in his causing to be published the transactions of the assemblies of the Plebs, as well as other important matters of public concern.

The first were the *Acta senatus*, the latter the *Acta diurna populi Romani*. The publication was made by painting the text on a white tablet smeared with gypsum. The tablet was displayed publicly, and for the inhabitants of the capital was thus what we call a placard. For those abroad copies were made by numerous writers and forwarded to their employers. After a certain interval the original was placed in the archives of the state.

This Roman Public Bulletin was thus not in itself a newspaper, though it attained the importance of such by what we would consider the cumbersome device of private correspondence to the provinces.

The *Acta senatus* were published for but a short time, being suppressd by Augustus. On the other hand, the *Acta diurna populi Romani* obtained such favour in the eyes of the people that their contents could be made much more comprehensive, while their publication was long continued under the Empire. They more and more developed, however, into a kind of court circular, and their contents began to resemble the matter offered by the official or semi-official sheets of many European capitals today. On the whole, they confined themselves to imparting facts; their one noticeable tendency was to ignore the disagreeable.

The contents still continued to reach the provinces by way of correspondence; and, as Tacitus tells us, the people had regard not merely for what the official gazette contained, but also for what it left unrecorded: people read between the lines. How long the whole system lasted we do not know. Probably after the removal of the court to Constantinople it gradually came to an end.

The Germanic peoples who, after the Romans, assumed the lead in the history of Europe, were neither in civilization nor in political organization fitted to maintain a similar constitution of the news service; nor did they require it. All through the Middle Ages the political and social life of men was bounded by a narrow horizon; culture retired to the cloisters, and for centuries affected only the people of prominence. There were no trade interests beyond the narrow walls of their own town or manor to draw men together. It is only in the later centuries of the Middle Ages that extensive social combinations once more appear. It is first the church, embracing with her hierarchy all the countries of Germanic and Latin civilization, next the burgher class with its city confederacies and common trade interests, and, finally, as a counter-influence to these, the secular territorial powers, who succeed in gradually realizing some form of union. In the twelfth and thirteenth centuries we notice the first traces of an organized service for transmission of news and letters in the messengers of monasteries, the universities, and the various spiritual dignitaries; in the fourteenth and fifteenth centuries we have advanced to a comprehensive, almost postlike, organization of local messenger bureaux for the epistolary intercourse of traders and of municipal authorities. Arid now, for the first time, we meet with the word *Zeitung*, or newspaper. The word meant originally that which was happening at the time (Zeit = time), a present occurrence; then information on such an event, a message, a report, news.

In particular do we find the word used for the communications on current political events which were received by the town clerks from other towns or from individual friends in the councils of those towns, either as letters or as supplements to them, and which are still frequently found in their archives. Thus the municipal archives of Frankfurt-on-Main possess as many as 188 letters relating to the raids of the Armagnacs in the early forties of the fifteenth century; they are mostly descriptions of sufferings and appeals for help from towns in Alsace and Switzerland. Among them are not less than three accounts of the battle of St. Jacob, one from Zürich, one from Strassburg, and one from the council of Basel[203].

This reporting is voluntary, and rests upon a basis of reciprocity. It sprang from the common interest uniting the towns against the noble and the territorial powers, and found effective support in the numerous town messengers who maintained in regular courses—for this reason, called "ordinary" messengers—the connection between Upper and Lower Germany.

In the fifteenth century we find a similar exchange of news by letter between people of high standing—princes, statesmen, university professors—which reaches its highest development during the era of the Reformation. It is now good form to add to a letter a special rubric, or to insert on special sheets, "*Novissima*," "Tidings," "New Tidings" or "News," "Advices." Moreover, we already notice how people have ceased to give each other mere casual information about the troubles and distress of the time, and aim at a systematic collection of news. It was especially to the great commercial centres and the trading towns which were the centres of messenger activity and the seat of higher education that news items flowed from all quarters, there to be collected and re-edited into letters and supplements, and thence to be diverted in streams in all directions. Everywhere these written tidings bear the name of newspaper (*Zeitung* or *neue Zeitungen*).

The largest part of this correspondence is of a private character. Men at the centre of political and ecclesiastical activity communicated to each other the news that had come to hand. It was a reciprocal giving and receiving which did not prevent those with

---

[203]Wülker, *Urkunden u. Schreiben, betreff. d. Zug d. Armagnaken*: in Neujahrsblatt d. Vereins f. Gesch. u. Altertumsk. zu Frankfurt-a.-M. for 1873.

On the following section consult: Hatin, *Histoire politique et littéraire de la presse en France* (Paris, 1859-61), Vol. I, pp. 28 ff., and his *Bibliographic historique et critique de la presse périodique française, précédée d'un Essai historique et statistique sur la naissance et les progrès de la presse périodique dans Us Deux Monies* (Paris, 1866), pp. xlvii ff.; Leber, *De l'état réel de la presse et des pamphlets depuis François I jusqu'a Louis XIV* (Paris, 1834); Alex. Andrews, *The History of British Journalism* (London, 1859), Vol. I, pp. 12 ff.; Ottino, *La stampa periodica, il commercio dei libri e latipographia in Italia* (Milano, 1875), p. 7; Rob. Prutz, *Geschichte d. deutsch. Journalismus* (Hanover, 1845), Vol. I: J. Winckler, *Die period. Presse Oesterreichs* (Vienna, 1845), pp. 19ff.; Grasshoff, *Die briéfliche Zeitmg d. XVI. Jahrhunderts* (Leipzig, 1877): *Steinhgusen*, in Archiv i Post u. Telegraphie, 1895, pp. 347 fi., and his *Geschichte d. deutsch. Briefes*, 2 vols.

a heavy correspondence from multiplying their news-sheets in order to append them to letters to different persons, nor the recipients from redespatching copies of them or circulating them amongst their acquaintances. Princes, it would seem, already maintained at important commercial points their own paid correspondents.

For a time these written newspapers did not find their way among the masses. The circles for which they were intended were: (1) princes and statesmen, as also town councillors; (2) university instructors and their immediate cooperators in the public service in school and church; (3) the financiers of the time, the great merchants.

Almost all reformers and humanists are diligent newspaper correspondents and regular recipients of newspaper reports. This is especially true of Melancthon, whose numerous connections throughout all parts of Germany and the neighbouring countries continually brought him a plentiful store of fresh news, with which he in turn supplied his friends, and certain princes in particular. In comparison with his, Luther's and Zwingli's correspondence is relatively poor in such matter. On the other hand, John and Jacob Sturm, Bucer and Capito of Strassburg, Oecolampadius and Beatus Rhenanus of Basel, Hatzer and Urbanus Rhegius of Augsburg, Hier. Baumgartner of Nuremberg, Joachim Camerarius, Bugenhagen, and others were very zealous and active in this direction.

The sources for their news are manifold. Besides oral or written communications from friends, we know of narratives of incoming merchants, particularly of book-dealers who had visited the Frankfurt fair, reports of letter-carriers, accounts from soldiers returning home from their campaigns, communications from strangers passing through their town or from visiting friends, and especially from students coming from foreign lands to study at German universities; finally, any items gleaned from foreign ambassadors who happen to be passing through; from chancellors, secretaries, and agents of important personages.

Naturally such oral news collected at random varied greatly in worth, and had first to undergo the editorial criticism of the correspondent before being circulated further. The news-items based upon written information were of much greater importance. It may be of some interest, by following Melancthon's correspondence, to inquire somewhat into the sources of them[204].

---

[204] According to Grasshoff, cited above, pp. 23 ff.

We soon perceive that there were a number of definite collecting centres for the various classes of news. In the forefront of interest at that time stood the Eastern question, that is, the threatening of the countries of Central Europe by the Turks. News of the engagements with the latter came either from Hungary through Vienna, Cracow or Breslau, or from Constantinople by sea by way of Venice. The reporters are mostly ecclesiastics, adherents of the New Learning.

On affairs in the South communications came from Rome, Venice, and Genoa, as well as from learned friends in Padua and Bologna. News from France and Spain was procured by way of Lyons, Genoa, and Strassburg; from England and the Netherlands by way of Antwerp and Cologne; from the countries of the North by way of Bremen, Hamburg, and Lubeck; from the Northeast by way of Königsberg and Riga.

In Germany, Nuremberg was the chief collecting centre for news, partly by reason of its central position, partly because of its extensive trade connections. Anyone desirous of receiving reliable and definite information on the doings of the world wrote to Nuremberg or sent thither a representative. Princes like Duke Albert of Prussia and Christian III of Denmark there maintained resident correspondents, whose duty it was to collect and report any fresh items of news. Town officials, councillors, and reputable merchants frequently undertook such an office. Besides Nuremberg, Frankfurt, Augsburg, Regensburg, Worms, and Speier were also important news centres.

The newspapers that Melancthon compiled from these various sources are simply historical memoranda, selected with some care and interspersed at rare intervals with discussions of a political nature, and more frequently with all kinds of complaints and fears, wishes and hopes. Along with the important news from the Emperor's court, from the various seats of war and on the progress of the Reformation, we meet with others reflecting the complete naivete and incredulity of the times: reports of political prophecies, strange natural phenomena, missbirths, earthquakes, showers of blood, comets and other celestial apparitions.

In the second half of the sixteenth century this species of news-agency received definite form and organization as a business, not merely in Germany, but, apparently even earlier, in Italy, especially in Venice and Rome.

Venice was long regarded as the birthplace of the newspaper in the modern acceptation of the word. This opinion was supported by the extensive use of the name *gazetta* or *gazette* amongst the Latin nations for a newspaper; and this word is to be found earliest in Venice as the name of the small coin.

We will not enter into the accounts—at times rather romantic—that have been given to justify the derivation (in itself improbable) of the name of the newspaper from the name of the coin.[205]

In itself, however, there is much to be said for the presujnption that journalism, as described above, was first developed as a business in Venice. As the channel of trade between the East and West, as the seat of a government that first organized the political news service and the consular system in the modern sense, the old city of lagoons formed a natural collecting centre for important news-items from all lands of the known world. Even early in the fifteenth century, as has been shown by the investigations of Valentinelli, the librarian of St. Mark's Library, collections of news had been made at the instance of the council of Venice regarding events that had either occurred within the republic or been reported by ambassadors, consuls, and officials, by ships' captains, merchants and the like. These were sent as circular despatches to the Venetian representatives abroad to keep them posted on international affairs. Such collections of news were called *fogli d'avvisi*.

Later on, duplicates of these official collections were made, though evidently not for public circulation, but rather for the use of prominent citizens of Venice who sought to derive advantage from them in their commercial operations, and also communicated them by letter to their business friends in other lands.

This appending of political news to commercial correspondence, or the enclosing of the same on special sheets, soon became the practice also among the large traders of Augsburg, Nuremburg, and the other German towns. By and by it occurred to some that the collection and transmission of news by letter could be made a source of profit. In the sixteenth century we find on the Venetian Rialto, between the booths of the changers and goldsmiths, an independent news-bureau that made a business of gathering and distributing to interested parties political and trade news: information as to arrival and clearance of vessels, on prices of wares, on the safety of the highways, and also on political events.[206] Indeed, a whole guild of *scrittori d'avvisi* grew up. In a short time we meet with, the same

---

[205]Comp. Hatin, *Bibliographie de la presse périodique*, p. xlvii.
[206]According to Prutz, *Gesch. d. Journalismus*, I, p. 212.

people in Rome, where they bear the name _novellanti_ or _gazettanti_. Here their activity, whether because they circulated disagreeable facts or accompanied their facts with their own comments, became discomforting to the Curia. In the year 1572 not less than two papal bulls were issued against them (by Pius V and Gregory XIII); the writing of "advices" was strictly forbidden, and its continuance threatened with branding and the galleys. Nevertheless we continue to meet numerous indications of a news service from Rome to the Upper Italian cities and to Germany.

In the meantime, newspaper writing had also become a business in Germany with an organization that, for the existing conditions of trade, is really wonderful. This organization is connected on the one hand with the further development of despatch by courier, and on the other with Emperor Maximilian's institution of the post from the Austrian Netherlands to the capital, Vienna, by which the regular receipt of news was greatly facilitated. We thus find, at various places, in the second half of the sixteenth century, special correspondence bureaux which collect and communicate news by letter to their subscribers. Several collections of these epistolary newspapers have been preserved: for instance, one from 1582 to 1591 in the Grand Ducal library in Weimar, and two in the University library at Leipzig from the two last decades of the same century[207].

Let us refer briefly to the oldest year of the Leipzig collection. It bears the heading: "News to hand from Nuremberg from the 26th of October Anno 87 to the 26th of October Anno 88." Then follow in independent groupings transcripts of the news received weekly from Rome, Venice, Antwerp, and Cologne at the office of the Nuremberg firm of merchants, Reiner Volckhardt and Florian von der Bruckh, and thence given out again either by the house itself or by a special publisher. The person who received the present collection was probably the chief city clerk of Leipzig, Ludwig Trüb.

The communications from Rome are as a rule dated about six days earlier than those from Venice, and the Antwerp correspondence about five days earlier than that from Cologne. All four places lay on the great post-routes from Italy and the Netherlands to Germany. Along with these periodical communications irregular ones appear now and then, for instance, from Prague and Breslau, and particularly often from Frankfurt-on-Main.

---

[207]Comp. Jul. Opel, _Die Anfänge d. deutsch. Zeitungspresse_ in Archiv f. Gesch. d. deutsch. Buchhandels, Vol. Ill (1859).

Examining the contents of these news items more closely we soon find that we have to do not with events occurring in Rome, Venice, Antwerp, etc., but with reports collected at these places. Thus the correspondence from Antwerp contained not merely news from the Netherlands, but also from France, England, and Denmark; by way of Rome came news not only from Italy, but from Spain and the south of France as well; from Venice came news from the Orient. The reports are soberly descriptive and commercial in tone. Political items preponderate; communications on trade and commerce appear less frequently. There is no trace of the favourite tales of wonders and ghosts.

But how was the news service in these four great collecting points organized? Who were the collectors and the intermediaries? How were they paid? What were their sources of information? Unfortunately we can answer only part of these questions.

In the first place, as to the sources from which the authors of the letters derive their information, they themselves appeal at times even to the last mail or to the regular messenger service, the "Ordinari". Thus we read in a letter from Cologne dated February 28, 1591: "The letters from Holland and Zeeland, and also from Italy, have not yet appeared." In a similar letter from Rome of date February 17, 1590, we are informed that the postmaster there has contracted with the Pope to establish a weekly post to and from Lyons; and at the close we read, "In this way we shall have news from France every week."

Nothing more than this is to be gleaned from the collection itself. When, however, we notice contemporaneously in several German cities that it is the heads of the town-couriers and the imperial postmasters who in particular devote themselves to the business of editing and despatching news-letters, the supposition gains greatly in probability that the collection of news is in most intimate connection with the mail service of the time. The messenger masters and the postmasters probably exchanged at regular intervals the news they had collected, in order to pass it on to their particular clients. But the whole matter stands greatly in need of closer investigation[208].

The relations between wholesale trade and newspapers are some-

---

[208]Steinhausen in Archiv f. Post u. Tel., 1895, p. 355, expresses merely a supposition, though indeed a very well grounded and probable one, on the course of development.

what clearer. Like the Nuremberg merchants mentioned above, some large trading houses in other localities had also organized an independent news service. Especially prominent were the Welsers and Fuggers, whose news reports we find in the celebrated letter-book of the Nuremberg jurist, Christoph Scheurl[209], along with the Nuremberg correspondence. In the second half of the sixteenth century the Fuggers had the news coming to them from all parts of the world, regularly collected and apparently also published. The title of the regular numbers was "*Ordinari-Zeittungen.*" There were also supplements, or "specials," with the latest items. The price of one number was four kreuzer; the yearly cost in Augsburg, including delivery, was 25 florins, and for the *ordinari* numbers alone, 14 florins. One Jeremiah Krasser, of Augsburg, burgher and newspaper writer, is named as editor. He informs us that he supplied many other gentlemen in Augsburg and district with his news. A file of this organ of publication, so rich in material, for the years 1568 to 1604 is found in the Vienna library[210].

The newspapers of the Fuggers regularly contain news from all parts of Europe and the East, and also from places still further removed: Persia, China and Japan, America. Besides the political correspondence, we have frequent reports of harvests and memoranda of prices, now and then even communications in the nature of advertisements, and a long list of Vienna firms—how and where all things could now be procured in Vienna. Even literary notices of recent and noteworthy books appear; and there is one account of the presentation of a new drama.

As in Augsburg, so in other places in Germany we meet individual correspondents—journalists (*Zeitunger*), novelists—who carry on their newspaper writing in the service of princes or of cities. Thus in 1609 the elector of Saxony, Christian II, made a contract with Joh. Rudolf Ehinger, of Balzhein in Ulm, whereby the latter undertook for a yearly fee of 100 florins to furnish reports upon events in Switzerland and France, Swabia naturally being included. In the year 1613 Hans Zeidler, of Prague, received from the Saxon court for similar service a yearly salary of 300 florins, together with 3319 thalers 6 g. gr. for expenses incurred in collecting his news[211].

---

[209]Christoph Scheurl: *Briefbuch, ein Beitrag z. Geschich. d. Reformation u. ihrer Zeit* (Sooden u. Knaake, Potsdam, 1867-1872).
[210]Sickel, Weimar. Jahrb. f. deutsche Sprache u. Litteratur, I, p. 346.
[211]C. D. v. Witzleben, *Gesch. d. Leipziger Zeitung* (Leipzig, 1860), pp. 5-6.

In the same year the sovereign bishop of Bamberg had newspapers forwarded to him by a Dr. Gugel, of Nuremberg, for a fee of 20 florins. In the year 1625 the town of Halle paid the news correspondent, Hieronymus Teuthorn, of Leipzig, the sum of two schock, eight groschen, as quarterly fee; and as late as 1662 the council of the town of Delitzsch was subscriber to a newspaper correspondence from Leipzig at a quarterly fee of two thalers. The postmasters and messenger chiefs appear to have been paid somewhat better for their services, which were indeed more valuable. At least, we know that in the year 1615 the postmaster at Frankfurt, Johann von der Birghden, who furnished a great number of German princes with news, was in receipt of a yearly salary of 60 florins for supplying the electoral court of Mainz with the weekly newspapers[212].

Even in the seventeenth century the written newspapers appear not to have made their way to wider circles. They were still too costly for that.

At the close of the sixteenth and in the seventeenth century we find written newspapers in France and England, as well as in Germany and Italy. In France they are called *nouvelles à la main*; in England, *news-letters*. In both countries they are confined to the capital city.

The line of development in Paris is the more interesting: it may be said indeed that the most primitive of all newspapers, the precursor of the written newspaper, is to be found there. It is the related, or spoken, paper[213].

In the turbulent times of the sixteenth and seventeenth centuries groups of Parisian burghers would assemble each evening on the

The Saxon court in 1629 maintained similar agents in Vienna, Berlin, Brunswick, Augsburg, Ulm, Breslau, Hamburg, Lübec, Prague, Amsterdam, at the Hague, and in Hungary.

[212]Faulhaber, *Gesch. d. Post in Frankfurt-a.-M.* (Archiv. f. Frankf. Gesch. u. Kunst, New Series, X), pp. 31, 60 ff.

[213]Comp. Hatin, *Histoire de la presse en France*, Vol. I, pp. 32-33. [An interesting present-day instance of the "spoken" newspaper, which may indeed not be so very rare a phenomenon, is given in a sketch of Swiss life in the little village of Champery by a recent writer in the Canadian Magazine. "On three of the houses of the village," it is stated, "are curious balconies, which are in reality old pulpits, once used for open-air preaching. They now serve the place of the country newspaper, for on Sundays, after mass, a man calls out from them the news of the week, what there is for sale, what cattle have been stolen or have strayed, and other items of interest to those who have come down for the day from the isolation of the high mountains."—*Swiss Life and Scenery*, by E. Fanny Jones. Can. Mag., Aug. 1898, p. 287.—ED.]

street corners, on the Pont Neuf, and on the public squares, bringing together the news of the day and making their own comments
upon it. As is easily conceivable, there were among these groups
individuals who became adepts in the collection and repetition of
news. Gradually method and organization were introduced; the so-
called *nouvellistes* held regular meetings, exchanged their news with
each other, and made comments thereon, discussed politics, and laid
plans.

The writers of the time treat these groups with never-ending
satire; the comic dramatists seize the fruitful theme, and even Mon-
tesquieu devotes to them one of the most entertaining of his *Lettres
Persanes*[214].

What was at the outset a mere pastime for news-hunters and
idlers, enterprising brains soon developed into a business. They
undertook to supply regular news to people of rank and standing.
Men in high station kept a *nouvelliste* as they kept a hair-dresser
or surgeon. Mazarin, for instance, paid such a servant 10 livres per
month.

These groups of *nouvellistes* soon began to seek customers in the
Provinces also, and these, of course, could be supplied only by letter.
Each group had its particular editorial and copying bureau, and its
special sources for court and official news. The subscribers paid a
fixed sum, according to the number of pages that they desired each
week. Thus originated the celebrated *nouvelles à la main*, which,
in spite of many prosecutions on the part of the government, lasted
till well towards the end of last century, and which were often sent
abroad as well[215]. That which gave them a firm footing along with
the printed newspapers was, to a certain extent, the circumstance
that they rendered the secrecy of the government system largely
illusory, and further, took the liberty now and then of animadverting
on public conditions[216].

In England likewise the *news-letters*, more especially devoted to
furnishing the country nobility with the news of the capital and
the court, maintained themselves well into the eighteenth century.
The printed newspapers of that epoch indeed adapted themselves

[214] *Œuvres complètes* (Paris, 1857), p. 87, Lettre CXXX.
[215] *La Gazette de la Régence, janvier 1715—juin 1719, publiée d'après le
manuscrit inédit conservé a la Bibliothèque royale de La Haye, par Le Comte E.
de Barthélemy* (Paris, 1887) gives a description of the contents of these sheets.
[216] Similarly in Austria: Joh. Winckler, *Die period. Presse Oesterreichs* (Vienna, 1875), PP- 28-9.

to the system to the extent of appearing with two printed and two unprinted pages, thereby enabling their subscribers to send them to others, enriched with additional notes in writing[217].

Thus we see that at about the same time in all the advanced countries of Europe the written newspaper arises as a medium—of course, as yet a decidedly restricted medium—of news publication, and maintains itself for more than two hundred years. It is, however, most remarkable that the production of these written news-sheets as a business can nowhere be traced beyond the period of the invention of printing. In this connection the question naturally arises, why the printing-press was not taken into the service of the regular news publication.

The question is answered by the simple fact that even in young colonial countries with an European population accustomed at home to printed newspapers, the written preceded the printed news-sheets. This was true of the English colonies in America at the beginning of the eighteenth century[218], and of the colony of West Australia in 1830[219]. This proves that it could not have been so much the pressure of the censorship, that so long delayed the employment of the press for news publication, as the lack of a sufficiently large circle of readers to guarantee the sale necessary to meet the cost of printing.

However, since as far back as the close of the fifteenth century, special numbers of those written newspapers containing matter of a presumably broader interest were frequently printed. These were the *one-page prints* issued by enterprising publishers under the name of "*Neue Zeitung*," and disposed of at fairs and markets. Collections are to be found in every old library[220]. The oldest of these prints

---

[217]For details: Andrews, *The History of British Journalism*, Vol. I, pp. 14 ff.; Hatin, as above, p. 51. Joachim von Schwarzkopf, U*eber Zeitungen* (Frankfurt-on-Main, 1795), p. 9, relates that likewise in Germany "in the case of some newspapers that in contents and form resembled manuscript sheets (for example in Mainz and Regensburg) the printing-press was occasionally made use of because of the large number of subscribers." He also mentions Vienna, Munich, Berlin and Hanover as places from which sheets filled with secret domestic news were distributed.

[218]Frederic Hudson, *Journalism in the United States from 1690 to 1830* (New York, 1873), pp. 51 ff.

[219]Andrews, as above, Vol. II, pp. 312 ff.

[220]Treated bibliographically by Weller, *Die ersten deutsch. Zeitungen* (Bibliothek d. literar. Vereins, Vol. LXI). Supplement to same in the "Germania," XXVI, p. 106.

is a report of the obsequies of Emperor Frederick III from the year 1493. From that time till the sixteenth century had run its course they continued to hold their own; but with the growth of periodical news-sheets, they became rarer, and finally, in the eighteenth, disappeared. The earliest numbers bear either no title at all or take their title from the contents. The name *Zeitung*, or newspaper, for such a loose sheet appears for the first time in 1505. We find, however, various other appellations; for example, Letter, Relation, Tale, News, Description, Report, Advice, Post, Postilion, Courier, Rumour, Despatch, Letter-bag[221]. To these all kinds of qualifying titles are frequently added, such as Circumstantial News, Truthful and Reliable Description, Faithful Description, Truthful Relation, Review and Contents, Historical Discourse, and Detailed Explanation; very often we have: New and Truthful Tidings, Truthful and terrible Tidings, Wonderful, terrible, pitiful Tidings. In England some of the titles are: Newes, Newe Newes, Thiding, Woful Newes, Wonderful and strange News, Lamentable News; and in France: Discours, Memorable Discours, Nouvelles, Recit, Courier, Messager, Postilion, Mercure, etc.

The titles, we notice, are sensational and pretentious. The contents vary greatly. In the great majority of cases they consist of political news; argument remains altogether in the background. The written news-letters are the chief, though not the sole, source for these fugitive productions of the printing-press. Ordinarily, the one page prints are independent of each other; and only here and there at the end of the sixteenth century can several consecutive numbers be instanced; but this is not sufficient to justify us in supposing a periodical issue. These loose sheets, however, at least prepare the way, as regards form and matter, for the printed newspaper with its regular issues. And they render a like service in so far as they awakened among the masses an interest in occurrences reaching beyond mere parish affairs.

The first printed periodical news collections begin as early as the sixteenth century. They are annual publications, the so-called *Postreuter* (postilions) or news epitomes whose contents may in a manner be compared with the political reviews of the year in our popular calendars[222].

---

[221] *Brief, Relation, Mär, Nachricht, Beschreibung, Bericht, Aviso, Post, Postillion, Kurier, Farna, Depesche, Felleisen.*

[222] According to Prutz, cited above, they appeared as early as the middle of

These are supplemented by semi-annual news summaries, the so-called *Relatiomes semestrales* or Fair Reports. They were begun between 1580 and 1590 by Michael von Aitzing. They drew their information chiefly from the regular post and traders' newspapers, and for more than two centuries formed one of the chief articles of sale at the Frankfurt fair, and later on at the Leipzig spring and fall fairs as well[223]. The first printed *weekly* of which we have direct information is a Strassburg sheet, whose numbers for the year 1609 are found in the University library at Heidelberg, while fragments of later years are preserved in the public library at Zürich[224]. It corresponds exactly in matter and form with the regular despatches which the post brought weekly from the chief collecting places of the news trade. It was soon imitated; and after the beginning of the Thirty Years' War the growth in the number of printed weeklies was particularly rapid. We have evidence of the existence of about two dozen in the second and third decades of the seventeenth century. They were established chiefly by book-printers; though in numerous places the post assumed, naturally with varying success, the right of printing despatches as a part of its prerogative. While in Frankfurt, Leipzig, Munich, Collogne, and Hamburg the old connection between post and newspaper continued for a considerable time, the publication of news was in many other towns completely absorbed by the book-printers, a fact of the greatest moment for its further development.

Germany is the first country that can show printed newspapers appearing regularly at brief intervals. The English and the Dutch claims to the honour of having produced the earliest printed weeklies are now generally abandoned. England can point to nothing similar before the year 1622: the first French weekly sheet appeared in 1631[225].

It will perhaps seem strange that a leap was made directly from

the sixteenth century.
[223] *F. Stieve, Ueber d. ältest, halbjährig. Zeitungen oder Messrelationen, u. insbesond. über deren Begründer.* Frhrn. Michael von Aitzing: Abh. der k. bayer. Akad. d. Wiss., Ill, CI. XVI, p. I (Munich, 1881). Comp. also Orth, *Ausführl. Abhand. von d. berühmten zwoen Reichsmessen, so in d. Reichsstadt Frankfurt-a.-M. jährlich abgehalten werden* (Frankfurt, 1765), pp. 714 ff.; Prutz, as above, pp. 188 ff; J. von Schwarzkopf, *Ueber politische u. gelehrte Zeitungen in Frankfurt-a.-M.,* 1802.
[224] Opel, as above, pp. 44 ff.
[225] [See article *Newspapers* in the Ency. Brit, and the literature there given.—ED.]

half-yearly reports to weekly publications without a transitional
stage of monthly reports. It must, however, not be forgotten that
the collection of news, as well as the distribution of the news-sheets,
had to conform to the peculiar commercial facilities of the time. The
most important of these were the fairs and the stage-posts. The
semi-annual fairs made possible the distribution of the printed news
from one great centre of trade and travel to even the most remote
points. But the stage-posts traversed the chief trade-routes once a
week each way. The leap from the half-yearly to the weekly reports
lay thus in the nature of things.

By the weekly newspapers the impetus was given to the essentially modern development of the press. Yet it was a considerable
time before the first daily newspapers appeared. This occurred in
Germany in 1660 (*Leipziger Zeitung*), in England in 1702 (*Daily
Courant*), in France in 1777 (*Journal de Paris*).

We need not pursue this theme down to our cosmopolitan papers that appear three times a day. The distinguishing feature of
the latter as contrasted with the written newspaper of the sixteenth
century is not so much the magnitude of the organization for procuring news and the rapidity in transmitting it, as the transformation
in the nature of the contents, particularly the advertising, and the
influence thereby exerted on public opinion, and, consequently, on
the course of the world's history.

For the sixteenth century the network of agencies for the regular
collection of news already described, was without doubt magnificent.
There runs through it a modern characteristic, the characteristic of
uniting individual forces in divided labour towards a single end. In
the department of news collection there has been little advance since
the sixteenth century. The whole subsequent development of the
newspaper in this direction rests on the separation of news collection
from news despatch (post), and on the commercial organization of
the former into correspondence bureaux and telegraph agencies. To
the telegraph agencies have fallen the duties of the earlier postmasters and news-scribes, but with this difference, that they no longer
labour directly for the newspaper readers, but supply the publish-
ing house with half-finished wares, making use in such work of the
perfected commercial machinery of modern times.

Again, the further development of news *publication* in the field
that it has occupied since the more general adoption of the printing-
press, has been peculiar. At the outset the publisher of a periodical

printed newspaper differed in no wise from the publisher of any other printed work—for instance, of a pamphlet or a book. He was but the multiplier and seller of a literary product, over whose content he had no control. The newspaper publisher marketed the regular post-news in its printed form just as another publisher offered the public a herbal or an edition of an old writer.

But this soon changed. It was readily perceived that the contents of a newspaper number did not form an entity in the same sense as the contents of a book or pamphlet. The news-items there brought together, taken from different sources, were of varying reliability. They needed to be used judicially and critically: in this a political or religious bias could find ready expression. In a still higher degree was this the case when men began to discuss contemporary political questions in the newspapers and to employ them as a medium for disseminating party opinions.

This took place first in England during the Long Parliament and the Revolution of 1649. The Netherlands and a part of the imperial free towns of Germany followed later. In France the change was not consummated before the era of the great Revolution: in most other countries it occurred in the nineteenth century. The newspaper, from being a mere vehicle for the publication of news, became an instrument for supporting and shaping public opinion and a weapon of party politics.

The effect of this upon the internal organization of the newspaper undertaking was to introduce a third department, the *editorship*, between news collecting and news publication. For the newspaper publisher, however, it signified that from a mere seller of news he had become a dealer in public opinion as well.

At first this meant nothing more than that the publisher was placed in a position to shift a portion of the risk of his undertaking upon a party organization, a circle of interested persons, or a government. If the leanings of the paper were distasteful to the readers they ceased to buy the paper. Their wishes thus remained, in the final analysis, the determining factor for the contents of the newspapers.

The gradually expanding circulation of the printed newspapers nevertheless soon led to their employment by the authorities for making public announcements. With this came, in the first quarter of last century, the extension of private announcements[226], which

---

[226]At first, it would seem, in special advice or intelligence sheets which in

have now attained, through the so-called *advertising bureaux*[227], some such organization as political news collecting possesses in the correspondence bureaux.

By admitting advertisements the newspaper fell into a peculiarly ambiguous position. For the subscription price it formerly published only news and opinions of general interest; now, through all sorts of advertisements, for which it receives special remuneration, it also serves private trade and private interests. It sells news to its readers, and it sells its circle of readers to any private interest capable of paying the price. In the same paper, often on the same page, where the highest interests of mankind are, or at least should be, represented, buyers and sellers ply their vocations in ignoble greed of gain. For the uninitiated it is often difficult to distinguish where the interests of the public cease and private interests begin.

This is all the more dangerous in that in the course of the past century the subjects discussed on the editorial page of the newspapers have grown to embrace almost the whole range of human interests. Statecraft, provincial and lo.cal administration, the administration of justice, art in all its manifestations, technology, economic and social life in its manifold phases, are reflected in the daily press; and since the development of the feuilleton, a good proportion of literary and even of scientific products flows into this great stream of contemporary social and mental life. The book as a form of publication—we may have no doubts on the point—loses ground from year to year.

It is impossible to enter into these matters at greater length. The sole aim of this cursory survey of the modern development of journalism has been to give, from the view-point of historical evolution, the beginnings of the newspaper press their proper setting, and at the same time to show how the gathering of news has been conditioned at each epoch by general conditions of trade.

The Roman newspaper is one feature in the autonomous administration of the wealthy and aristocratic household. A news-clerk was kept, just as was a body-surgeon or a librarian. In most cases he is the property, the slave, of the news-reader, working according to the directions of his master.

In the written newspaper of the sixteenth century there is ex-

---

many cases come from general agencies (Inquiry offices, Bureaux of Information). Comp. F. Mangold, in Basler Jhrb., 1897.
[227] *Annoncen-Expeditionen*

hibited the same handicraft character then dominating all branches of higher economic activity. The news-writer, on demand and for a definite price, furnishes directly to a circle of patrons the news that he had gathered —in which proceeding he doubtless suits the amount to the latter's needs. He is reporter, editor, and publisher in one.

The modern newspaper is a capitalistic enterprise, a sort of news-factory in which a great number of people (correspondents, editors, typesetters, correctors, machine-tenders, collectors of advertisements, office-clerks, messengers, etc.) are employed on wage, under a single administration, at very specialized work. This paper produces wares for an unknown circle of readers, from whom it is, furthermore, frequently separated by intermediaries, such as delivery agencies and postal institutions. The simple needs of the reader or of the circle of patrons no longer determine the quality of these wares; it is now the very complicated conditions of competition in the publication market. In this market, however, as generally in wholesale markets, the consumers of the goods, the newspaper readers, take no direct part; the determining factors are the wholesale dealers and the speculators in news: the governments, the telegraph bureaux dependent upon their special correspondents, the political parties, artistic and scientific cliques, men on change, and last but not least, the advertising agencies and large individual advertisers.

Each number of a great journal which appears today is a marvel of economic division of labour, capitalistic organization, and mechanical technique; it is an instrument of intellectual and economic intercourse, in which the potencies of all other instruments of commerce—the railway, the post, the telegraph, and the telephone—are united as in a focus. But our eyes can linger with satisfaction on no spot where capitalism comes into contact with intellectual life; and so we can take but half-hearted pleasure in this acquisition of modern civilization. It would indeed be difficult for us to believe that the newspaper in its present development is destined to constitute the highest and final medium for the supplying of news[228].

---

[228][Comp. Mr. Alfred Harmsworth on *The Newspapers of the Twentieth Century* in North Amer. Rev., Jan. 1901.—ED.]

Chapter VII. Union of Labour and Labour in Common

THERE is in Germany perhaps scarcely a modern textbook or contemporary course of university lectures on political economy in which some mention is not made of the principle of *union of labour* and some remark offered thereon. No one has really much to say about it. Yet it is there, and has its traditional place after the section on the division of labour, where, if it be thought at all worthy of it, it receives with regularity its paragraph, to come to light no more in the later text of the book or lecture.

And so it has been for more than half a century. But as science cannot be lenient with concepts that are not fitted to give a deeper insight into a series of phenomena, simply because they have once gained currency, it is at length time for a closer investigation of this ancient inventorial item in order, if it is really unserviceable, to discard it, or to assign it its proper place should it be found useful in furthering our knowledge.

According to the text-books, union of labour is nothing more nor less than "the other side of division of labour;" or "division of labour viewed from the standpoint of the organizing unit;[229]" the "correlative of division of labour;[230]" "the reverse side of the medal whose obverse side is the division of labour.[231]" These are all somewhat vague expressions, which on the whole seem to have their origin in

---

[229] Both in Philippovich, *Grundriss d. polit. Oek.* (2d ed), p. 78.
[230] Mangroldt, Grundriss d. Volkswirthschaftslehre, § 29.
[231] Kleinwachter, *Die volksw. Produktion* in Schonberg's Handbook, § 13.

the view that if labour is divided it must also be reunited, since the separate parts cannot exist independently. Here then the idea of division of labour is either conceived of very restrictedly—somewhat after the manner of Adam Smith's pin-manufactory—in which case the unifying force is supplied by the capital of the entrepreneur; or the conception is broadened to embrace the so-called social division of labour, in which case the labour-uniting element must be furnished by trade; so that union of labour would be synonymous with commercial organization generally.

In fact, Roscher, who gives the most detailed treatment of the subject, and to whom all later writers resort, regarded the subject in this light[232]. Division of labour and union of labour are in his view, "but two different aspects of the same conception, namely, *social labour*: separation of tasks so far as they would incommode one another, and their union in so far as they aid one another." "The vinedresser and the flax-grower," he continues, "would necessarily die of hunger if they could not count for certain on the grower of grain; the workman in the pin-factory who merely prepares the pin-heads must be sure of his comrade who sharpens the points if his labour is not to be entirely in vain; while the labour of a merchant simply cannot be conceived of without that of the different producers between whom he acts as intermediary."

The whole phenomenon is thus shrouded in the mists of processes of commerce and of organization; it is made synonymous with economy generally. In particular it altogether loses its correlation with the notion of division of labour. For the rest, Roscher discusses at length only the constancy of the progress of civilization—which is realized by each generation leaving to its successors the augmented inheritance of its predecessors; and further, the advantage of large undertakings and the association of small ones whereby labour ultimately disappears almost completely from the horizon.

Roscher in all this goes back to Frederick List[233], who, in his theory of the development of national productive powers, was the first in Germany, as far as I am aware, to use the expression "union of labour." Moreover, he turned it to peculiar account. Starting from a criticism of the "natural law" of division of labour, neither Adam Smith nor any of his successors have, in List's opinion, thoroughly investigated the essential nature and character of this law or followed

---

[232] *Principles of Political Economy* (New York, 1878), I, pp. 203-4.
[233] *The National System of Political Economy* (London, 1885), pp. 149 ff.

it out to its most important consequences. The very expression "division of labour" was inadequate, he says, and necessarily produced a false conception. He then continues: "It is division of labour if one savage on one and the same day goes hunting or fishing, cuts down wood, repairs his wigwam, and makes ready arrows, nets, and clothes; but it is also division of labour if, as in the example cited by Adam Smith, ten different persons share in the different occupations connected with the manufacture of a pin. The former is an objective, and the latter a subjective division of labour; the former hinders, the latter furthers production. The essential difference between the two is that in the former one person divides his work so as to produce *various* objects, while in the latter several persons share in the production of a single object."

"Both operations, on the other hand," we read further, "may with equal correctness be called a union of labour; the savage unites various tasks in his person, while in the case of the pin-manufacture various persons are united in one work of production in common. The essential character of the natural law from which the popular school explains such important phenomena in social economy, is evidently not merely a division of labour but a division of different commercial operations among several individuals, and at the same time a federation or union of various energies, intelligences and powers in a common production. *The cause of the productiveness of these operations is not merely the division, but essentially this union.*"

This latter List develops further, and upon it endeavours to base the demand for the establishment of a *harmony of the productive powers* in the nation. The highest division of occupations and the highest unification of the productive powers in material production are found in agriculture and manufacturing. "A nation devoting itself exclusively to agriculture is like an individual engaged in material production with one arm gone," etc.

Free these explanations from the ingenious rhetoric of the great agitator, and we find, as so often, that he has been unjust towards Adam Smith. The latter in no way overlooks the fact, as List is frank enough to admit, that division of labour postulates a cooperation of forces; and at the close of his celebrated chapter on division of labour he explains expressly that by means of this joint labour the meanest person in a civilized country may attain a more ample accommodation than an African king[234]. But he was keen-sighted enough not to regard this fact, which was involved in the nature of division of labour and identical with it, as an independent economic phenomenon. What purpose would it serve to call the same thing at one time division of labour and at another union of labour, according as it was viewed from one side or the other? In a young science that would have been only a source of confusion.

Of course the procedure of the Indian who successively hunts, fishes, fells trees, etc., would never have been recognised by Adam Smith as a particular instance of division of labour. On the contrary, he would have designated it undivided labour[235], a condition such as preceded division of labour throughout society. Division of labour is for him something else than division of time.

Of the factor of time in the disposal of labour List speaks more at length in another place. He there explains that the individual branches of industry in a country only gradually gain possession of improved processes, machinery, buildings, advantages in production, experiences and skill, and all those details of information and connections that insure to them the profitable purchase of their raw material and the profitable sale of their products. It is easier, he believes, to perfect and extend a business already established than to found a new one; easier to produce superior goods at moderate prices in a branch of industry long domiciled in a country than in a newly-established one. "As in all human institutions, so in industry there lies at the root of important achievements a law of nature that has much in common with the natural law of the division of labour and of the federation of productive forces. Its essential feature consists in several successive generations as it were uniting their forces towards one and the same end, and as it were dividing among them the expenditure of energy necessary to its attainment." List calls this the *principle of stability and continuity of work*, and seeks to prove its operation in history by a series of examples: the superiority in strength of a hereditary over an elective monarchy, the transmission of the acquisitions of human knowledge through printing, the influence of the caste system upon the maintenance and development of industrial skill, the building of cathedrals in the Middle Ages during several generations. The system of public debts by which "the present generation makes a draft on a future generation" is also

---

[234]Book I, Chapter I, towards end.
[235]On his conception of division of labour, compare following chapter.

182

cited as a peculiarly apt instance of the application of the principle of continuity in work.

It is easily seen that List here is dealing only with a rhetorically clad *analogy* to union of labour. This, however, has not prevented later writers from forming out of "continuity of work" a special *type* of union of labour, although a little reflection might have taught them that it is a phenomenon not at all peculiar to economic activity. Continuity of work is the universal historical principle of social development by which man is distinguished from the animal. With each lower animal begins anew a similar existence which runs its course, so far as we know, today as thousands of years ago, leaving not a record, not a trace. But each human generation takes over the fruits of the civilization of all preceding generations, and hands them down with an increase to the succeeding age. This is true not merely of material production but also of art, science, religion, law, and custom. Continuity of work thus forms one of the essential conditions and first postulates of human existence; and there is no reason for giving it special treatment in the theory of the economic employment of labour, particularly since it offers for the latter no new instructive points of view.

Sundry text-books recognise still a third type of union of labour, which is said to arise "when several do similar work concurrently, and by virtue of union obtain a greater result than would be possible to them working individually." Heinrich Rau, who incidentally mentions this case[236], instances temporary companies of forest wood-cutters, of raftsmen, and of reapers. In reality he here singles out a procedure that is not division of labour, although an increased productivity in the labour of the individual results from the simultaneous cooperation of several. This case then, like the one of the varied activity of the Indian mentioned by List, cannot be summarily dismissed as already embraced under the conception of division of labour and as ill-adapted to special scientific treatment.

Without doubt the real reason for the formation of the concept union of labour and for its long retention in the literature of the

---

[236] *Grundsätze der Volkswirthschaftslehre*, I, § 116 (a). Rau appeals to Gioja, who had studied the matter somewhat in his *Nuovo prospetto delle scienze economiche*, I, 87 ff. Moreover Hermann, *Staatsw. Untersuchungen*, new edition, p. 217, had also given it some attention. He designates it as "the simplest combination of labour." Similarly by the French who distinguish *co-opréation simple* and *co-opération complexe*, and make the latter identical with division of labour. Comp. Cauwès, *Cours d'Econ. pol.*, I, § 225.

science is the vague feeling that there must be *an economic principle forming the counterpart of division of labour.* Cooperation it cannot be, for that is identical with certain forms of division of labour[237], its "other side." What then is this principle?

All *division* of labour is an accommodation of work to limited human capacity. It takes place when a *qualitative disproportion* exists between the work to be done and the individual's capability[238].

But there may also be a *quantitative disproportion* between the two factors in two ways: (1) the quantity of work to be done may be less than the available labour-power, and it may also (2) be more than equal to the strength of a single individual.

In the *first* case the physical force would not be completely utilized if the labourer confined himself to this one line of work. His capacity for work would in part lie fallow, and an uneconomic squandering of strength would result. The work in question could not, perhaps, form the basis for a life-supporting vocation. The labourer, even in his own private interest, will be driven to help himself by combining or uniting with the first a second activity to fill out his leisure time. We may suitably call this *union* or *combination of labour*[239].

In the *second* case the individual by himself cannot possibly perform the task, or can do so only with a disproportionate expenditure of time and energy. A single workman, for instance, might, if necessity demanded, succeed in cutting the trunk of a large tree into boards with a handsaw; but with what trouble and needless expenditure of time! If two men and a whip-saw are called into service, however, the work goes forward not only absolutely but relatively better. The picture of the saw-pit then arises, which at times can still be seen in rural timber-yards. The union of the workers organizes the labour of each individual more productively. If we are to avoid the most lamentable confusions we must no longer designate this procedure union of labour[240], but at most union of labourers.

---

[237]For example, subdivision of labour and division of production, but not division of trade. If various specialists take the place of a general practitioner no cooperation takes place amongst them either in commercial dealings or in any other way similar to that amongst the different workers in a factory.

[238]Comp. following chapter.

[239] *Arbeitsvereinigung.*

[240]To distinguish from the first case we would then have to say "subjective" (personal) union of labour; while the first case would be designated as "objective" (material) union of labour

More accurate does it seem, especially in view of the varieties of this process to be mentioned later, to employ the expression *labour in common*[241]. In this phrase the personal element, which here comes into prominence, is more clearly expressed.

Union of labour is then the union of different classes of work in one person; labour in common is the concurrent employment of several workers in the accomplishment of one task. In union of labour the same producer turns out various products or combines production with trading or with personal service; in labour in common various labourers produce in common the like product. In the one case the uniting point is in the subject of the work, the labourer, in the other the community lies in the object of the labour.

The two processes are independent of each other and of division of labour. They, of course, play their chief role during primitive stages of development and in the lower strata of economically organized society. Two great stages in the economic life of nations might indeed be distinguished: a lower one, in which the principle of union of labour and labour in common comes preeminently into play; and a higher one, with the principle of division of labour predominant. In the same way two spheres of social existence may be distinguished in contemporary economic life: one with pronounced division of labour, the other with union of labour and labour in common.

In a separate consideration of each of these two phenomena we had better begin with *union of labour*. It appears early in the history of peoples. It is universally met with directly the stage of individual search for food is passed, and when economic motives, be they even of the crudest kind, become discernible in men's transactions. For at that point we everywhere notice the sharp separation of two distinct spheres of production, each of which again contains many subdepartments. One embraces men's work, the other women's work. Essentially the same arrangement, with unimportant variations in detail, is found among all more advanced primitive peoples, and we cannot deny that there is a certain instinctive system about it. Of a *division* of labour between man and wife one cannot seriously speak, for from all we know none of the occupations assigned to either of the two sexes has ever been carried on by the other.

It must be assumed that this condition of things developed quite naturally. In any case the statement is false that the stronger man "imposed" upon the woman the tasks falling to him. Much rather is

---

[241] *Arbeitsgememschaft.*

it correct to say that each sex has of its own impulse—it might perhaps be said under the stress of environment—created in the course
of time its own department of production, developed the technical
details connected with it, collected the experiences, and transmitted
them to the following generation of the same sex. Thus these two
combinations of tasks, through continued hereditary transmission
within the same sex, have almost been evolved into sexual characteristics or functions. The hereditary task of the woman, in which
the man was not instructed, formed a species of natural equipment
that made her valued by the man and gave her a price. Though it
is true that from this grew the conception of the wife as property of
the husband, it is none the less true that the important part played
by the wife in production has been not the least important factor in
the gradual elevation of the rude primaeval union of the sexes to a
community of life in which the woman has finally raised herself to
equality of rights with the husband.

The economic importance of the union of various tasks in the
hands of each sex is essentially of an educational and disciplinary
nature. It compelled as it were of itself, at least on the part of the
wife, attention to the elements of time at seed-time and at harvest,
and finally to a division of time, very crude though it was, for the single day. It is a matter of particular moment in this connection that
the preparation of grain by means of the primitive rubbing-stone,
which is the method employed by most primitive peoples down to
the present day, makes exceedingly heavy demands upon the oper-
ator's time, so that the mere maintenance of three or four persons
required the labour of one woman[242].This is one of the most important supports of polygamy among these peoples, and renders it
tolerable for the wife. For a new spouse brought home by the husband always appears to the other wives as a helper to lighten their
lot. It is thus comprehensible that the possession of numerous wives
must serve as an indication of wealth. We may even assert that the
careful employment of time, with which systematic economic action
first begins, finds its starting-point in the union of labour on the
part of the women.

Moreover, when in the course of subsequent development considerable shiftings took place in the boundaries of the spheres of work
of both sexes, forcing the wife ever more towards the side of super-

---

[242]Comp. Dr. W. Junker's *Travels in Africa*, II, pp. 170, 171, and my *Arbeit
u. Rhythmus*, pp. 18, 60, 61.

vising consumption within the household and placing almost all the production in the hands of the husband, the principle of division of labour made itself felt almost solely in man's sphere of work, while to the wife's household management remained the most varied duties of preparing, disposing, cleaning, and repairing. The course of these latter really determines the division of time in our daily life.

To be sure, union of labour has not on that account disappeared completely from the economic world. *Agriculture* still embraces occupations varying greatly from one another; everywhere in civilized lands its development has been intimately connected with cattle-raising, while subsidiary industries are often included within its sphere. It is indeed one of the most important tasks of the farm-director so to arrange matters that the working powers of man and beast can be turned to full account in as many ways and in as regular a manner as possible. In the change of activity following the seasons of the year there is, even in large agricultural undertakings, but little room for subdivision of work and specialization; different kinds of occupations must always be united in *one* person, and among the women workers a clear division into farm hands and household servants is not feasible.

Similar considerations hold for *forestry*, in which keen practical men condemn the system still common in many places of having specialized labour for each season[243], and demand the employment throughout the whole year of a permanent staff of all-round workmen. Such a requirement can be met only on the basis of union of labour.

In *industry* handicraft has from time immemorial been founded on union of labour. It was not the highest productivity that determined the mutual delimitation of the departments of production, but regard for the daily bread which each master was to find in his craft. The numberless disputes between different guilds as to the limits of their trade which fill the pages of industrial history during the last few centuries continually raised discussions on the practicableness of this or that combination. In the age of industrial freedom handicraft has also advanced in the large cities in the direction of specialization; in the smaller towns the old combinations have been retained, and in country parts new ones are still arising each year. The mason is here often plasterer, painter, and paper-hanger as well,

---

[243]Comp. Fr. Jentsch, *Die Arbeiterverhält. in d. Forstwirth. d. Stoats* (Berlin, 1882).

while in winter he serves for wage as butcher; the smith is at the same time locksmith and chief engineer of the threshing-machine; paper-hanging is cared for now by the saddler, now by the painter, now by the bookbinder. In the towns the greatest variety of combinations are made by the new occupations. Gas-fitting and plumbing are undertaken now by the locksmith, now by the tinsmith, and electric services are installed in houses by craftsmen of most diverse types. Everywhere the craftsman appears willing to add to his workshop a small counter trade, especially with wares of his own department of labour no longer produced by hand-work, but often with various other articles as well. Justus Moser long since remarked the sound economic idea realized in this union; and would willingly have seen all petty retailing transferred to handworkers and their wives[244]. If we add to this the various alliances that handicraft makes with services of a personal character, especially minor civil offices, and in the country as a regular thing with agriculture, we are readily convinced that the union of labour still commands a very extended field[245]. Men of "modern mind" may deplore the great number of such "backward trades" pessimists may see in them a sign of the "distress in handicraft"; fanatics on production may regret that un-der such conditions the highest possible measure of productivity is not realized in every branch of industry. But an unprejudiced judg-ment, based upon an investigation of the facts, will find that in the union of labour the middle class of small independent workmen has its firmest footing; it will find too that in the majority of cases the due observance of sound business principles has not been wanting. For as a rule it is really a question of making use of time that is not taken up by the chief occupation, and of giving employment to capabilities that would otherwise lie dormant.

Union of labour is relatively still more common in *house industry* where the women employed at the same time attend to their domes-tic duties, and where the men often follow agriculture or some other business as primary occupation. Indeed the origin of many com-mission industries rests finally upon the consideration that persons not fully occupied could profitably combine them with their other

---

[244] *Patriotische Phantasien*, Vol. II, No. XXXVII.

[245] Copious material on the combinations of trades and secondary occupations of handworkers is offered in *Untersuchungen über d. Lage d. Handwerks in Deutschland*, edited by myself, in Schriften d. Vereins f. Socialpolitik, Vols. LXII—LXX, especially in the descriptions of industries in small towns and coun-try districts.

business.

Trading primarily is always union of labour, since in the earlier stages of its development it regularly includes transportation. Caravan trade is an example. In modern commercial life division of labour has strongly asserted itself in wholesale trade, and also in the retail trade of large cities. But along with these are numerous businesses, such as hardware and house-furnishing shops, which bring together the most varied articles. In the wholesale warehouses and export businesses, in the sixpenny bazaars and cash stores this development has reached its highest point. These giant undertakings of course lie beyond the range of our study, since with them the work is generally arranged in strict accordance with the principle of division of labour. On the other hand, the numerous small retail businesses carried on in suburban places, in small towns, and in the country usually as the sole occupation of one person lie within its survey, because here the owner deals in every possible article that will bring in money. Indeed one would have to write a detailed account of the sale shops to explain all that is to be found gathered together there. Certain wares are specially prized for filling out the stock, such as canes, cigar-holders, combs, brushes, and straw hats; and it is often difficult to learn how they have come into the company they keep. Many tradesmen of such a class at the same time carry on commission businesses, insurance and news agencies, sell lottery and theatre tickets, receive advertisements and savings-bank deposits, and the like.

In the great world of commerce there are various specialized occupations that can hardly be carried on with profit by themselves, and therefore are always followed in conjunction with another pursuit. What village could support a special precentor, village clerk, or sexton; what rural loan association maintain a treasurer; what insurance company pay its army of subagents sufficient for their support? Without the possibility of union of labour these and many other economic functions would simply have to remain unperformed.

The consideration determining the combination in each case could only be gleaned from a minute statistical and descriptive investigation. In most cases the influence that decides the person devoting himself to different kinds of work is the full employment of his time and the gaining of a full livelihood. For the method of combination, however, many other considerations come into play. Now it is to take advantage of a *clientèle* already existing, now to utilize a particular

189

talent or skill possessed by the workman for a further object. The economic principle will in these cases in one way or another always come into play.

The actual *extent* of union of labour in national economy is not easy to determine. Statistics have sought to answer the need by creating the rather unsatisfactory category of the auxiliary occupations; but it is easy to see that this designation does not exhaust the total number of cases that come here into question; it gives at most only those in which the auxiliary occupation ranks in some degree as an independent vocation. A *union of occupations* might be spoken of in this case[246]. Yet some conception of the immense economic importance of the union of labour may be gained when we learn from the results of the last German industrial census that on June 14, 1895, there were almost five million persons in the German Empire who had some secondary occupation, and that agriculture alone was an auxiliary pursuit for 3,648,237. Of 3,999,023 proprietors and managers in some branch of agriculture, industry, or trade, 36.9 per cent. (1,475,023) had an auxiliary occupation, while 2,928,530 carried on these branches as auxiliary work.

The following table gives a survey of the whole field of industrial activity covered by that census. In it those carrying on independent and dependent work are grouped together.

---

[246]On the occurrence of combined occupations in town life in the Middle Ages there are some details in my *Bevölkerung von Frankfurt*, I, pp. 232 ff., 417 ff.

Class of Occupation	No. of persons who-se chief occupation (1)	No. of persons having a secondary occup. (2)	No. of persons having no secondary occup. (3)	No. of persons making their occup. in col. 1 secondary (4)	Total No. (5)
A. Agriculture, forestry, stock-raising, fishing	8,292,692	1,049,542	7,243,150	3,643,237	11,940,929
B. Mining and industries	8,281,220	1,491,865	6,789,355	619,386	8,908,606
C. Trade and commerce	2,338,511	384,105	1,954,406	569,877	2,908,388
D. Domestic service, hired labour (various)	432,491	31,333	401,158	16,765	449,256
E. Public service, liberal professions	1,425,961	115,266	1,310,695	95,436	1,521,397
Total	**20,770,875**	**3,072,111**	**17,698,764**	**4,949,701**	**25,720,576**
Of these were:					
Males	*15,506,489*	*2,816,655*	*12,689,827*	*3,203,375*	*18,709,857*
Females	*5,264,393*	*255,456*	*5,008,937*	*1,746,396*	*7,010,719*

From this table we find that out of every 100 persons pursuing their chief occupation in one of the classes indicated, whether as proprietor or workman in any capacity, a second or third (auxiliary) occupation was added—

In agriculture, forestry, stock-raising, fishing, by............. 12.6 persons
In mining and industry by ....18.0 persons
In trade and commerce by ....16.4 persons

In domestic service and hired labour of various kinds by......7.2 persons
In public service and liberal professions by ....8.1 persons

Of the total number of persons following an occupation (either chief or auxiliary) in one of the said classes, a secondary pursuit from the same class was chosen—

In agriculture, forestry, stock-raising, fishing, by....................... 30.6%
In mining and industry by 6.7%
In trade and commerce by 19.6%
In domestic service and hired labour of various kinds by 3.7%
In public service and liberal professions by.................................. 6.2%

Even from the returns of occupations, which unfortunately are not sufficiently detailed for this purpose, it is clear that many occupations are carried on chiefly in conjunction with other pursuits. For example, in the table next presented the total number of persons following the vocation are contrasted, by percentages, with those following it either as principal or subsidiary, along with another occupation[247].

Stock-raising 83.4%
Inland fishing 69.3%
Turf cutting and preparing 93.9%
Stone cutting and carving 57.2%
Marble, stone, and slate quarrying and
the manufacture of rough wares from these materials 78.6%
Manufacture of fine stone wares 50.2%
Brick and clay-pipe making 86.9%
Butchering 58.1%
Insurance 68.7%
Personal transport and post 53-2%
Freight delivery 75.7%
Pottery 57.5%
Manufacture of earthenware and glass toys 56.0%
Nail-manufacture 67.0%
Blacksmithing 76.8%
Wagon-making 74.8%
Flaying 85.9%
Charcoal-burning 81.2%
Flour-milling 91.6%
Baking 61.6%
Turning 52.7%
Advertisement and labour-agency work 54-4%

Inn-keeping and refreshments 64.4%

These figures naturally are far from giving a true picture of the results of combined and divided labour in the occupation classes

---

[247]Columns 6 and 8 of *Reichsstatistik*, Tab. I.

indicated. It is at once apparent that in a statistical return on extractive production a country shoemaker who devotes a quarter of his time to land-cultivation n has necessarily the other three-quarters of his time left out of account. This, however, is not the point; it is rather the question of the number of human beings to whom a combination of occupations assures more abundant sustenance and also in most cases a more satisfying existence, both as regards health and morals, than a onesided employment in full agreement with the principle of division of labour. In the German Empire this number is large beyond expectation, amounting almost to one third of all persons engaged in earning their living.

The principle of union of labour, despite the wealth of forms in which it appears, is quite simple: how shall surplus strength be productively employed? The principle of *labour in common* cannot be reduced to such a smooth formula. In general, its aim is so to supplement the insufficient strength of the individual that the task presented can be accomplished. But the individual workman's insufficiency of strength may again have different causes. It may be based on a definite mental disposition that prevents the workman labouring continuously by himself; it may rest on lack of bodily strength; or, finally, it may result from technical conditions rendering it impossible for one piece of work to be performed unless accompanied by a second of a different character. Each of these three cases produces a distinct kind of labour in common. The first may be called *companionship* or *fraternal labour*, the second, *labour aggregation*, and the third, *joint labour*. We will consider them in order.

1. *Companionship or fraternal labour*[248] occurs when several workers come together and labour without the individual becoming in the progress of his task in any way dependent upon the others. Each thus labours for himself independently and adopts any tempo he pleases. The sole aim in union is to have the company of fellow-workmen, to be able to talk, joke and sing with them, and to avoid solitary work alone with one's thoughts.

The student whose work thrives best in undisturbed solitude will on hearing this probably shrug his sympathetic shoulders in pitying contempt, and find the subject hardly worth serious consideration. But anyone who has ever observed a group of village women braking flax, or doing their washing at the brookside, or watched a troop of

---

[248] *Gesellschaftasarbeit or gesellige Arbeit.*

Saxon field-workers hoeing turnips, or a line of reapers at work, or listened to the singing of a group of house-painters, or of women at work in an Italian vineyard, will be of a different opinion. The lower the stage of a man's culture the more difficult is it for him to stick to continuous and regular labour, if he is to be left by himself.

But the best proof of the importance of fraternal labour lies in its having found some sort of organization in all parts of the earth. We may call to mind the public working-places and common-houses of the savages[249], the common workrooms of the house-workers in Russia, the spinning-rooms of our peasant girls which the bureaucracy of the eighteenth century so fatuously opposed, but which live on in many villages to the present day in the evening gatherings for work in common. Custom everywhere joins to these gatherings dancing, feasting or other practice tending to make the work more agreeable. A few instances will serve to show the wide extent of such institutions.

In the Fiji Islands "several women always unite in the preparation of tapa; frequently all the women of the place sit together," and in net-fishing "women always work together in small groups; the work is at the same time a recreation, and there is often a merry time in the cooling bath."[250] Among many negro tribes in Africa women can be seen at public work-places pounding or grinding corn in common. A more circumstantial report is given by a missionary as to the North American Indians:[251] "The tilling of the ground, getting of the fire-wood, and pounding of corn in mortars is frequently done by female parties, much in the manner of . . . husking, quilting, and other frolics. . . . The labour is thus quickly and easily performed; when it is over, and sometimes in intervals, they sit down together to enjoy themselves by feasting on some good victuals prepared for them by the person or family for whom they work, and which the man has taken care to provide beforehand from the woods; for this

---

[249] K. v. d. Steinen, *Unter d. Naturvolk. Brasil.*, p. 374. Erman in Ztschr. f. Ethnol., II, p. 378 (on the Coljusches in Sitka). Jacobsen, *Reise in d. Inselwelt d. Banda-Meeres*, p. 213. Finsch, *Samoafahrten*, p. 357. Burton, as above, pp. 54, 297, 461. Nachtigal, *Sahara u. Sudan*, II, p. 624; III. pp. 146, 244. Count Schweinitz, *Durch Ostafrika im Krieg u. Frieden*, p. 171. Stanley, *Through the Dark Continent*, II, p. 82, and *How I found Livingstone*, pp. 546 ff. Semon, *In the Australian Bush*, p. 324. Comp. also *Arbeit u. Rhythmus*, pp. 38, 39, 71; and above, p. 37.

[250] A. Bässler, *Sudsee-Bilder*, pp. 224-6.

[251] Heckewelder, as above, p. 156. Similar report from South America in Ehrenreich, *Beiträge z. Völkerkund. Brasil.*, p. 28.

is considered a principal part of the business, as there are generally more or less of the females assembled who have not, perhaps, for a long time tasted a morsel of meat, being either widows or orphans, or otherwise in straitened circumstances. Even the chat which passes during their joint labour is highly diverting to them, and so they seek to be employed in this way as long as they can by going round to all the villagers who have ground to till." The same linking of work and pleasure is found in the *public social houses* that are met with almost universally among primitive peoples. Divided regularly according to the sexes, they are most frequently built for unmarried men and girls. They serve not merely as places of resort for common tasks, but often as sleeping places as well, and always as places for dancing and play. There singing and joking and chatting go on; the fruitless efforts of the awkward are ridiculed and the successful work of the diligent and skilful applauded.

A distant parallel to this institution has been retained among ourselves almost down to the present in the spinning-rooms of peasant girls[252]. These rooms had in every part of Germany their well-defined though unwritten rules and laws. "In Brunswick the spinning-rooms began with the approach of winter, when the field-work was ended. In many villages this occurred at Martinmas. They lasted then till Lent, or at latest till Palm Sunday, when other work had to

---

[252]But with similar conditions these are met with everywhere. Henry Savage Landor (*In the Forbidden Land, an Account of a Journey in Tibet,* I, pp. 109 ff.) found them even in the southern Himalayas among the Shokas, where girls and young men come together at night in particular meeting-places (Rambangs), for the sake of better acquaintance, prior to entering into matrimony. "Each village possesses one or more institutions of this kind, and they are indiscriminately patronized by all well-to-do people, who recognise the institution as a sound basis on which marriage can be arranged. The Rambang houses are either in the village itself, or half-way between one village and the next, the young women of one village thus entering into amicable relations with the young men of the other and *vice versâ*. I visited many of these in company with Shokas, and found them very interesting. Round a big fire in the centre of the room men and women sat in couples, spinning wool and chatting merrily, for everything appeared decorous and cheerful. With the small hours of the morning, they seemed to become more sentimental, and began singing songs without instrumental accompaniment, the rise and fall of the voices sounding weird and haunting to a degree. . . . Smoking was general, each couple sharing the same pipe. . . . Signs of sleepiness became evident as morning came, and soon they all retired in couples, and went to sleep in their clothes on a soft layer of straw and grass. . . . At these gatherings every Shoka girl regularly meets with young men; and while she entertains the idea of selecting among them a suitable partner for life, she also does a considerable quantity of work with her spinning-wheel."

195

be done. The evening gatherings were held in rotation at the houses of the different members of the particular weaving-circle. The membership of such a circle was made up of four, or at most of eight girls, who were friends or relatives of each other. The majority consisted of servants, though the daughters of peasants also joined in. The old folks spun by themselves. In the early part of the evening the girls were alone; for not till later on, about eight o'clock, did the male visitors, who by that time had finished their work, put in an appearance and take part in the company, at first with reserve, and then more and more boldly. The institution has as its basis a laudable diligence on the part of the girls."[253] Generally there was a fixed amount of work for the week reckoned in yarn; anyone not doing it received a nickname. At times a spinning contest was arranged, while a feeling of lively emulation always prevailed.[254] Indeed a species of labour police was maintained over the individual members. In the district of Nassau a moustache was painted with a piece of charcoal on the spinner who fell asleep; if she let the thread break and slip from her a lad might take her distaff, which she had to redeem with a kiss.[255]

The spinning-room has fallen a sacrifice to the technical revolutions of modern times; but all through the country during long winter evenings the young girls still congregate with their work in the house of a friend. This is also the case with several *house industries* carried on in the country, for instance, with lace-making in the Erz mountains, where this kind of gathering of working girls is still referred to as "go spinning."[256] This practice is fully developed in the system of house industry in Russia.[257] Here male and female

---

[253]R. Andree, *Braunschweig. Volkskunde*, pp. i68ff. Comp. K. Freiherr v. Leoprechting, *Aus d. Lechrain*, pp. 201-2; Ztschr. d. Ver. f. Volkskunde, III, pp. 291, 292, VIII, p. 366; and in detail Böckel, Volkslieder aus Oberhessen, pp. cxxiii ff.

[254]Interesting notes on competitive games in spinning in Ztschr d. Ver. f. Volksk., VIII, pp. 215, 216. Comp. *Arbeit u. Rhythmus,* p. 91 ff.

[255]Among the Wends in Lusatia on the last spinning night before Christmas the slow and lazy ones are brought to trial: Haupt and Schmaler, *Volkslieder d. Wenden in d. Ober- u. Nieder-Lausitz,* II, p. 220. Similar instances of labour supervision by comrades are found in other classes of peasant working groups. Comp. Hörmann, *D. Tiroler Bauernjahr* (Innsbruck, 1899), pp. SO, 52, 66, 70, 71, 75, 129.

[256]*Arbeit u. Rhythmus*, pp. 99, 100.

[257]Details in Stellmacher, *Ein Beitrag z. Darstellung d. Hausindustrie in Russland, pp. 106 ff.* M. *Gorbunoff, Über russische Spitzenindustrie* (Vienna, 1886), pp. 23 ff.

Kustaris frequently work together outside their homes. Large companies, often composed wholly of house-workers of the one village
engaged in a similar trade, gather together in a particular workroom, which is either a large room rented in a peasant's house or
a shop erected for the purpose. Such a common workroom is still
most frequently termed "spinning-room"(*Swetjolka*), and often "factory." It is to be found, for instance, in domestic cotton-weaving,
cloth-making, silk-spooling, and the making of shoes and toys. In
women's work only young girls, as a rule, attend, while the married
women work at home.

"According to the statements of the oldest people, cotton-weaving
was at first carried on exclusively in the swetjolka, because the technical handling of the loom could be learned more quickly and easily under the constant supervision of one skilled in weaving. The
living-room of the house served at first as swetjolka, but later on
a swetjolka separate from the house was built. Today the young
people and the diligent weavers still prefer to work in the swetjolka
rather than at home; the former because it is more sociable, the
others because they can work more regularly and to greater advantage. At home the weaver is often called away to domestic affairs;
the living-room there is not so spacious and bright, the air not so
pure, since calves and lambs are not infrequently codwellers with the
folks; in the swetjolka, also, the cotton, which at home is very liable
to become moist and mouldy, can be better preserved."

Thus fraternal labour accords very well with the economic principle, even though it originates primarily in the social instinct. In the
company of others people work with greater persistence than they
would alone, and in general because of the rivalry, also better. Work
becomes pleasure, and the final result is an advance in production.

2. By *labour aggregation*[258] we mean the engaging of several
workmen of similar capacity in the performance of a united task,
such as loading a heavy burden, shifting a beam, mowing a meadow,
beating for the hunt. In order to make the employment of a plurality of workers profitable, the work to be done need not be of itself
too heavy for the strength of one person; it is only necessary that it
cannot be done by such an one in a reasonable time. Labour aggregation is of special importance for seasonal work or for work that is
dependent upon the weather. Social conditions can also play a part
in expediting certain tasks.

---

[258] *Arbeitshäufung.*

These circumstances have early led to a species of social organization of aggregated labour, founded on the duty recognised the world over of mutual assistance among neighbours. We may use the expression current among the south Slavs and call it *bidden labour*[259]. Whenever anyone has work to be done for which his own household is not adequate, the assistance of the neighbours is sought. They give it at the time without further reward than their entertainment, which the head of the house offers in the accustomed way, solely in the expectation that when need arises they, too, will be aided by their neighbours. The work is carried out in sprightly competition amid jokes and song, and at night there is often added a dance or like merry-making[260].

This is a world-wide practice. Traces of it can even be found among the South Sea Islanders. In New Pomerania, for example, it is the custom for several families to cooperate in plaiting the fishing-baskets and large fishing-nets. "Before the basket receives its first dip in the water a meal in common is given, in which all who were engaged in the making participate."[261]

In Djailolo (Halamahera) when a piece of land belonging to a local community is to be cleared, ten to twenty relatives are called together to assist in felling the trees, their services being compensated later in other work. So it is at the planting of paddy, and at the rice harvest[262]. "Whenever anyone wants to build a house he solicits some of his relatives to help cut the building material while the tide is out, he providing them the while with food. For the roofing, which is done with sago leaves, more helpers are invited. These then hold a feast, at which the chiefs are generally present."[263]

Among the Madis or Morus in Central Africa each cultivates his own land; if it is of considerable extent, and requires more hands than his family can furnish, he calls his friends and neighbours to his assistance. On such occasions payment is neither given nor expected,

---

[259] *Bittarbeit.*
[260] Numerous instances of this custom in Chapter V of my *Arbeit u. Rhythmus.*
[261] Parkinson, *Im Bismarck-Archipel,* p. 115.
[262] Riedel, in Ztschr. f. Ethnol., XVII (1885), pp. 70 ff. Similarly in New Guinea, Finsch, *Samoafahrten,* pp. 56 ff. *Among the Bagobos in South Mindanao*: Schadenberg in Ztschr. f. Ethnol., XVII, pp. 19 ff.
[263] Riedel, as above, p. 61. *Kubary, Ethnogr. Beiträge z. Kenntnis d. Karolinen-Archipels,* p. 264. C. Hose, *The Natives of Borneo,* in Journ. of Anthrop. Inst., XXIII (1894), pp. 161, 162.

but all are ready to render such help and to receive it[264].This custom appears to be prevalent throughout Africa; the possessor of the
land has, as a rule, to supply generous entertainment to the whole
company[265]. Among the Gallas the inhabitants of a village assemble on the threshing-place to thresh the panicles of the durra and to
root up the corn amid the singing of melodious songs adapted to the
strokes in threshing[266]. Bidden labour is also common in building
a house[267]. Among the Hovas of Madagascar when the grave of an
important man is to be built, not the relatives and members of his
tribe alone assist in transporting the heavy rocks, but all the inhabitants of the village in which he lived. There is no money-payment
for such services; in its stead, however, great masses of provisions
must be supplied during the transport of the heavy stones, which
usually lasts many days, often for long intermediate periods; and
above all many oxen must be killed. As the people are accustomed
to help one another, no inconsiderable part of their time is spent
in such services. On the highways of the country one often meets
great processions of two to three hundred men, women and slaves,
who pull by starts on the strong ropes by which means the stone,
placed on a rough boat, is drawn forward[268]. The Georgians (Central Transcaucasia) resort to bidden labour at the vintage, in sowing and harvesting maize and wheat, in hewing and drawing wood
from the forest. In Servia it is customary at grass-mowing, maize-
cutting, plum harvest, the vintage, and also with spinning, weaving
and carpet-making; in many parts of Russia at the hay and grain
harvests, in hoeing turnips, felling timber, transporting manure and
in ploughing, as well as with the women in spinning and even in
scrubbing the house. In Germany it remains quite general in the
country in house-building and locally in minor agricultural tasks
(flax-pulling, bean-cutting, sheep-washing). It is an expedient of independent household economy, as is readily seen, and recedes more
and more with the appearance and advance of the entrepreneur system.

But in most cases where bidden labour was formerly usual the

---

[264]Robert Felkin in Proceedings of Roy. Society of Edin. 1883/4, p. 310.
[265]Endemann in Ztschr. f. Ethnol., VI, 1874, p. 27. Pogge in Wissmann,
Unter deutsch. Flagge quer durch Afrika, p. 311. Nachtigal, *Sahara u. Sudan.*
Ill, p. 240. Post, *Afr. Jurisprudenz*, II, p. 172.
[266]Paulitschke, Ethnogr. *Nordost-Afrikas*, I, pp. 134, 217.
[267]Schurtz, *Afr. Gewerbe*, p. 21.
[268]Sibree, *Madagaskar*, pp. 255, 256

large landowner will still engage a number of labourers if he is not able to hurry along the work fast enough with his machines. Labour aggregation becomes particularly important for him in the early stages of a process of production whose final stages can be more cheaply completed when carried on concurrently. A meadow could perhaps be mowed by one labourer in three days. Yet where possible the owner will employ six or more mowers who dispose of the work in a forenoon, because all the grass should be dried uniformly and all the hay drawn in at once. Frequent drawings would increase the costs of production.

Even where there are no such reasons the farmer whose fields are intermixed with those of others will always prefer to undertake the fields in succession with all his help rather than divide it among the different fields. The work goes forward better and more briskly in company than in solitude, for no one will lag behind the others; moreover, of itself the rapid progress of the work enlivens the workers, while a piece of work in which no progress can be recognised, and the end is not in sight, always disheartens. Thus the six mowers in the instance just given will, with average diligence, finish the meadow not in one-sixth of the time that the single mower with the same diligence would require, but in a shorter time. Moreover with large undertakings in which the proprietor does not work along with the others, it has further to be considered that with dispersion of the workers the costs of supervision per unit of acre increase[269].

Labour aggregation belongs almost exclusively to the class of work requiring little skill, and which can be executed with simple manual implements, or even without any tools whatever. It is thus found in

---

[269] Even in the *Grundsätze d. ratiowllen Landwirthschaft* (4th edition, Berlin, 1847), I, pp. 112ff., of A. Thaer we find the following rules: "Large tasks are never to be undertaken many at a time, especially in places at a considerable distance. As far as possible they must be finished in succession, and in every case with all possible energy, partly on account of the superintendence, partly because a certain rivalry can be awakened among the workers if many of them are under supervision together. On the other hand, if the task is extensive and only a few of them are set to work, they become almost frightened at its extent and its slow progress and even lose Courage, and believe that, because of its magnitude, their absence will not be noticed. In such extensive tasks one man or one team too many is always better than one too few. In smaller tasks, on the contrary, care must be taken not to employ more than are necessary. ,The men easily get in each other's way, depend upon one anothes, readily believe that their work has been thought heavier than it really is." Similarly, H. Settegast, *Die Landwirthschaft u. ihr Betrieb*, I, p. 313; 111, P. 138.

its widest extension in epochs of undeveloped technique[270], declining as the implements of labour are improved. Yet a considerable sphere still remains to it. The grandest instance of labour aggregation is at all times presented by the standing armies.

When a large number of persons labour together two kinds of labour aggregation are possible. In the first the individual workmen remain independent of one another during the moments their strength is called into play, and work together only for the more speedy disposition of the task. We will designate this first species *simple aggregation of labour*. Instances are presented in several masons working on a new structure, a number of pavers on a road, a group of diggers or snow-shovellers, a row of mowers or turnip-hoers. An intermediate form is offered by a band of African carriers marching one after the other in single file, by beaters at a hunt, by several ploughers in a field.

In the second case the activities of the different workmen do not proceed independently of one another, but either simultaneously or with regular alternations, that is, they always proceed rhythmically. We will name this kind of labour agglomeration *concatenation of labour*, because it, so to speak, links each one taking part in the work to his neighbour through the succession of his movements, and combining all by means of the tempo into unity of system, makes it, as it were, an automatically working organism. All tasks falling under this head must, if continued for some time, adopt a rhythmical course. There are some, to be sure, that are completed with a single exertion of strength, such as several lifting a heavy weight by word of command or pulling down the trunk of a tree with a rope.

The tasks of this class, which are performed rhythmically, can be sub-divided according as the powers of the individual workers are exerted simultaneously or alternately into *labours with concurrent tempo* and *labours with alternate tempo*[271].

Labours with concurrent tempo are performed, for instance, by the two lines of rowers in propelling a boat by oars, by sailors in heaving an anchor, in hoisting sail, in towing a boat against the stream, by carpenters, who, in laying a foundation with a pile-driver, drive

---

[270]This was the case especially among the ancient Egyptians. Some details on this have been gathered together in *Arbeit u. Rhythmus*, pp. 109, 110.

[271]More in detail in my paper already frequently mentioned, *Arbeit u. Rhythmus,* to which reference may once for all be made for the following paragraphs as well.

great posts into the earth, by those drawing up barrels, and generally by all groups of workmen who have to move a weight by pulling together on a rope, by the two, four, six, or eight people carrying a hand-barrow or a sedan-chair, and by soldiers on the march. Very frequently the keeping of time during the work is assisted by simple counting, by a chorus among the workers, or by the sound of a musical instrument, especially of the drum.

Examples of workmen labouring with *alternate tempo* are: three stone-setters hammering in time the pavement stones with their paving-beetles; three or four threshers on the barn floor, two smiths hammering, two woodmen in the saw-pit or chopping a tree, two maids blueing linen or beating carpets.

In tasks to be performed with concurrent tempo the problem is to accomplish by combination a task far surpassing the strength of one person, with the smallest number of labourers possible, so that all taking part in the work shall be led to apply the utmost amount of energy at the same moment.

In tasks with alternate tempo we meet as a rule with labours that in themselves could be performed by a single individual. Generally they are fatiguing tasks in which the various motions, such as raising and lowering the arms in striking with the threshing-flail, require more or less time. The individual worker here is always tempted to allow himself a brief pause for rest after each stroke or thrust, and thus loses the rhythm of the movements. The strokes or blows then succeed one another with unequal force and at irregular intervals, whereby the work is much more tiring in its results. If now a second or third workman be added, the motions of each individual will regulate themselves by the rhythmic sound that the instruments give forth in striking the material worked upon. A quicker tempo is realized, which can be maintained with little difficulty. Each workman remains indeed independent, but he must adapt his movements to those of his comrades. The import of the matter is thus not that the magnitude of the task demands a doubling or tripling of forces, but that a single person working alone cannot maintain a definite rhythmical motion.

To be sure, the sole consequence of calling in a second or third workman one would imagine to be the doubling or tripling of the effect of one workman's expenditure, yet this kind of labour concatenation results in a heightened production, inasmuch as it regulates equably for each the expenditure of force and the pauses for rest.

The single workman lets his hands fall when he grows tired, or at
least lengthens the tempo of his movements. Quick tempo in work
enlivens; the men working in common are stimulated to rivalry; none
will fall behind the other in strength and endurance.

This pressure upon the weaker workman to equal the stronger
becomes prominent in some tasks with a somewhat free rhythm in
which the concatenation is realized by grouping the workmen in rows
and making the progress of the work of the one row dependent upon
the activity of the other. In a line of mowers in a meadow each man
must perform his task uniformly with the rest if he is not to retard
the man following him or run the risk of being struck with his scythe.
In a line of labourers handing or tossing each other the bricks for
building, each one in a series must receive with equal speed if he
does not want to bring the whole work to a standstill.

This mutual accommodation of workmen to each other, which is
peculiar to all kinds of labour concatenation, thus becomes a disciplinary element of the greatest importance, especially for unskilled
work, such as preponderated at primitive stages of economic and
technical development. It can, indeed, be instituted also as a means
of discipline to accelerate the work in those cases of labour aggregation that in themselves do not require such a linking of movements.
For these there are artificial means of marking the tempo (counting,
singing, accompaniment of music), by means of which simple labour
aggregation is changed into labour concatenation. This is the case
with slave labour, which, for obvious reasons, must always be carried
on by gangs, and with the public labours of primitive people.

In Camerun "the chief Ngilla, a well-known Mohammedan slave-
hunter, drew up his people in companies of one hundred, and had
his hoeing done to the beat of music which followed. Behind these
workmen marched the sowers to the same beats, throwing seeds from
a sack which was hung about them."[272] The Basutos assemble every
year to cultivate the fields necessary for the personal sustenance of
their chief and his principal wife. "It is a remarkable picture," writes
the missionary Casalis,[273] "to see on such an occasion hundreds of

---

[272]Meinecke, *D. deutsch. Kolonien in Wort u. Bild,* p. 35, with illustration.
[273]*Les Bassoutos,* p. 171, with illustration. Another can be seen in Gerland,
Atlas d. Ethnographie (Leipzig, 1876), Tab. XXII, No. 25. Similar reports by
K. Endemann of the Sotho negroes in Ztschr. f. Ethnol., VI, pp. 26 and 30;
Paulitschke, as above, I, p. 216; from the Gallas by Harar; and on the Bagabos
in Southern Mindanao by Schadenberg in the same publication, XVII, pp. 19,
20.

black men drawn up in straight lines moving their hoes up and down in unison. The air resounds with the songs by which the workers are enlivened, and by which they can keep the proper time. The chief makes a point to be present and sees to it that several fat oxen are killed and made ready for the labourers. All classes adopt the same plan to lighten and expedite their work; but among the common people it rests on reciprocity."

The last example shows very clearly the transition from bidden to manorial labour. We find the same thing in the Soudan, where the erection and repairing of the village walls in particular is carried out to the accompaniment of music; and again among the Malays and the Chinese, who, since early times, have directed the public manorial services by the beat of the drum. In Europe also this means has been essayed. In the Baltic provinces down to the end of the eighteenth century landowners had their harvesting done by the serfs to the rhythm of the bagpipes, and traces of similar usage are at hand from other countries. In our modern States we meet with this species of labour concatenation brought about by artificial means only in the measured cadenee of military forces, where the aim is always to train a number of men to complete unanimity in their exercise of strength, and where the breaking of the tempo by a single person detracts from the general effect.

3. We come now to the last kind of labour in common, which we have designated *joint labour*[274]. Certain tasks in production require for their performance the simultaneous cooperation of various classes of labour. These latter supplement one another, and may be called complementary phases of labour. Since they cannot possibly be performed by one workman, several workmen of various kinds must be combined in one group to form an organized and indivisible whole. Such a group is sometimes called gang, company, band. (In Bavaria and Austria Pasz[275]; in other parts, *Rotte, Truppe, Bande.*)

Instances from agriculture are quite numerous. Thus in drawing in hay or corn, the load-builder, the pitcher, the after-raker, in binding, the binder and the gatherer, form natural groups; in mowing grain a second person is required to glean, in digging potatoes another gathers them up. From the sphere of industry may be mentioned the smith and the bellows-man, the rope-maker and the

---

[274] *Arbeitsverbmdung.*

[275] Comp. Schmeller, *Bayer Worterbuch*, I, p. 409. The origin of the words is not clear.

man who turns the wheel, mason and hod-carrier, those placing and those pounding in the paving-stones; from other spheres: the cook and the turnspit; inn-keeper, waiter, and house-boy; on the street-car, driver and conductor; in the row-boat, oarsman and steersman, likewise hunters and beaters, musician and dancer, blower and organist, drummers and pipers, judge, bailiffs and clerk, doctor and attendants, a theatrical troupe, an orchestra. The list could be continued much further.

In all these cases it is not a question of processes that have arisen through division of labour and then been reunited, but of activities of quite different kinds, none of which could ever exist by itself, and which, therefore, have come conjointly into being. In their advancement these occupations are dependent on one another, support one another and only together from a coordinated whole. The workers engaged must therefore accommodate themselves to each other; the one must work into the hands of the other, without whom he could accomplish nothing at all. In most cases his labour by itself would be quite unproductive.

As a rule there will be in such associations of labour an activity that can be designated the leading or dominant one, while the other is subordinate and auxiliary. Accordingly the personal relationship between the workmen employed will also take the form of a dependent relationship. If the directing workman is independent, the workman who in technical matters is dependent will frequently stand in the relation of employee. If the associated labour is made part of an undertaking it is usual for the whole work ("team-work," collective piece-work) to have assigned to it a collective wage, as is the case with the cigar bunch-breaker and roller, the glass-blower and attendant. The plan thus offers a means of applying the system of piece-wage even in cases where the work of one labourer cannot be separated from that of another or of several others; but it results in most cases to the disadvantage of those who perform the subordinate labour[276].

On the whole, this form of labour in common belongs also to the stage of undeveloped technique in the instruments of production. With advancing development the supplanting of the subordinate labour by animal or mechanical power is aimed at. The most familar example is offered by the plough, which was formerly drawn by human beings, later by oxen. In this, however, the combination

---

[276]Comp. Schloss, *Methods of Industrial Remuneration*, pp. 61 ff.

of labour endured some time longer, inasmuch, as a second driver or several drivers were required besides the ploughman, until at length a more perfect construction of the plough made them superfluous[277].

In conclusion, it is again to be emphasized that the whole sphere of labour in common belongs, like that of union of labour, preeminently to the departments and the epochs of labour possessing little or no capital. They are the resource of the economically frail. As such, however, their great evolutionary and historical importance lies in their training of man to methodical division and economy of time, to self-subordination to a general aim, and to regular and intensive labour. These supplement each other in that the inherent weakness of union of labour, pervading the life of each man in primitive times, everywhere finds its counterpart in the temporary communities of labour that arise wherever the variously employed skill of the individual is inadequate to a given task. Resting originally on custom alone, they lead in course of time to relationships capable of legal compulsion, such as slavery and serfdom. The principles of union of labour and labour in common have in other respects contributed little to the creation of permanent organizations, but they have left permanent works. The pyramids and stone monuments of Egypt, the ruins of the giant cities of Mesopotamia, the structures of the peoples of early American civilization must be observed if we would know what human beings are capable of performing, even without the knowledge of iron, without draught animals, and without such simple mechanical expedients as lever, screw, or pulley, when united by one mighty mind in community of work.

For science also the two phenomena here referred to, now that they have been defined, may prove themselves upon unbiassed testing not altogether useless building stones. The theory of labour still stands in need of further extension. The development of the points of view, which in this chapter it has been possible in most cases

---

[277]Interesting modifications of the system of combination of labour are found in the cases where more expensive implements are necessary, and only one of the parties possesses them, while the others merely contribute their labour. In North Russia this is particularly the case in fishing, and again in the work of ploughing, where the hitching together of six to eight animals is rendered advisable from the heaviness of the soil. Examples from Wales, Ireland, and Scotland in Seebohm, *Village Communities* (4th ed.), p. 81. Meitzen, *Siedelung u. Agrarwesen d. Westgermanen u. Ostgermanen, d. Kelten*, etc., I, pp. 212 ff.; II, pp. 129, 130. Similarly on the Bogos in the mountains of Abyssinia, in Post, *Afr. Jurisprudenz*, II, pp. 184, 185.

only to indicate, would probably show that there is still much to be harvested in this region. For we have even now an inkling of the truth, that ini union of labour and labour in common much more subtle psychical influences cooperate than in the division of labour, which has hitherto been the almost exclusive object of our attention. To discover them all is, indeed, possibly only to the reflecting and self-observant worker.

Chapter VIII. Division of Labour.

I N most of the sciences nowadays there are popular truths. They consist as a rule of general principles, to which their propounders have given such initial completeness of form and substance that it would seem as if they might be added at once to our store of knowledge as an assured acquisition of the human mind incapable of being either shaken or lost. Such truths become the mental property of the educated with a rapidity often surprising. The convenient impress they bear from the beginning makes them coins for intellectual exchange that gain currency far beyond the department of knowledge for which they were issued. On the other hand, their passage over into the intellectual and linguistic circulation of the educated world serves again to confirm their validity within the narrow department of study from which they have sprung. If knowledge is making rapid progress in this department it comes to pass that these now popular truths remain inviolate while all the remaining structure of the science is demolished and rebuilt. They are like inorganic bodies overrun and enveloped by the luxuriant growth of living organisms.

Such is the case, if we are not mistaken, with the theory of division of labour in political economy. In its present form this theory dates from Adam Smith, and its popularity is indeed due in no small measure to the external circumstance that it is presented in the first chapter of Book I of his classical work, where it could not escape even the legion of those who merely "read at" books. Adam Smith is, of course, not the originator of the theory. He borrows it in its essential features from the *Essay on the History of Civil Society*, which his countryman, Adam Ferguson, published in 1767. Yet the

theory has been adopted by all later students in the agreeable form
in which Smith presented it. In this form it has also gone over into
other sciences and become familiar to every educated person.

In essaying then to subject the economic theory of division of
labour to a critical examination, and to supplement this examination by the application that this theory has quite recently received
in the department of sociology, we count upon dealing with a circle
of ideas familiar to many[278]. For this last application marks at the
same time one of the few attempts made by economic science to advance on this point beyond Adam Smith. In other respects students
have contented themselves with correcting Smith's theory of division of labour in subsidiary points, tracing it back historically and
dogmatically to the ancient Greeks, adapting explanatory examples
to the technical advances of the present, and besides its bright sides,
bringing forward the dark sides as well. On the whole, however, our
remarks on popularized scientific truths hold good for this theory.
While round about it the structure of economic theory has been diligently altered and extended, it has remained intact. Only recently
a reputable economic writer, in a critical survey of the progress of
political economy since Adam Smith, stated that the subject is exhausted; that regarding it one can but repeat what has been already
said by others[279].

Under these circumstances it will suffice for us to discuss the
subject in direct connection with the celebrated Scotchman's presentation of it. We will, however, not cover the whole subject, but
attempt merely to answer the two questions: *What is division of
labour?* and *How does it operate?*

What division of labour is we can nowhere learn from Adam
Smith. He illustrates the process that he designates by this name
only by individual examples, and from them deduces directly the
statement which has since been termed the "law" of division of
labour, and which can be summarized in the words, that in every
industry the productivity of labour increases proportionately with
the extension of labour[280]. His examples, however, when closely
scrutinized by no means illustrate similar economic processes.

---

[278]Comp. following chapter.
[279]M. Block, *Le progrès de la science economique depuis Adam Smith* (Paris,
2d ed., 1897), I, p. 533.
[280]The correctness of this sharp formulation is manifest from the words of the
first chapter: "The division of labour, so far as it can be introduced, occasions
in every part a proportionable increase of the productive powers of labour".

There is first the celebrated instance of the pin-manufactory. With the ordinary workman, who is not particularly adept at this special branch of business and who perhaps could, with his utmost industry, make scarcely one pin in a day, and certainly could not make twenty, Smith contrasts the factory in which a considerable number of workmen with divided labour produce similar wares. "One man draws out the wire; another straights it; a third cuts it; a fourth points it; a fifth grinds it at the top for receiving the head; to make the head requires two or three distinct operations," etc. In this manner there result up to the completion of the pin eighteen distinct operations, each of which can be transferred to a particular hand. Smith finds that in such a cooperating group of workers the output of each individual, as compared with that of the labourer working separately and producing the whole product, is increased a hundred, indeed a thousandfold.

This example has been repeated even to weariness; it has become, in general, the classic type of division of labour. Most people can conceive of it only in this one form, the form of a factory in which the total labour necessary to the production of the ware is divided into as many simple operations as possible, carried on simultaneously by different persons in the same establishment[281].

But Adam Smith has not confined himself to this example. He calls it also division of labour when a product has to pass through various trades and employments in a country, from the procuring of the raw material till it is ready for use; as, for instance, the wool through the hands of the sheep-breeder, the spinner, the weaver, and the dyer. In a rude state of society all this, he points out, is the work of one man; in every improved society, on the contrary, the farmer is generally nothing but a farmer; the manufacturer nothing but a manufacturer. The labour, too, that is necessary to produce any complete manufacture, is almost always divided among a great number of hands.

Smith makes no distinction between the two kinds of division of labour, and ascribes to both the same effects. But it does not require lengthy consideration to recognise that we are here dealing with two

---

[281]Helmolt, *De laboris divisione*, 1840, (a Doctor's Dissertation from the University of Utrecht,) pp. 38, 39: "Ubi plures operarii simul opus quoddam conficiunt, singuli vero continue eadem operis parte sunt occupati, ut, si aliquid perfecerint eandem rem de novo aggrediantur." And yet Ferguson had previously entitled his chapter on the division of labour: "On the Separation of Arts and Professions."

distinct processes. In the case of the manufacture of woollen cloth a whole process in production is separated into various departments. Each of these departments becomes an independent economic organism; and a ware must, from the procuring of the raw material on, pass through a series of trades before it can be offered ready for consumption, each change in ownership involving a charge for profits. In the case of the pin, on the contrary, the manufacture of the object of the division of labour does not constitute a complete process in production, but merely a single department. For its raw material, the wire, is already well advanced towards completion. The result of the division is not a series of new trades, but a chain of dependent employments whose successful utilization under present conditions postulates the existence of wage-workers held together by one entrepreneur. The product, before it is completed, passes, it is true, through a larger number of hands than previously, but it undergoes no change of proprietorship.

Two industrial processes so thoroughly different demand different names. We will designate the division of a whole process of production into several industrially independent sections division of production; and the breaking up of a department of production into simple dependent labour elements *subdivision of labour*[282].

Finally Adam Smith cites a third example that is neither division of production nor subdivision of labour. He compares three smiths: a common smith, who can handle the hammer well, but has never been accustomed to make nails, a second smith who has been accustomed to make nails, but has not this for his sole or principal occupation, and finally a nail-smith who has never followed any other calling. He finds that if all three make nails for a definite period the work done increases according as the workman limits himself to the production of one product. It is this limitation to the exclusive production of a single line of goods that he calls division of labour.

The justification for this nomenclature is not at once apparent. What is divided? Where are the parts?

Manifestly Smith conceives the whole business of a smith who, as in olden times, makes horseshoes, ploughshares, and wheel-tires, as well as axes, spades, and nails, as the subject of the division. From this comprehensive department of production a line of products is separated, and their production taken over by a special workman, the nail-smith, while the remaining products continue to form part

---

[282] *Produktionsteilung* and *Arbeitszerlegung.*

of the smith's work. The articles formerly produced jointly in the one business of the smith are for the future manufactured in two different businesses. In the place of one industry there are now two; and each forms for an individual a separate business or vocation.

It is clear that in this case it is neither a question of cutting a somewhat extensive process of production into various sections, nor of subdividing such a section into its simplest elements. For, as Smith himself explains, the labour process of the nailer is neither shorter nor less complex than the smith's: each for himself blows the bellows, stirs the fire, heats the iron, and forges every part of the product. A change has taken place only in one respect: each applies this process to fewer classes of goods. Under the system of divided labour, however, the goods produced, taken singly, do not pass through more hands than formerly. We will call this third species of division of labour *specialization* or *division of trades*.

How specialization is distinguished from subdivision of labour is readily perceived. The one is a division of the whole task of production between different businesses; the other takes place within a single business. It is perhaps more difficult at first sight to distinguish division of production and specialization of trades. In division of production cross-cuts, as it were, are made through a somewhat extensive process of production; in specialization a distinct department of business is split lengthwise.

To offer a simple example, the production of leather articles of use was originally confined to the one establishment. The Siberian nomad and the Southern Slav peasant still procure the hides, tan them, and out of the leather make footwear, harness, etc., within their own household establishment. In the countries of Western Europe the trades of the tanner and the currier had arisen by the early Middle Ages. Leather goods down to their finished condition then passed through three trades,—that of the furnisher of the hides, of the tanner, and of the currier. That was division of production. In time the special handicrafts of the shoemaker, the saddler, the strap-maker, the maker of fine leather goods, etc., have separated themselves from the large industry of the currier; and each produces a particular class of leather wares by approximately the same process of work. That is specialization, or division of trades.

In division of production, to use a simile, the whole stream of production of goods is from time to time dammed up by weirs; with specialization it is diverted into numerous small channels and rivulets.

In his explanatory examples Smith goes no farther than this. We may also for the present pause here and lay before ourselves the question: What led the "father of political economy" to embrace under the one name division of labour three processes so different as division of production, subdivision of work, and specialization? Wherein are these processes, whose fundamental differences we have been able only briefly to indicate, essentially similar?

The true response to this question will at the same time furnish us with the simplest and broadest definition of division of labour, a definition which must be accepted by all who, on this point, have followed Adam Smith, that is, by all scientific political economists[283].

Manifestly those three different kinds of division of labour have only the following in common with each other: all three are *processes in the economic evolution of society which have originated through acts of human volition, and in which an economic task is transferred from the one person hitherto performing it to several persons, the transfer being so made that each of these performs but a separate part of the previous total labour.* Division of labour will accordingly always be characterized by an increase in the number of labourers necessary for the accomplishment of a definite economic end, and at the same time by a differentiation of work. The economic tasks become simplified, better adapted to limited human capacities; they become, as it were, individualized. Hence division of labour is always at the same time classification of labour, organization of labour in accord with the economic principle; its result is ever the cooperation of varied energies in a common work which could formerly only be performed by a single pair of hands.

---

[283]Those savants of course excepted who no longer define at all. Most later definitions overlook the causal force of the word division, and in place of the process of division put the realized condition. Schmoller, for instance, understands by division of labour "the permanent adaptation of the individual to a specialized life-work affecting and dominating the whole life" (Jhrb f. Gesetzg., Verw. u. Volksw., XIV, 47). He thus forces under division what can be but its result. E. v. Philippovich states in his *Grundriss d. Pol. Oek.*, I, 50: "Division of labour is the actual divided performance of tasks leading to a common end. It assumes, like every division, a unity from whose standpoint the labour of the individual appears not as something exclusive and self-contained, but as a part of a larger whole. This unity is determined either by society as a whole, or by some organization of society into separate parts." But why first construct this totality? Why not begin with it? Society and the business undertaking have surely not been divided; they are but results of the division of labour.

Keeping this clearly in mind, and passing in review from this standpoint the whole field of the economic employment of labour in its historical and contemporary development, we soon recognise that with the typical examples of Adam Smith and the three kinds of division of labour deduced by us from them, the range of the latter is by no means exhausted. We find, on the contrary, a fourth and a fifth type of division of labour, which we will designate respectively the *formation of trades and the displacement of labour.*

Let us begin with the *formation of trades*, which should indeed rank first in an enumeration of the kinds of division of labour. For it forms the beginning of all economic development. To understand it one must start from the conception, that before the origin of a national economy the different peoples pass through a condition of pure private economy in which each house has to produce through the labour of its members all that is required. This labour can be divided among the members of the household in various ways, according to age, sex, and physical strength, and according also to their relation to the father of the family. But this distribution of labour is not division of labour from the standpoint of society, for its effects remain restricted to the household and exert no creative influence upon other economies; nor does it influence the formation of classes in society. At this stage there are, therefore, all varieties of agricultural and industrial technique; but there is no system of agriculture, no industry, no trade as a separate branch of business; there are no peasants, no industrial classes, no merchants as social business groups.

This state of affairs is altered as soon as individual tasks separate from this many-sided activity and become subjects of vocations, the bases of particular business occupations. The way for this advance is prepared by the division of labour of the great slave and serf husbandries. We cannot, however, treat of these here. The part that detaches itself from the range of work of the autonomous domestic establishment and becomes a separate and independent business is at one time a complete process of production, for example, pottery; or again, a single section in production, for example, cloth-fulling, corn-grinding[284]; or still again, a species of personal service, for example, surgical work. Most frequently, however, it is the productive part of the domestic labours that is abridged through the forma-

---

[284]In this case the formation of a trade is at the same time division of production.

214

tion of trades; and in the course of centuries these labours are more and more restricted to the province of consumption. On the other hand, there arise the different branches of production and the various industries which through specialization and division of production become multiplied *ad infinitum*.

It would be a mistake, however, to imagine that this process of the formation of vocations which begins with us in the early Middle Ages has long been completed. Parts of the old domestic economy are still falling away; in the country, slowly; in the towns, more rapidly. Every city directory can disclose to us a series of independent industries which have come into existence only within the present century, through the splitting up of former single phases of domestic activity.

Of course it would be erroneous to assume that each instance of a new trade which is not division of an old trade or of a branch of production is to be traced back to division of labour between household and new business occupations. A bicycle-factory, a galvanizing or electrical establishment, an ice-factory, and a photographic atelier are industrial undertakings owing their origin not to division of labour, but to the rise of entirely new species of goods. They must accordingly be excluded from this survey. Yet they are not on that account beyond the influence of division of labour, since from the beginning they accommodate themselves to the forms of production conditioned by such division.

Connected only externally with this process is the phenomenon that we have already termed *displacement of labour*. It accompanies the invention of new machines and other fixed tools of labour. The division of labour here operates in the following manner:

With the introduction into a branch of production of a newly-invented machine there is a complete displacement of the previous organization of work. As a rule the mechanism undertakes only separate movements that until then have fallen to the human hand; and in the business installing the machine the sole initial change is generally the transfer of the workman, who formerly performed those muscular motions, to attendance upon the machine, which demands from him other muscular motions. In this way, for instance, after the introduction of the sewing-machine, the labourer in the tailoring establishment works with hand and foot, while formerly his hand alone was called into action, and then, moreover, in a different manner.

215

But even previously to that there were many more persons engaged in the making of a coat than the tailor. There were in the first place the producers of the materials used by the tailor: the wool-producer, the spinner, the weaver, the dyer, etc.; then the producers of fine implements: the needle-manufacturer, the scissors-manufacturer, and many others. All these producers still continue active after the introduction of a sewing-machine. But a new one is added, the machine-manufacturer; or, since the machine is produced through subdivision of work, at once a whole group: the machine-fitter, the founder, the metal-turner, the carpenter for the models, the mounter, the varnisher, etc. We have, if we embrace under our view the whole process of production, a part of the total labour pushed back from a later to an earlier stage. The work of tailoring is in part transferred from the tailoring establishment to the machine factory.

The whole process is typical, and undoubtedly exhibits the characteristics of division of labour. If we employ for it the expression *displacement of labour* the phrase must be understood in a local and temporal sense. As regards locality, displacement of labour means the partial transference of the manufacture of an article from one place of production to another; as regards time, it signifies the substitution of work that has been previously performed for work being performed now, the pushing back of a section of the work that was formerly devoted to the production of consumption goods to the furnishing of the means of production. In this, however, it is not at all necessary that a new untiertaking should be formed to produce the new implement of labour exclusively. For, as in the case of the sewing-machine, a machine-factory already in existence can undertake its production. The essential thing to note is that the new process for the production of clothing contains an increased number of different employments, and accordingly claims the service of more labourers.

We have now become acquainted with five different kinds of economic processes falling under the head of division of labour, which are still in operation every day before our eyes. This is of course saying very little as to their relative importance in modern industrial life. For the latter is itself the result of a long process of development; and he who regards it with the eye of an historical student will find everywhere side by side the most primitive and the most modern: the one with a modest, the other with a ubiquitously prominent sphere of influence. Society in its long evolution from the isolated to the social economy has ever been seeking and finding new methods of organization in work. But it has not on that account discarded the old, nor will it discard them so long as their roles have not been completely played. For here too the great law of economy prevails; nothing is lost that is still capable of being at any point advantageously employed.

This also holds for the various forms of division of labour. Even though subdivision of work and displacement of labour at present surpass in importance specialization and division of production, and even though formation of trades as a species of division of labour need hardly be longer taken into account, none of these principles of economic organization has ceased to operate. Each continues active in the places where it can still assert its force.

In economic history each of them has had a period of preponderance. Formation of trades appears with tis in the early Middle Ages. The chief activity of specialization is coincident with the prime of municipal development. Division of production begins at the same time. Its whole force in the economy of capital, however, is developed only after subdivision of work and displacement of labour begin to operate, and neither of these can with certainty be traced back beyond the seventeenth century.

It is with reluctance that we refrain from a detailed presentation of the historical conditions governing them, as well as of the causes and consequences of their appearance. We are the more loth because only in this way can the sharp distinctions we have made between the different processes find their full justification, and the traditional abstract treatment of the whole matter its refutation. We must, however, devote a few general words to the cause and result of division of labour. For the distinguishing of those five kinds of the latter would necessarily appear scientifically unimportant, or an idle nicety of refinement, if all stood in like casual connection with the economic phenomena that precede or follow them.

Adam Smith derives all division of labour from one common *origin*: man's natural propensity to trade. He does not determine whether this is the result of instinct or of conscious mental action. He thus renounces a sharp psychological analysis of economic action, and contents himself with considering division of labour as deep-rooted in the dark depths of instinct.

In this, however, he falls foul of his own examples. For if division of labour has its origin in an immemorial instinct of man, then it is a fundamental factor of economic life, which must assert itself whenever and wherever men exist. Yet Adam Smith's examples regularly set over against the condition of divided labour a condition of undivided labour, and deduce the former from the latter. For this has to be inferred from the dynamic employment of the word division. There actually existed for centuries, as we already know, a condition of society in which division of labour was wanting: and the different kinds of the latter can be pretty definitely determined by the time of their origin. Social division of labour is thus generally a historical category, and not an elemental economic phenomenon.

The same is true of exchange. Just as there have been epochs without economic division of labour, so there have been epochs without exchange. The first acts of trade do not appear simultaneously with division of labour, but long precede it. They serve the purpose of equalizing casual surpluses and deficiencies that have made their appearance in otherwise autonomous economies. Exchange is here something accidental; it is not a necessary concomitant of the husbandry of the time. Even when with the formation of trades social division of labour arises, exchange is still very active in forms which it is the evident purpose to exclude as far as possible. The housewife of early time uses the hand-mill to grind the corn she herself has grown, and from the flour thus produced she bakes her bread. After the industries of the miller and the baker have been established the grinding is turned over to the miller, and the baker then receives the flour to make bread of. From raw material to finished product the new article of consumption has never changed its proprietor. For their pains, miller and baker are allowed to retain a definite part of their product. In the whole process of production with divided labour this is the sole occurrence partaking of the nature of exchange.

From this one readily recognises that the alleged propensity to trade is for Adam Smith only a means of extricating himself from an embarrassment. We can the more readily spare ourselves the trouble of entering further into this point since recent economists have not accepted this tenet of their Scottish master. They rather prefer to regard exchange as the unintentional result of division of labour. This we can accept, with the limitation that with divided labour exchange becomes necessary from the moment that the producer possesses all the means of production. It then becomes a vital

218

element of each economy; and from this point on almost every advance in division of labour increases the number of necessary acts of exchange. But this stage of development is not reached till centuries after the earliest origin of economic division of labour. Even today, for example, it is by no means the rule in country parts for the miller to own the corn and the baker the flour, and a triple exchange to be necessary before the consumers can come into possession of the bread.

If then exchange is merely a secondary phenomenon in the evolutionary processes of social division of labour, we are by this very fact compelled to seek another motive for man's efforts toward this division.

In this we are led back directly to the fundamental facts of economy: the boundless extent of human needs, and the limited means of satisfying them. Human needs are capable of an infinite multiplication and subdivision; they are never at rest; they increase in degree and extent with the progress of civilization. The material suitable for human ends is limited, as is also human labour which invests it with the qualities of a marketable ware and increases its quantity. With the increase in the number of human beings the relation of the total demand to the mass of raw material capable of profitable utilization which nature can offer becomes even more unfavourable. The quantity of labour necessary to satisfy the total requirement thus increases for a double reason: more and better goods are to be produced; and they are to be turned out under more unfavorable conditions. The share in head-work falling to each one engaged in the undertaking would thus become at length intolerable were it not possible to reduce it through an economic employment of labour.

Now simple observation teaches that every person is not equally qualified by nature for every employment. The differing bodily and intellectual tendencies of individuals necessarily occasion important differences in the products of labour; and these differences become ever more marked with advancing social development or, what is the same, with increasing variety of work to be performed. The principle of economy requires that everyone's employment befit one's capabilities; for only in this way can labour yield its highest service. To have "the right man in the right place" becomes all the easier as the tasks increase in number and each is permanently consigned to a special hand.

Along with the multiplication of occupations comes a simplification. Every composite work means for the individual executing it a frequent change of motions, and every such change a waste of energy. For passing from one kind of movement to another calls for mental and bodily accommodation to the new class of work, which means an outlay of strength yielding in itself no useful return. With muscular movements pursuing a uniform course, however, the mind's share in the work can be eliminated, and an automatic performance of those movements soon enters, which, with increasing practice, removes farther and farther the limits of fatigue. At the same time the intensity of automatic labour can be greatly increased, so that not only can the movements be continued longer, but a larger number of them is possible within a given unit of time. An extraordinary advance in the effectiveness of labour is the result[285].

All this makes it, as it were, a command of economy to narrow the labour tasks if we are to utilize every kind of endowment, and avoid every bootless waste of strength. In most processes of production, however, we find decidedly heterogeneous employments united: hand-work and head-work; operations demanding great muscular power along with those in which suppleness of the finger, delicacy of touch, keenness of sight come in question; tasks requiring a skill gained through theory and practice, and those that even the unpracticed is in a position to undertake. In early times when these different tasks were placed in one hand a great waste of skilled labour resulted, and the productive part of the population was limited to those who had mastered some one branch of technique in all its parts. By separating the qualitatively unequal labour elements from one another, division of labour succeeds in utilizing the weakest as well as the strongest workers, and in inciting them to the development of the highest special skill.

Thus division of labour is, in the last analysis, nothing but one of those processes of adaptation that play so great a part in the evolutionary history of the whole inhabited world: adaptation of the tasks of labour to the variety of human powers, adaptation of individual powers to the tasks to be performed, continued differentiation of the one and of the other. Therewith the whole process advances out of the twilight of instinctive life into the bright day of conscious human activity.

Yet one fact still requires special mention. It is, that the *personal casual element* in division of labour stands out more clearly

---

[285]More in detail in *Arbeit u. Rhythmus*, pp. 24 ff.

the further back we go in the history of man-kind. For this reason the predominant forms of division of labour in the early stages of development are those in which the individual is assigned an independent task that can be carried out without any extensive material equipment. It is more especially the intellectual and artistic activities that expand earliest into vocations. The priest, the prophet, the magician, the singer, and the dancer are the first to gain a separate position on account of special gifts.

If an unfree system of labour exists, division of labour develops first within the slave family; and it is with the assistance of a personal and moral feature hitherto hardly heeded that it comes into being. Wherever the system of supervised labour in common is inapplicable, the master must provide every unfree worker with a particular range of duties, for which he can be held responsible. He must impose on him a single definite kind of work if he wishes to profit by his labour. Hence among the Romans that almost over-refined specialization of work in the *familia urbana*, the careful selection of slaves according to bodily and mental endowment for the different agricultural employments[286]; and among the serfs of the Middle Ages the extreme frequency with which the rent paid in kind was fixed in very special products of domestic work. The man acting in the slave household exclusively as field-worker or smith, barber or scribe, the rent-collector and the man whose sole duty it was to supply the court with casks or vessels, knives or linen cloth, acquired a special dexterity wherewith, when the hour of emancipation sounded, they entered society as professional workers. Thus in the individual task rendered necessary by the slave economy of the stage of exclusive domestic husbandry, and in the specialization that it conditions, lay the seedtime for the social division of labour of the following stage.

It is at a much later date that *material elements* supplement the personal element of endowment and adaptation in originating division of labour[287]. Formerly it was men alone, now things also

---

[286] Comper on this the fine remarks of Columella, I, 9: "Sed et illud censeo, ne confundantur opera familiae, sec ut omnes onmia exsequantur; nam id minime conducit agricolae, seu quia nemo suum propium aliquod esse opus credit, seu quia, cum enisus est, non suo sed communi officio proficit ideoque labori multum se substrahit, nectamen viritim malefactum deprehenditur, quod fit a multis," etc.

[287] On what follows compre *Arbeit u.Rhythmus* Chap. IX. How strongly the personal element still predominated in the division of labour in the town economy of the Middle Ages is seen from the conditions for admission into a guild. As

become differentiated,—tools, raw materials, products. Each advance in division of labour seeks to adapt itself to the existing tools and implements, or to provide new ones for the particular task. Let one but think of the innumerable kinds of hammers, tongs, and chisels used in the different branches of metal and wood-working! The division of labour among persons finds its counterpart in a division of use among the instruments of work. But as long as the tool is merely a reinforcement of the human agent, the personal adjustment will dominate the process of production. It is only when artificial appliances are introduced which enable man to subdue natural powers to his service that the labour instrument gains control over the labourer's social individuality, as well as over his bodily movements. And now the impetus for a fresh advance along the path of division of labour can as readily originate in a newly-invented implement of labour as in the possession or acquisition of a particular personal qualification. Most newly-invented machines require the attendance of workmen possessing a qualification not previously represented in the business. Then, joined to this, comes the saving consequent upon the growing extension of production, a feature of importance from the standpoint of capital. But this saving can take place only on the assumption of a unification and concentration of demand sufficient to make the wholesale production, which perhaps has long been technically possible, economically possible also. Many labour-processes cause approximately the same costs whether they embrace many or few pieces, as is the case, for example, with dyeing, grinding, drying, postal delivery. But if the method of work can be so contrived that masses of the raw or half-manufactured material which are to be worked over are collected at definite points, the employment of hands at these points solely for this purpose becomes profitable, with, on the whole, a considerable saving in costs.

How far in such matters the social principles of immobility of labour and of free competition may cooperate to retard or to advance is not to be investigated here. A warning is merely to be given against observing and judging these matters solely in the light of modern industrial conditions. Division of labour reaches out far beyond the sphere of material things. It can show in recent times,

---

far as the carrying on of a trade come in question only personal requirements were made - ability to do the work with one's own hand. Material requirements had to be met by the person seeking admission only as a citizen - possession of a house and of arms; and as a Christian - entrance-fee in wax.

especially in the field of intellectual work, advances and results far surpassing those in the department of manufacturing technique. Indeed, the former are largely the direct cause and occasion of the latter. On the other hand, in the whole broad field lying beyond the limits of material production the material aids to labour play only an unimportant part. The personal element is here continually decisive for the further development of division of labour; and we thus have to recognise it as paramount in the whole great process of advancing civilization.

As to the universal originating cause of division of labour more than this cannot be said. The particular conditions of origin under which the various kinds and forms make their appearance will be briefly discussed in another place.

At this point we can make but like cursory reference also to the *economic consequences* of division of labour, although it is in this very particular that the various forms most widely diverge.

Adam Smith knows but one effect of division of labour: the increased productivity of labour. He thus restricts its influence to the sphere of production. In this he is right. Division of labour permits the production of more and better goods with a given expenditure of human strength than was possible with undivided labour. Production becomes cheaper; its costs diminish as far as labour is concerned. And since Smith considers labour the true measure of exchange value, he can dispense with investigating whether under all circumstances division of labour also insures a cheaper satisfaction of the wants of the customer. However narrow this conception may appear, it is certainly more reasonable than the unlimited extension given by many recent economists[288] to the effects of division of labour when they derive the whole of our present commercial organization directly from division of labour, and think to characterize it sufficiently by calling it, as they commonly do, the "economy of divided labour." In this they allow themselves to be guided by the opinion that in their present form and method of action the most important economic phenomena are determined by division of labour; that in the highly refined subdivision of trades occasioned by it division of labour is, so to speak, the skeleton supporting the economic organism, while trade and commerce represent the ligaments and muscles that hold it together and enable it to functionate like a great living body. Commerce, however, they say, is occasioned

---

[288]Schmoller may again serve as an example: *Grundriss*, I, pp. 364 ff.

directly by division of labour; division of labour is its cause. Therein lies a great mistake. By itself, division of labour does not create trade. And inversely, a condition of undivided labour may easily be imagined concurrent with a relatively well-developed trade.

Let us elucidate the last sentence first. We may recall that peoples standing at the stage of private domestic economy can have a relatively well-developed exchange of goods—for profit or otherwise, if smallness of the household membership or extraordinary inequality in the distribution of the gifts of nature give occasion for it. Each house and each worker produces, in a condition of complete union of labour, everything that the natural advantages of the place of habitation permit of. Exchange but fills up the gaps of home-production; its objects are merely surpluses of otherwise autonomous establishments. The weaker the different households are numerically and the oftener unfavourable seasons—dying of cattle, spoiling of the stores, or sickness of members of the household— threaten at particular points the satisfaction of their needs, the more frequently will surplus ware be drawn from an outside source in exchange for the excess commodity in one's own sphere.

Thus the negro races of Central Africa have a great number of weekly markets, which are usually held under special peace protection in the midst of the primaeval forest. Yet among them there is scarcely a single industry carried on as a business; and every species of division of labour is lacking, save the separation of the spheres of work according to sex. The same state of things has been observed in different parts of Oceania. Even in the countries of Western Europe a fairly brisk market trade must seemingly be assumed for the early Middle Ages, notwithstanding the complete absence of a developed subdivision of labour.

On the other hand, as already frequently remarked, when the existence of slavery or serfdom calls into being households numerically extensive, division of labour can establish itself at the same stage of domestic work without giving rise to exchange. On the estates of wealthy Romans there were workmen of very different grades of skill, perhaps even some who produced according to the principle of subdivision of work; but exchange neither united them with each other nor with the consumers of their products. The power holding them together was the authority of the head of the family. Under slavery this power lay in the ownership of the persons, under serfdom, in the ownership of the soil. An establishment thus organized is a *permanent community for production and consumption.* What it produces it also consumes. Indeed, division of labour really appears for it a welcome means of avoiding exchange.

In such large households regular division of labour according to employment paves the way for the succeeding economic stage. It is the starting-point for the formation of trades. On the latter is based the origin of special economic life-vocations. It liberates a section of humanity from the soil, on the possession of which its existence had solely depended. It furnishes the burgher as well as the peasant with the means of livelihood. Specialization increases the number of opportunities for trade, it supplies the framework within which higher mechanical skill is developed. And at first division of production has no other effect. Formation of trades, specialization, and division of production—all three together—are indeed able of themselves to create an economy based upon divided labour, but this economy is not at once national economy. For, first of all, it still lacks the circulation of goods.

The whole process of division of labour up to this point proceeds, as we know, by the method of workers separating from the independent household of the proprietor of the soil, and in the service of other households turning to account any special skill in the form of wage-work. They are, it is true, tradesmen living from the earnings of their special trade; but the raw material that they work up is owned by the person who will finally consume the product in his own house. Now there are certain cases in which several of such wage-workers must cooperate in one process of manufacture if the commodity is to be completely finished; for example, in preparing bread, the miller and the baker; in making a garment, the weaver, the dyer, and the tailor. In the exercise of their technical skill all these labourers engaged in independent trades are united with one another through the product which passes through their hands in different stages of its manufacture. The whole employment of the one is to continue the work of the other. Their economic cooperation, however, is effected by the owner of the raw material, who has himself generally produced it, and to whom the finished product returns—that is, by the consumer. The means, however, by which same person attracts to his service the various part-producers is the wage that he pays to each. This payment, moreover, represents the sole commercial act involved in this kind of division of labour.

In building a house one employs successively on wage the mason, the carpenter, the roofer, the glazier, the joiner, the locksmith, and the decorators, and supplies them with the material necessary for their work. Their objective point of union they all find in the new structure; their personal point of union they possess in the builder. He unites them, so to speak, into a *temporary community of production*. But their union is a loose and constantly changing one. No permanent economic organization of society arises from it. Today they serve this builder, tomorrow that. Division of labour makes the producers socially dependent neither upon one another nor upon the contractor. They remain "master workmen."

Nor is there much change in this regard when the wage-worker rises to the position of craftsman and himself supplies the raw material for his labour. A wagon, for instance, is ordered from the wagon-maker, is ironed by the smith, and painted by the painter. The wagon-maker furnishes the wood, the smith the iron, the painter the paint. The payment that they receive at this stage is a remuneration for the labour and the material furnished by each. But the one guiding the production is still, as ever, the consumer of the commodity produced by divided labour.

Through all earlier forms of division of labour, as one perceives, there runs an obvious endeavour to restrict the number of commercial transactions evoked by it to those absolutely necessary. In the midst of all trades originating in division of labour stands domestic work, the mother of them all, with its primeval community of labour dissolving but slowly. Alongside it, even throughout the stage of town economy, the particular manufacturing establishments and professional workmen called forth by formation of trades, specialization, and division of production continue to be firmly and closely united. From the customer's house they receive the commissions which they execute; and even then during the performance of the work they frequently enter into a temporary *consuming community*. In the stage of national economy the consumer withdraws more and more from his century-old position as director and uniter of divided production. These duties now develop into a vocation. This vocation, however, can be independently exercised by those alone in whose hands the means of production—or at least the circulating means of production—are at the same time found, that is, by the capitalists. Because of the double duties that thus fall to them—procuring capital and directing the production—they are called *business undertakers* or *entrepreneurs*.

In their hands the division of labour undergoes a complete transformation. In so far as it is division of production each part-producer
now disposes of the products of his own raw material to his succes-
sor. They become for each a source of profit, that is, circulating
capital. Thus arises along with the trade in certain classes of finished wares, a series of exchanges of raw material or unfinished goods
with no other aim than to unite the various stages of division of
labour with each other. This exchanging is in character quite unlike
the one between the consumer and the various producers in succession, which previously held exclusive possession of the field. The
earlier exchange, at least for the one acquiring the product, is pure
exchange for use, in which he is concerned with the commodity as
an object of consumption. The later exchange is for purchaser and
seller always a business transaction in which the utility of the object
of exchange is of secondary, and its character as capital—the profit
to be gained by it— of primary, importance. The forms of division
of labour, displacement of labour, and subdivision of work now arising for the first time have by their mutual relationship the effect of
imparting the quality of capital to the fixed means of production
as well. The subdivision of work makes necessary a permanently
dependent labouring class. It alone gives to the method of capitalistic production its full expansion. Although, on the other hand, it
largely destroys, in the department accessible to it, that which the
formation of trades and specialization had previously created—the
independence of the petty traders.

This new phase of division of labour, accordingly, raises commerce to a height unknown before. In trade, in transportation, in
credit negotiation, in insurance, it calls forth numberless other phenomena of division of labour under the shadow of the entrepreneur
system, which lead in turn to fresh commercial services of a manifold kind. But in itself division of labour does not create this new
commerce. The impelling and creative element in modern national
economy is not division of labour, but *business capital*, and commerce is its spring of life.

The point at which capital in its primal form of money first displayed its earning power was *trade*. From there it has encroached
upon production by enabling the trader to take the consumer's place
as director of production. In this way that commission system first
took its rise in the world of industry in which the commission man-

ufacturer enters into the same outer relationship with wage-worker and craftsman that the father of the household formerly held. To the one he advances the raw material, from the other he purchases the finished products made from self-supplied material, with the object of further disposing of them. Where a productive process falls into different sections he guides the product from one to the other, and finally places it on the market as finished ware. As a rule, he operates merely with circulating capital. He has to do permanently with fixed capital only when it becomes profitable to pass over from commission to factory production. While, however, in the province of industry trading capital was merely a transforming agency, in the departments of banking, transportation, and insurance it has been creative. These departments of business are really, when we consider them from the side of division of labour, only ramifications of trade.

Thus, it seems to us, we have to recognise *capital as the creative influence in modern national economy, and division of labour as the medium* through which it operates. Its support and representative is the entrepreneur.

That the latter has been able to utilize this medium of division of labour to much greater purpose than the head of the household before him is plainly evident. Today the entrepreneur determines what we shall eat and drink, read in the papers and see at the theatre, how we shall lodge and dress. That means everything. For a great part of the goods we consume the right of self-determining is taken away. And since uniform production on a large scale is most advantageous to the manufacturer, there is operative in the sphere of *consumption* an increasingly active *uniforming process.*

In contrast with this the province of labour exhibits a continually advancing differentiation. The field of work of each individual is ever growing more restricted. It is only when broken up on the basis of technique into its parts, that labouring skill can furnish workable building material for the task of the entrepreneur. Every business establishment is a union of various fragmentary activities, originating through division of labour, into an organic whole. It unites workmen economically and technically dependent into a permanent community of production. This community of production, however, has ceased to be at the same time a community of consumption. On the contrary, its members belong to distinct households which have been freed from all the burdens of production, and which are in no wise connected with one another or with the employer's household.

In the formation of those communities of production the entrepreneur's plan of action varies according to the presence or absence of the earlier forms of division of labour in the manufacture in
which he wishes to place his capital.

In the first case he absorbs into his undertaking all the independent branches of business that up to that time had to do with the
wares to be produced. He specializes their workers and permanently
allots to them the performance, side by side, of the part-tasks required by the business. As an example, take the furniture-factory, in
which joiners, turners, wood-carvers, upholsterers, glaziers, painters,
and finishers are *incorporated* in a common productive process.

In the second case he first *organizes* the work according to the
principles of subdivision of labour, in the branch of production concerned, and furnishes the business with a comprehensive outfit of
machinery.

In both instances there are in the fully-equipped business, in
addition to the entrepreneur, only subject part-workmen whom the
technical arrangement of the work renders dependent. In the one
case they have been independent craftsmen, and the task of the
entrepreneur consists in combining them into one industrial unit; in
the other the business unit already exists, and its component parts
are to be sought. Very soon the employees of either origin are no
longer to be distinguished from one another.

Early handicraft had as a basis a few workmen of similar training
who, even though at different stages (apprentices, journeymen, master workmen), worked side by side. The qualifications of the groups
so composed bear, from handicraft to handicraft, no resemblance
to each other. It is impossible for a transfer to be made from one
species of employment to another; for instance, the smith cannot be
wheelwright. The law recognises this by the sharp dividing lines it
draws between them.

Modern industrial activity unites workers differing in skill and
strength into cooperative harmony within the undertaking. Their
grouping for business purposes follows the same principles of organization from branch to branch of production: there are no sharp
boundary lines between industries. A distinction of vocations hardly
occurs among entrepreneurs, though to a certain extent it exists
among the workmen. As far as the entrepreneur's functions are
concerned, it is almost a matter of indifference whether he man-
ages a street-railway, iron-works, or a weaving factory. Among the

employees, on the contrary, in consequence of the continued subdivision of work, there are now numerous specialists who are required in very different branches of production. The locksmith, the
metal-turner, the moulder, the planer, and the cutter appear in all
branches of well-advanced metal industry, in each special department of machine-construction, in railway workshops, etc. Fireman
and engineer are necessary in every large establishment, whether
it produces cotton thread or illustrated papers. Joiners, tinsmiths,
coopers can be incorporated into or attached to undertakings of the
most varied type, and office-clerks, pattern-artists, and engineers
have a similarly varied usefulness. To these is to be added the mass
of unskilled labour that is swallowed up by the large manufacturing
establishments. For many entrepreneurs almost the sole remaining
question is how to apportion and arrange these labour elements in
such a way that they may cooperate as a mechanical unit.

This cursory survey has taught us how at different epochs division of labour has exerted an influence upon the industry of peoples,
and upon the existence of individuals, varying according to the organizing principles dominating the different economic stages.

During the stage of independent household economy there prevails either union of labour in the hands of the father and mother of
the family, or division of labour developed upon the basis of slavery
or serfdom. In both cases the household represents a permanent
community of production and consumption. The principle holds
good: who works with me shall eat with me.

In the stage of town economy specialization and division of production predominate. The part-producers are personally free; but
the consumer of their wares, who unites them under favourable circumstances into temporary communities of production, determines
in the main the nature and time of their production. During the period of common production he often provides them with their keep.

During the stage of developed national economy the entrepreneur
controls the production of wares under division of labour. The part-
producers are personally free labourers. They are united by the employer into permanent communities of production. All other community of living is excluded; and if perchance on occasion of a business
jubilee the entrepreneur gives a dinner to his workmen, the newspapers report how he ate and drank with them at the same table, and
consider it a particular condescension on his part.

These are different economic worlds, separated from one another

230

by a deep gulf. If there breathes in the primitive union of labour of the home, and, in part, in the earlier division of labour as well, a warm breath of social fellowship, there surge through the modern division of labour the cold, cutting winds of calculation, contract, and greed of gain. If the older division of labour was the caryatid of economic independence, the modern is ever forcing large masses into a condition of dependence. The pressure of capital is making men's occupations increasingly dissimilar; it is making the men, as consumers, ever more alike. If in the olden time the individual's portion of goods was shaped by his own hands and head, and was, so to say, a component part of his being that had taken objective form, the consumption goods surrounding us today are the work of many hands and heads. As to the workers, we are supremely indifferent; and as to their work, when once we have paid its last possessor the market price, we for the most part reck but little. In the narrow circle of a life-vocation the mind becomes narrowed, frequently to obtuseness. In our sphere of activity we have lost in fulness of life, and the worker has not the old joy in his work. Are we sufficiently compensated for these losses by the variety of articles which it is ours to use because thousands of hands labour for us, because thousands of heads think for us? Or has division of labour merely made life richer in pleasures, but poorer in real joy?

Chapter IX.
Organization of Work and the Formation of Social Classes.

THE economic processes involved in the organization of work are processes of adaptation. Whether they fall under the head of union of labour, of labour in common, or of division of labour, they all originate in the effort to remove the disproportion perchance existing between the labour to be performed at a given moment and the powers of the individual labourers, and to bring them into agreement with each other. They must accordingly react upon the individual in compelling him to adapt, to accommodate himself mentally and physically to a definite work. In this adaptation certain resistances on the part of human nature are first to be overcome. Once vanquished, however, this negative element is, usually by virtue of continued practice, replaced by a positive one. The individual gains insight into the special character of his work; he develops a particular dexterity for it; his mental powers are directed continuously towards the same goal, and therefore expand in a definite direction in short, his adaptation to the work becomes a part of his being and distinguishes him from other individuals.

If, then, the class of work to which the workman devotes himself be of such a nature as to accentuate the special character of the individual man in society, the question naturally arises, how far such individual characteristics arising from work react upon the social life of the species. More specifically stated, the question would be: Is there a definite organization of society corresponding to a definite organization of work; and what is the nature of the influence exerted by the one upon the other?

The question is not so simple as it may perhaps at first sight appear. Nothing, for instance, seems easier than to trace back the caste system of India to the hereditary character of occupations, and accordingly to seek its origin in division of labour. But we know positively that the lower and the higher castes have different origins; and many indications favour the view that place of residence and possession of property have cooperated in the genesis of that hereditary stratification of society. Finally we see that the essential nature of the caste lay in purity of blood and of social relationships. Difference in caste excluded eating in common especially, although it does not seem to have prevented a similarity of occupation. All this gives good ground for the assumption that the separation according to employments was only a result of the division into castes which had originated in differences in race. A similar course of development can be shown for the social classes of the Middle Ages.

In considering the relations between economic activity and society generally, it is never to be forgotten that they are reciprocal, and that with them we can seldom determine with certainty action and reaction. Just as a particular kind of organization of work, when it lays hold of the individual for life, furnishes specially differentiated men to society, so society on the other hand has from its stratifications and its individuals to provide the plastic material used by organization of work. Certain strata of society will favour distinct forms of labour in common and division of labour, others will place obstacles in the way of their operation. Slavery, for instance, encourages the concatenation of labour; the presence of a numerous class of unpropertied wage-workers promotes subdivision of work. But those social influences alone are not able to produce these results; others of a technical and a general civilizing nature must be assumed, for instance, with subdivided labour, a highly specialized equipment of instruments of production.

All these relationships are thus of an extraordinarily intricate nature and demand the most circumspect treatment. As a rule we can tell what features in the economic and social world are found side by side, but it is seldom that we can determine how they are mutually connected. In attempting, then, to discover the social bearings of

233

organization of work in its various forms, we enter a field as yet little investigated, in which each step aside from the path leads into an impenetrable thicket of confused ideas.

At first the oldest system of organization of work, *union of labour*, seems to have been socially unimportant. Its earliest appearance reaches back into the pre-economic period where the individual has to perform all the labour necessary to his maintenance. It is to be found more extensively, then, in the earlier stages of independent domestic economy. The tools are simple and few, each must serve the most varied purposes, and everyone must be acquainted with their use. From work of such a type the impulse to a division of society, to a formation of relations of social dependence, manifestly cannot come. Society, it appears, must consist of a uniform mass of individual households; and such is its actual constitution as long as collective ownership of the soil prevails. Within the individual households, on the other hand, a separation of male and female work can take place. But this is not transferred to society; each household is in this respect an exact replica of the other. If social differences nevertheless exist, their cause is to be sought in other conditions.

Union of labour maintains this [socially trivial] character in the higher stages of development even up to the highest. Today it is met with almost exclusively in the humbler spheres of economic life and in the lower strata of spciety. Here it arises in most cases from the striving for independence; it is the support, the stay, and the comfort of the common folk. Indeed, it can appear here even as recoil from an excessive division of labour[289]. If it were the sole active factor in the economic life of a people, it would lead to a society of lifeless uniformity and render a successful struggle from the lower to the higher impossible.

With *labour in common* it is different. To be sure, in its loosest form of fraternal labour it exists between equals only temporarily, and therefore can have scarcely any effect upon the organization of society. At the most, it can but suggest it. The two forms of labour aggregation, on the contrary, become a means to the formation of special groups; they create and maintain relations of social dependence or, at least, assure their continuance where they have been developed from other causes. The same can be said, although not with equal definiteness, of many forms of union of labour. In both

---

[289]Comp. our remarks in the Händwort. d. Staatswiss., IV, p. 377.

cases cooperation amongst a plurality of persons depends upon the extent of the work to be performed as compared with the imperfect nature of the tools; and where those tasks are of a permanent nature or, at least, are frequently repeated in any one department of economic labour—for example, in agriculture—they require for their stability permanent social groupings secured by sortie controlling power.

On this rests, in large part, the long continuance of slavery and serfdom, although it cannot be said that the necessity for union of labour originally created these institutions. Nevertheless wherever property in man and hereditary dependence of the labouring population have existed, we notice in the early stages that master and slave are distinguished but slightly from one another; that they perform their work together; that the dependent class is, in numbers, hardly stronger, indeed often weaker, than the ruling one. But in the course of time this is changed; the enslaved part of the population becomes more numerous, though less through natural internal increase than artificial augmentation from without by means of wars of conquest, men-stealing, the slave trade, and misuse of power against weaker freemen. At the same time the class of propertied freemen is ever more sharply distinguished from that of the unfree; labour becomes in the eyes of the former a disgrace, while for the latter it develops into a burden of constantly growing oppressiveness. A deep gulf rends society, and there is no means of bridging it other than release from the condition of compulsory labour. Frequently even this does not suffice, as is shown, for instance, by the sharp distinction between freemen and freed men among the Romans.

The necessity for this graded progress lies in the technical conditions affecting the developed forms of labour in common. The natural consequence of the imperfect character of the implements[290] is that larger tasks can be accomplished only through the application of combined human labour on a large scale. Each advance of the household economy thus necessarily presupposes an increase in the number of its unfree workers. Each rise in the standard of life of the ruling class involves a waste of human material, which, according to our conceptions, is monstrous. To realize an effective union of labour this material must be organized and disciplined. The necessity of working slaves in gangs has from time immemorial been

---

[290]Comp. also A. Loria, *Die Sklavenwirthschaft im modern. Amerika u. im europaisch. Altertum*, in Ztschr. f. Sozial. u. Wirthschaftsgesch., IV, pp. 68 ff.

deduced from their unreliability and laziness which compelled the strict supervision of their work. It is indeed true that these features everywhere characterize servitude. But not it alone; they are rather phenomena incident to a half-developed culture in general, which at such a stage may be found even among free people. Moreover the slave-holder applies the system of division of labour along with labour in common whenever this can result in such an assignment of definite duties to the individual workman that he can be made responsible for the performance of them. But in the sphere of production the allotment of particular tasks to the individual is usually either impossible or inadvisable, because profitless.

Thus at this stage we see labour in common assuming extensive proportions and becoming by far the most potent organizing principle of unfr.ee labour.

David Hume long since remarked[291] that slavery necessitated a strict military discipline; and our investigations are corroborative of this observation.

In early Egypt "each of the great administrative offices possessed its own craftsmen and workmen. These were divided into bands. We even meet with such a company on the estates of the more prominent men of the ancient empire, and notice how, led by their ensign, they draw up on parade before the lord of the estate. The galley-slaves of every larger ship likewise form a company, and even the demons that nightly propel the ship of the sun through the lower world bear this name. The craftsmen of the temple and of the necropolis are similarly organized. The Egyptian magistrate cannot think of these people of lower rank otherwise than collectively; the individual workman exists for him no more than the individual soldier exists for our high army officers. Just as these free or half-free workers always appear in companies, so the slaves of the temple and the necropolis and the unfree peasants of the manors are duly organized in military fashion and regarded as a part of the army."[292] The large Roman slave estates exhibit like phenomena. On the rural estates the unfree workers are divided into groups according to their occupation; each group falls again into trains of not more than ten men under a "driver"; the *villicus* is commander-in-chief over all. Their day's work is performed with military discipline; at night they are lodged in barracks. In the wealthiest homes the urban family likewise ex-

---

[291] *Essays*, p 252.

[292] Erman, *Aegypten und agypttsches Leben im Altertum*, pp. 180-186.

hibits such ordered groups; in the Imperial household the separate slave groups are expressly designated colleges or corporations[293]. We see here how the need for labour in common led to permanent organizations among the unfree; and this need was met in the same way by the agriculturalist of later Roman times, by the manorial constitution of the Middle Ages, and by the more modern servile tenure. In each of these the labourers necessary for the large rural estates were united into distinct corporate groups attached to the soil, in order that they might always be ready for seed-time and for harvest. One can really say that manorial servitude, attachment to the soil, and personal subjection[294] owed their ascendancy to the necessity of labour in common, and that their great extension and long duration were conditioned by this necessity. A reaction of labour in common upon the organization of society is thus established beyond doubt, giving it not merely a peculiar socio-judicial impress, but also deeply influencing the mental disposition of the associated workers. One of the keenest observers of agrarian conditions in North Germany[295] found as a prominent trait in the character of the peasants "that they cling very closely to each other." They live much more sociably among themselves than the ordinary citizens of the towns. They see each other daily at each piece of demesne work, in summer in the field, in winter in the barn and in the spinning-room. Like soldiers, they constitute a corps, and like them gain an *esprit de corps*. The same may be said of all unfree conditions; uniformity and the disciplining of work create uniform herd-like masses which become more dull and indolent the more hopeless their condition.

This explains the small productiveness of their labour, which in turn leads to inhumanly harsh treatment, reducing the labourers to the level of the animal. Generation after generation of like labour perpetuates the same way of thinking, the same feelings and sensa-

---

[293] Thus mention is made of collegia (*corpora*) *lecticariorum, tabernaclarwrum, cocorum, prcegustatorum, decuriones or propositi cubiculariorum, velariorum, tricliniariorum, structorum, ministratorum, balneariorum, unctorum*, etc. On all this comp. Marquardt, Privatleben der Römer, pp. 144 ff., 154. The remarks in text do not contradict what was said above regarding division of labour in the slave family of the Romans. This sprang from the necessity of having for each piece of work required by the household a responsible person—not from the knowledge of the greater productivity of divided work—while labour in common had its basis in technical considerations.

[294] *Hörigkeit, Schollenpflichtigkeit, Leibeigenschaft.*

[295] Christian Garve, *Ueber d. Charakter d. Bauern u. ihr Verhaltnis gegen d. Gutsherrn u. gegen d. Regierung* (Breslau, 1786), pp. 14 ff.

tions towards the oppressors. The ruling race is now markedly distinct, both intellectually and physically, from the subject one, just as the vigorous tree in the forest stands out from the weakling. But in this evolutionary process causes and consequences are confused as in a tangled skein; one perceives only a labyrinth of economic and social factors, acting and reacting, and nowhere a thread to guide with certainty the investigating eye. There are close relationships existing between the two spheres; that is all that we can with some measure of assurance determine.

The problem offered by the third primal form of organization of labour, division of labour, would seem relatively much easier of solution. Moreover, each individual in the world of today has a certain interest in it, inasmuch as he is personally affected by it. For everyone, if he does not wish to be a useless member of society, has to accommodate himself to a particular task; and the more completely he succeeds in this, the more diversified do men themselves become in their every action and thought.

The German census of occupations of 1895 recorded in all 10,298 distinct trade designations. Now one may assume that different names are current for many trades in different parts of the country, and that a deduction is accordingly to be made for double counts. On the other hand, one must also remember that very different kinds of work, especially in the public service and the liberal professions, are designated by the same name, and that the numerous individual tasks which have arisen within the separate industrial undertakings through division of work and which have been transferred to special workmen, can be but imperfectly taken into account in the returns. Thus the census figures should rather be increased than reduced. We have thus in round numbers 10,000 kinds of human activity, each of which can become in our modern society a life-work, and subject the whole personality to its sway.

New special trades, moreover, are being formed continually[296]. Each new process of production, each advance of technique and science, is subjected to the universal division of labour. Thinking and feeling men are thus forced into the restricted field of trade interests of the narrowest and pettiest sort. The time foreseen by Ferguson, when even thinking would become a special business, has long

---

[296]From 1882 to 1895 the number of trade designations in the German census of occupations has been increased by 4119. The returns were as follows:

238

since been reached[297]. The scope of universal human interests grows narrower the greater the divergence of the special interests of the numerous spheres in life from one another, and the greater the severity of the struggle for existence.

The differences among men due to nature and culture without doubt assist this divergence in the most varied spheres of life; yet, in our opinion, this is true to a much smaller extent than is frequently assumed. Of course, as everyone knows, a jockey must differ from a carrier, a brewer from a tailor, a dancer from a singer, a poet from a merchant, if he is to be competent for his vocation. But what natural talents cause one man to appear destined to be an inspector of diseased meat, another a bookbinder, and a third a chiropodist, hosiery manufacturer, or tobacconist, will likely be as difficult to fix as to determine beforehand the success of a particular individual in any given liberal profession.

Although, then, many classes of occupations are adapted to bringa particular talent to the highest development, with many others the presence of such a talent will be of no perceptible importance. All, however, through continuous practice and use, will produce a certain differentiation of the men devoting themselves to them; certain organs will become enfeebled through lack of use, while others, through constant exercise, will be developed to greater perfection; according to his task the individual will be attuned physically, intellectually, and morally, to a definite key; through his occupation he

For the Class of Occupations	Census of Occupations for	
	1882	*1895*
A. Agriculture, gardening, cattle-raising, forestry, fisheries	352	465
B. Mining and quarrying industry, and building trades	2,661	5,406
C. Trade and commerce	1,315	2,216
D. Domestic services and other wagework	75	82
E. Military, court, civil, and ecclesiastical service, liberal professions	1,876	2,079
Total	**6,179**	**10,298**

How far this growth in figures is to be traced to an actual increase in trades, how far to greater exactness in statistical census work, cannot be determined. A part of the difference, however, is certainly to be attributed to increasing division of labour.

[297]Most notoriously in politics, where the majority of men procure their ideas ready made from some newspaper editorial. But also to no inconsiderable degree in scientific circles, where on this account the last is always right; for example, the reviewer of a book over the author.

will be given a particular impress which will often be even externally discernible. This we all recognise when we come into contact with strangers and involuntarily classify them to ourselves according to callings.

With this personal differentiation, however, the economic graduation is transferred also to society at large. Similar occupations and views of life, similar economic position and social habit lead to a new distribution of social groups. They produce classes based on occupation and a community of interests which dominate them even in their most minute social ramifications, and are strong enough to cover up inherited differences in position due to birth, or to reduce them to insignificance. We have even seen how these new social aggregations reach out beyond the political boundaries, and how the social interests and feelings of kinship resting on division into trades overtop those of nationality based upon similarity of blood.

Under these circumstances we may raise the question, which recent biology has brought into close connection: whether, and to what extent, in a society with free choice of occupation, the personal variations developed through division of labour are *hereditary*, just as under the system of castes and of classes according to birth such peculiarities are transmissible. In this it is not merely a question of natural capacities which may be utilized in one's occupation and in which the possibility of hereditary transmission—though not more—is readily admitted. It is a question rather of the whole physical and mental aptitude for a vocation, of the skill gained through accommodating oneself to a circumscribed task, of the intellectual plane consequent upon such work, of the conception of life, and the direction of the mind resulting from the character of one's vocation.

From the latter point of view, ever since Shakespeare's "Winter's Tale," the problem has frequently been treated in literature. Generally this has been done by making educational influences that counteract upon the character and social position of the parents determine events. Views as to the issue have greatly changed in the course of the last century. It would certainly be a profitable undertaking for a literary historian to take up this problem of education and heredity, and investigate more closely the dependence of literature upon the spirit of the times and upon the position in life of the writers[298]. While Lindau in *Countess Lea* makes the daugh-

---

[298] The latest treatment of this subject is to be found in Ludwig Ganghofer's tale, *Der Klosterjäger* (Stuttgart, 1893). It is exceptionally healthy and subtle.

ter of the usurer develop, in spite of the paternal education, into a paragon of nobleness, in a story by Arsene Houssaye (*Les trois Duchesses*), of three children interchanged directly after birth, the son of the peasant woman remains peasant in understanding and in way of thinking, although educated as a prince; the daughter of the frivolous actress becomes a courtesan, and the daughter of the duchess, even in humble surroundings, displays the native elevation of her character.

The question has also been touched upon in numerous ways in more serious literature. But a short time ago W. H. Riehl, in his *Culturgeschichtliche Characterköpfe*, drew a contrast between the "peasant youngsters with limited capabilities" who had graduated from the gymnasium with highest standing and the "intellectually highly trained sons of cultured parents," between whom, class for class, there arises an insurmountable wall. The former, he believes, would develop at the university into mediocre students, whom the "cultured son of cultured parents," if he went to the university at all, would soon overtake. Finally the former peasant youth becomes "a very mediocre though clerically efficient civil servant." What becomes of the son of the cultured parents, "who has already been favoured by the manifold educational interests of his parents' home," we are, unhappily, not informed.

The first to discuss the subject with a claim of strict scientific treatment[299], which, to be sure, is not made in the above case, was Professor Gustav Schmoller, who, in a very confident manner, rendered his decision that "the adaptation of individuals to various activities, increased through heredity during centuries and thousands of years, has produced men of ever more individual and diverse types." All higher social organizations, it is claimed, rest upon continued differentiation produced by division of labour. "The castes, the aristocracies of priests, of warriors, of traders, the guild system,

---

[299]Schmoller has objected to this expression in his review of my book in Jhrb. f. Gesetzg. Verw. und Volksw., XVII (1893), pp. 303 ff. He desires to have his remarks regarded as but "a kind of essay in philosophical history." I can perceive in this characterization no repugnancy to the expression used by myself. Nor can I discover that the further remarks of Schmoller in the paper cited have furnished proof that I have misunderstood him in essential points. I believe, therefore, that I am acting most correctly in allowing the following remarks to appear again word for word as they stood in the first edition, and in directing the attention of the reader to Schmoller's remarks on the same in the article indicated.

the whole constitution of labour today are but forms differing according to the times, which division of labour and differentiation
have imprinted upon society; and each individual has arrived at his
peculiar function not merely through individual adroitness and fate,
but also through his physical and mental disposition, his nerves,
and his muscles, which rest upon hereditary tendencies and are determined by a causal chain of many generations. *The differences in
social rank and property, in social esteem, and in income are only a
secondary consequence of social differentiation.*"[300]

One will perhaps expect that the proof for these surprising sentences has been attempted with the help of biology. But, aside from
cursory reference to biological analogies, that path is avoided. Yet
it would certainly have been useful to pursue it further, because it
must have led inevitably to a point where the conception of heredity
must needs have been defined and its sphere marked off from that
of imitation and education[301].

On this account we also will have to avoid this path, and enter
upon an examination of the elaborate historical and ethnographical
material that Schmoller adduces for his assertions.

Such historical proofs are of a nature peculiar to themselves.
To the eye, of one gazing backwards things get shifted from their
proper place. Cause and effect appear equally near in point of time.
One finds oneself in a position similar to that of the man who looks
away into the distance and sees a church steeple that really rises
far behind a group of houses apparently standing directly over the
nearest building.

After a similar fashion, we fear, Schmoller in the critical instances
of his comprehensive investigations has viewed the causal relationship of the historical processes in an inverted succession as regards
reality. So far as these are occurrences that do not reach back into
epochs beyond the range of historical investigation, such as the ori-

---

[300] Comp. Schmoller's articles on the division of labour in his Jhrb., XIII, pp.
1003-1074; XIV, pp. 45-105; and a short summary of his conclusions in the
Preuss. Jhrb., LXIX, p. 464. [See further his *Grundrisz*, pp. 395-411.—ED.].

[301] Such an attempt, though indeed with but meagre results, is to be found in
Felix, *Entwickelungsgesch. d. Eigenthums*, I, pp. 130 ff. Among the more recent
biologists this point in the problem of heredity is really no longer a matter of
controversy; especially Weismann (*The Germ-plasm*, Eng. ed., London, 1893)
has decidedly contested the transmissibility of acquired characteristics. Comp.
also Galton, *A Theory of Heredity*, in Journal of Anthropolog. Institute, V, pp.
329 ff.; James, *The Principles of Psychology*, II, 678.

gin of castes, of the priesthood, of the oldest nobility, we would venture to believe that one might unhesitatingly reverse his surprising conclusion and say: the diversity of possession and of income is not the result of division of labour, but its chief cause.

For the past, in so far as it lies open to our eyes, this can be demonstrated with absolute certainty. Inequality in the extent and tenure of landed property forms among the ancient Greeks and Romans, and even among our own people from the early Middle Ages onward, the basis of class organization. The noble, the peasant class, the class of villeins and serfs are at first mere classes based on property; it is only after a considerable time that they develop into a species of classes based on occupation[302]. When in the Middle Ages along with the rise of the craftsman class the definite formation of trades sets in, it proceeds again from distribution of property. The demesne servants, the landless villeins who have learned an industrial art, begin to turn their industrial skill to independent account. The industrial process followed must adapt itself to their poverty; it is pure wage-work, in which the work-man receives the raw material from the customer. Only later do we have a real division of production between agriculturalist and craftsman. The latter acquires a business capital of his own. But how trifling this is, is best indicated by the circumstance that, as a rule, the craftsman works only on ordered piece-work, and that the whole industrial process for transforming the raw into the finished product lies usually in one hand[303]. The industrial undertakings were exclusively small undertakings. Where the great extent of the sphere of production of a handicraft called for an increased supply of capital, men did not turn to production on a large scale with subdivision of work, but

---

[302]The presence of the unpropertied noble in the service of others (*Dienstadel*) is a proof, not against, but for, this conception. It would be inconceivable that the landed noble had not preceded him.

[303]The longer the duration of the process of production the smaller the business capital that the single producer requires, but the greater the mass of labour which the completed product contains. In the Middle Ages, to cite a very familiar example, the shoemaker was frequently tanner as well. The whole process of industrial elaboration from the raw hide to the finished footwear thus lay in one hand. Assuming now that the tanning of the hide required half the time that was necessary to its transformation into shoeware, a shoemaker desiring to carry on tanning alone would have required three times as much business capital as the tanner who at the same time made shoes. But if he wished merely to make up into shoes leather already tanned, his business capital must amount to one and a half times the former, together with wages and profits.

to specialization which limited the demand for capital and kept the business small.

As one observes, each step taken by mediaeval division of labour in industry was conditioned by the possession of wealth. It is the same with trade. The trading class of the Middle Ages is derived from the class of urban landowners, who had become, through the introduction of rents on houses and the practice of rent-purchases, possessors of movable capital. It is from this class of stockholders and tradesmen that the present manufacturing class has sprung since the seventeenth century. Through the fertilizing of industry with their capital, the two new forms of division of labour—subdivision and displacement of labour—arise, and the division of production for the first time realizes its full efficiency. Half-manufactured products now wander in masses from workshop to workshop; in each place they become capital, in each they yield a return; from one department of production to another fresh outlays in interest and other charges are added, and through them profits on capital are made[304]. Subdivision of labour presupposes a class of non-propertied wage-workers. This class comes from that section of the craftsmen who, through the capitalistic character assumed by division of labour, have become incapable of competing, and from the landless peasant population.

In industry, indeed, the dependence of division of labour upon possession of property becomes especially manifest. In the Middle Ages each advance of industrial division of labour augmented the number of urban "livelihoods," because it diminished the business capital; at the present time the progress of division of labour diminishes the num-ber of independent existences since it increases either the fixed or the business capital, or both. In the Middle Ages the effort was made to keep each industrial product as long as possible in one establishment in order to embody in it as much labour as was feasible; nowadays, by division of work, the business capital is carried with the utmost rapidity through the separate stages of production in order to make the relation between interest expended and profit realized the most favourable possible. In the Middle Ages dearth of capital led to specialization; in our time abundance of capital impels to subdivision of work and displacement of labour.

Thus from the varied distribution of property have the general

---

[304]The connection of capital with division of labour has been presented in a masterly manner by Rodbertus (*Aus d. litter. Nachlass*, II, pp. 255 ff.); but in this he has not adequately distinguished the different kinds of division of labour.

features of our organization of society according to occupation been developed historically; and on this foundation, which our present industrial organization is ever strengthening and solidifying, they continue to rest. The latter is explained very simply from the following circumstance: 1. Every vocation under our industrial organization yields an income; and only the propertied person is in a situation to seek out for himself the more lucrative positions within the universal organization of labour, while the unpropertied person must be content with the inferior positions[305]. 2. Property itself, by virtue of its capitalistic nature, furnishes an income to its owner, even without work on his part, and transmits itself from generation to generation with this capability. In so far as our propertied classes are also social classes according to occupation, they are not such because their occupation creates property, but rather because property determines the selection of a vocation, and because as a rule the income that the calling yields is graded much the same way as the property on which the vocation is founded.

True, there is no novelty in this statement. Each of us acts conformably to this view. Daily experience readily suggests it; and scientific political economy has always recognised it. The whole wage-theory itself rests on the assumption that the son of the workman can become nothing else than a workman. This is a consequence of his poverty, not of hereditary adaptation to his trade. Must one then really prove now for the first time that occupations whose inception and conduct require capital, or whose acquisition demands large outlays, are as good as closed to those without capital? The much-boasted "freedom of enterprise" thus exists only within very narrow limits. In very exceptional cases these indeed are now and then transgressed; but as a rule it is not the particular vocation, but rather the general *vocational class*[306] to which the individual is to belong in society that is indicated for each person by the wealth of the paternal house. The "social rank" that in popular estimation is enjoyed by a particular class, however, can hardly be maintained without corresponding financial equipment—a proof that it also is not a secondary consequence of social differentiation (resting upon

---

[305]This means, then, "that those whom poverty drives to seek a profitable vocation are compelled by their very poverty to abandon that vocation" Lotmar, *Die Freiheit d. Berufswahl* (Leipzig, 1898), p. 27.

[306]On this concept, in which we attempted to express the reciprocally conditioned existence of property and vocation long before we were acquainted with Schmoller's work, compare my *Bevölkerung d. Kantons Basel-Stadt*, p. 70.

division of labour), but essentially a child of the rational union of wealth and vocation.

No matter how many vocational classes may be distinguished in society, occupations of very diverse character will still be represented in each, and between these callings a continuous exchange of labour will take place. This exchange extends as far as the classes of work demand approximately the same equipment of wealth, and as far, therefore, as they stand in the same "social rank"; one might also say that it extends as far as people marry among each other, or regularly associate with one another, or as there is approximately the same plane of culture. All these things stand together in a mutual relationship. It is an everyday occurrence for a high public official to destine his son for agriculture in order, later on, to purchase him an estate, for the son of a large landholder or manufacturer to enter upon an academic career, for the son of a clergyman to become a civil engineer, the son of the engineer a physician, the son of the physician a merchant, the son of the merchant a lawyer or an architect. Just as easy and frequent is the transition from peasant to schoolmaster or to brewer, from baker to watchmaker, from blacksmith to bookbinder, from miner to factory-hand, from farm-hand to station-hand or coach-man, etc. We all look upon these transitions, in spite of the great differences in labour skill, as socially proper and industrially unobjectionable, although there can hardly be men "differentiated" more widely through division of labour than a statesman and a farmer, a manufacturer and a professor, a merchant and an architect, and so forth. When the son of the manufacturer in turn becomes manufacturer, and the son of the peasant again a peasant, we know that in many cases the financial means once consonant with this vocation have dictated the occupation without regard to the fitness or unfitness of the individual for the role thrust upon him.

This glance at practical life must restrain us from conceiving in too narrow a sense Schmoller's theory of the hereditary transmission of personal differentiation consequent upon division of labour. That the son of the shoe-maker by virtue of inherited adaptation should be in a better position to produce shoes than, let us say, picture-frames; that the clergyman's son, though his father had been taken from him on the day of his birth, will, of all classes of occupation, exhibit the greater natural aptitude for the clerical calling, cannot possibly be meant by that theory, even if in the last-mentioned case

246

the forefathers of the clergyman during the previous two centuries had handed down the spiritual office to each other from generation to generation. For if we hold strictly to the biological idea the adaptation to occupation would necessarily increase from age to age, and reveal itself in continually improving performance of duties. It will, however, hardly be seriously maintained that the numerous clerical families of Protestant Germany, who are in the position just described, furnish today relatively better pulpit speakers and more efficient pastors than in the seventeenth century.

In the domain of the guild handicraft of our towns, in consequence of the jealous exclusiveness of the different trades, the positions of master-craftsmen, with but few exceptions, have been actually passed down from father to son from the sixteenth to the eighteenth century. The technique, however, not only has not improved, but has lamentably degenerated, and now languishes, as Schmoller himself in an earlier treatise has shown[307]. Far from augmenting the technical acquisitions of their fathers, the sons have not even been able to maintain the standard of professional aptitude reached by them.

We must therefore look upon the new theory, if we would not be unjust to it, as referring to the *inheritance of bodily and intellectual characteristics by the members of social classes grouped according to occupation.* But these classes are, as a rule, likewise based upon property and income, since the standard of their life, both material and intellectual, is conditioned by property and income. Accordingly one must demand of the originator of the theory to distinguish between the consequence of the character of sustenance and education rendered possible for each class by the possession of wealth, and the result of hereditary adaptation to occupation. If such a distinction of the probable and possible causes is not undertaken, or if without examination there is ascribed to division of labour that which can be traced back with greater probability to the apportionment of wealth, the whole theory must be content in its undeniable weakness in "historical proof" to be treated as an inexact Darwinian analogy, as a thesis advanced without proof.

That within a whole social class of this kind a transmission of the "bodily and intellectual constitution," of the "nerves and muscles" takes place from one generation to another no one has as yet doubted. One may indeed term this heredity, but in this he must

---

[307] *Zur Gesch. d. deutsch. Kleingewerbe im ip. Jhdt.*, pp. 14, 667 ff.

247

not overlook that each fresh generation must be raised through theoretical and practical education to the intellectual and moral level
of the parents. Though in this the elements of culture "fly to" them,
to use Riehl's expressive phrase[308], though the example of their surroundings incites them to imitation, though much is appropriated
without trouble which under other conditions must first be learned
with effort, it is still a question of the acquired, not of the innate.
This holds to a certain extent even of the bodily constitution—the
"nerves and muscles"—so far as it rests upon the character of sustenance and education[309].

Elements of adaptation to a vocation can certainly be transferred
by the indicated paths of "unconscious absorption" and imitation,
just as well as other elements of education. But this process is
fundamentally different from inheritance in the biological sense[310].
That which in this sense is said to be hereditary must make its
appearance even when the offspring are completely removed at the
moment of birth from the influence of their progenitors.

We know not whether there are people who consider the physical
and intellectual peculiarities constituting the plane of culture of our
six or eight vocational classes in society as transmissable in the sense
that they must appear among the descendants of each class even
when brought up within another class. It is only individual instances
of this kind that practical life is ever presenting; and as yet no one
has taken the trouble to collect them. They are generally cases
of children of the humbler classes who are brought up or formally
adopted by members of a higher class. There will scarcely be anyone
bold enough to maintain that these persons, artificially united to
social groups of higher rank, are later on distinguishable from the
members of these groups by birth by reason of less business ability
or of a lower plane of culture.

A further series of observations of this nature is offered by the

---

[308] *Anfliegen.*

[309] Schäffle, *Bau u. Leben d. soz. Körpers* (1. AufL), II, p. 201, designates that
the physical side of pedagogy. He says: "The physical education of each new
generation and its schooling in the external graces of the parents or ancestors
comes as an immense additional task to the procreative activity of the sexes. ...
In this second act physical adaptations are obtained that were unknown to the
parents themselves."

[310] This latter is the real question with Schmoller, as he plainly indicates in
Preuss. Jhrb., Vol. 69. p. 464. The sociological conception of inheritance
which Schaffle has constructed in works cited (II, pp. 208ff) is not treated by
Schmoller, thousgh many of his remarks recall it.

instances in which descendants of one class have by their own energy raised themselves into a higher class. Everyone knows what difficulties the era of capitalistic production opposes to such an attempt, and frequently only too successfully. Everyone, too, can readily call up the picture of the "upstart" who, with all the technical ability he shows for his trade, is defeated in his effort to reach the intellectual and moral level of his new class. This serves again to illustrate the truth that the adaptation to an occupation enjoined by division of labour—the prime condition of business success—is accomplished by each individually, and without too much difficulty. But the moral and intellectual adaptation demanded by the plane of culture of the class ripens slowly even amid favourable surroundings, and comes to full maturity only in the second or third generation.

A strict proof of the fallacy of Schmoller's theory of heredity cannot be adduced; but the proofs hitherto advanced in favour of its accuracy fall equally short of conclusiveness. Before venturing to dogmatize one would perhaps have to pass in review the great men of a nation and note the vocations of their parents, and the number who have issued from classes of humble occupation. At the same time one would need to determine for the different classes the degree of probability of their members attaining a prominent position in which they alone could display high ability. Finally one would have to ascertain what relation the number of prominent men who have actually come forth from any given class of tradesmen bears to the number obtained by the calculation of probabilities. It does not need to be demonstrated that for such an investigation all the data are lacking.

But it may be maintained that the new theory contradicts the belief of modern civilized people based, as it is, upon the observation of many generations.

How often the complaint is made that so much talent pines under the weight of adversity? If to this dictum we oppose the other that real talent will always find a way, we may indeed offer a formula to flatter the egoism of successful competitors, though in reality it meets all too rarely with confirmation.

Our whole socio-juridical development since the French Revolution is based on the assumption that admission to every free calling and to all public offices, which latter, after all, we still regard as *the pinnacle of class divisions*, shall be free to all. This principle of free choice of vocation, whose recognition has been gained only after severe struggles, would be a great mistake, and every endeavour towards its realization lost labour, if beside the inequality in distribution of wealth the hereditability of vocational aptitudes likewise stood in the way of its establishment.

Even many of our oldest academic arrangements must, in the light of this theory, necessarily appear fundamentally erroneous. To what a high degree the costliness of preparation narrows admission to the favoured positions of the business world is well known. From time immemorial, however, a great peril to the efficiency of the official and the scholastic class has likewise been perceived; and an effort has been made to obviate this danger through scholarships, free board, remission of fees, and similar arrangements for rendering study possible to those without means. The practical results of these arrangements may be a subject of dispute. Yet in judging them it is essential to remember that advancement in the vocation enjoying popular esteem depends not only upon personal integrity, but also upon the social education of the individual, upon his ability to make his own strength felt; that in this imperfect world even the capable man who too modestly holds back may all too easily be outdistanced by the mediocre man who is boldly self-assertive; that he who seeks to climb the social ladder from the lower rungs will find it much more difficult to reach the top than the man who starts halfway up. The German language has an expression for denoting distinction in a line of business which happily characterizes the importance of the personal element in the achievement of success. It is *sich hervorthun* [literally, to do oneself forward]. Thus it may indeed be that the student sons of the peasant in Riehl's story failed to distinguish themselves in their vocations because they lacked capacity. It is none the less true that many of them missed success because they did not know how to "do themselves forward" in the right place, how to bring their personality into play.

In every social grouping in which the occupation exerts an influence there is generally formed within the different classes a community of feeling that turns instinctively against the intruder, and in spite of all his talent frequently dooms him to failure; while, on the other hand, it supports and carries along weaklings belonging by birth to the group in question. Thus, as concerns advancement in the public service, which still bears in a preeminent degree the sign manual of a class characterized purely by its vocation, personal and family connections often play, along with financial standing, a decisive part. Where these become a cloak for nepotism they can indeed impress upon it the characteristics of an hereditary class. In the broad realm of labour, organized according to occupation and extending beyond it, property will indeed remain, as long as the present economic system lasts, the prime cause of social class-formation. And just such an accessory importance as fell in the stages of unfree labour to community of labour, will here attach to division of labour. If the employment is inherited it is not because the adaptation to the vocation has been inherited, but because the property is transmitted by which membership in it is conditioned.

The above theory of heredity consequently bears, though certainly unknown to its originator, the cheerless lineaments of a social philosophy of *beati possidentes.* It calls to the man of humble birth who thinks he has in him the power to occupy a higher position in life: "Abandon all hope; your physical and intellectual constitution, your nerves, your muscles, the causal chain of many generations, hold you fast to the ground. For centuries your ancestors have been serfs; your father and grandfather were day-labourers, and you are destined for a like position." We need not recite how the consequences of this new theory do violence to our moral consciousness, to our ideal of social justice.

In the state of improved thesis in which it at present stands, the theory, in our opinion, falls to the ground from the very fact that, as is frequently enough observed, in a single generation the whole road from zero to the highest point of modern culture, from the lowest to the highest stage of division of labour, from the foot to the summit of the social ladder is traversed, and vice versa. One must indeed wonder that such a theory could originate among a people who count among their intellectual heroes a Luther the son of a miner, a Kant the son of a saddler, a Fichte the son of a poor village weaver, a Winckelmann the son of a cobbler, a Gauss the son of a gardener, not to mention many others[311].

There is an old anecdote of a cardinal whose father had tended

---

[311]Valerius Maximus wrote a chapter (III, 4), *de humili loco natis, qui clari evaserunt,* that begins thus: "Saepe evenit ut et humili loco nati ad summam dignitatem consurgant et generosissimarum imaginum foetus in aliquod revoluti dedecus acceptam a majoribus lucem in tenebras convertant."—In the most recent presentation of his theory, which shows considerable modification, (*Grundriss,* pp. 396 ff.,) Schmoller rests the fact "that talents and great men come from all classes of a generally highly cultured society "upon" *the peculiar influences of variation.*" But this explains nothing.

swine, and a French ambassador filled with the pride of noble birth. In a difficult negotiation in which the cardinal represented the interests of the church with adroitness and tenacity the ambassador was so carried away that he taunted the other with his origin. The cardinal answered: "It is true that my father tended swine; but if your father had done so, you would be tending them too."

This little story has perhaps expressed better than a long disquisition could have done what the observation of many generations has established: that the virtues by which the fathers rise are as a rule not handed down to grandson and great grandson; that even if the occupation is inherited, the ability to carry it on disappears. Each aristocracy, be it aristocracy of property or of occupation, degenerates in the course of time like the plant growing in too fertile soil. In this it is not at all necessary to think of a moral decay; it suffices if the physical and intellectual powers decline, and procreation grows weak. The introduction of uncorrupted blood, ascending from the lower to the higher vocations, appears then a condition fundamental to the healthy exchange of social material. The great problem of the century, indeed, we have always considered to be the ensuring that a gradual rise in the social scale is made possible; that a continuous regeneration of the higher vocational classes takes place. In the caste system, which would be a necessary consequence of the theory of heredity, we have ever seen the beginning, not the end of the progress of civilization.

We will not allow ourselves to be led astray in this conception. The solution of the problem just mentioned is for modern civilized peoples a question of their very existence. For if history has taught anything with insistence it is, that for a people that can no longer be renewed from the fresh spring of pure physical and intellectual strength flowing in the lower classes, the statement once made by B. G. Niebuhr with regard to England and Holland holds good: the marrow has departed from their bones, they are doomed to inevitable decay.

Chapter X. Internal Migrations of Population and the Growth of Towns Considered Historically.

LL prehistoric investigation, as far as it relates to the phenomena of the animate world, necessarily rests upon the
hypothesis of migration. The distribution of plants, of the
lower animals and of men over the surface of the earth; the relationships existing between the different languages, religious conceptions,
myths and legends, customs and social institutions; all these seem
in this one assumption to find their common explanation.

In the history of mankind we have, to be sure, abandoned the
view that nomad life is to be regarded as a universal phase in the
growth of civilization, which each people necessarily traversed before
making fixed settlements, and which served, along with the taming
of domestic animals, as the "natural" pathway of a people passing from the hunting stage to agriculture. Ethnographic research
has made it sufficiently clear that all primitive peoples, whatever
the economic foundations of their existence, readily, often, indeed,
for very insignificant reasons, shift their habitations, and that they
exhibit an extraordinary number of stages intermediate between nomadic and settled life[312]. The northern and southern limits of the

---

[312]Comp. Z. Dimitroff, *Die Geringschatzung d. menschlichen Lebens u. ihre*

inhabited world are still peopled by races without fixed abode; and even in its midst there are broad areas in which a condition of continual migration prevails. Most civilized peoples have proverbs or other historic bequests from such a time.

In the German language this far-distant period of universal mobility has left distinct traces. The word for "healthy" (*gesund*) meant originally "ready for the road."[313] *Gesinde*, signifying today household servants, is, in the olden speech, a travelling retinue; companions (*Gefahrte* and *Gefährtin*) means, in the strictly literal sense, the fellow-traveller. *Erfahrung* (experience) is what one has obtained on the journey (*fahren*); and *bewandert* (skilled) is applied to the person who has wandered much. With these the list of such expressions is far from exhausted. In the general significance attached to them today the universality of the concrete range of conceptions and observations from which they originally sprang finds expression.

It is natural to suppose that this condition of general nomadic wandering, with its deep-rooted nomadic customs, did not suddenly cease; that, in all probability, the whole course of further development down to our own day has been a gradual progress towards a settled condition and an ever-closer attachment of the man to the spot where he was born.

Various indications support this view. Among our forefathers the house is reckoned movable property; and it is demonstrable that many settlements have within historic times changed their locations. Despite the lack of artificial roads and comfortable means of transportation, the individual appears in the Middle Ages much more migratory than at a later time. This is supported by the numerous pilgrimages that extended as far as St. Iago, in Spain, by the crusades, by the great bands of travellers, the migratory life of king and court, the rights of hospitality of the marquisates and the developed system of escorts.

Each fresh advance in culture commences, so to speak, with a new period of wandering. The most primitive agriculture is nomadic, with a yearly abandonment of the cultivated area; the earliest trade is migratory trade; the first industries that free themselves from the household husbandry and become the special occupations of separate individuals are carried on itinerantly. The great founders of religion, the earliest poets and philosophers, the musicians and actors of past

---

Ursachen bei d. Naturvölk. (Leipzig, 1891), pp. 33 ff.
[313] [From *senden*, meaning to go, to travel.— ED.]

epochs are all great wanderers. Even today, do not the inventor, the preacher of a new doctrine, and the virtuoso travel from place to place in search of adherents and admirers—notwithstanding the immense recent development in the means of communicating information?

As civilization grows older, settlement becomes more permanent. The Greek was more settled than the Phœnician, the Roman than the Greek, because one was always the inheritor of the culture of the other. Conditions have not changed. The German is more migratory than the Latin, the Slav than the German. The Frenchman cleaves to his native soil; the Russian leaves it with a light heart to seek in other parts of his broad Fatherland more favourable conditions of living. Even the factory workman is but a periodically wandering peasant.

To all that can be adduced from experience in support of the statement that in the course of history mankind has been ever growing more settled, there comes a general consideration of a twofold nature. In the first place the extent of fixed capital grows with advancing culture; the producer becomes stationary with his means of production. The itinerant smith of the southern Slav countries and the Westphalian ironworks, the pack-horses of the Middle Ages and the great warehouses of our cities, the Thespian carts and the resident theatre mark the starting and the terminal points of this evolution. In the second place the modern machinery of transportation has in a far higher degree facilitated the transport of goods than of persons. The distribution of labour determined by locality thereby attains greater importance than the natural distribution of the means of production; the latter in many cases draws the former after it, where previously the reverse occurred.

To these statements there are, of course, some considerations and facts opposed. First, the extent to which man was by law tied to the soil in the earlier agrarian period— the unfree nature of all his economic and legal relationships in contrast with the modern freedom of person and property. Further, and in part as a result of this, we have in modern times the entire dependence of many individuals upon movable capital or personal skill. Still further, the growing ease of transfer of landed property which today allows the peasant to convert house and land into money and on the other side of the ocean to start life anew; while the villein of the Middle Ages could at most attach himself as an extra-mural citizen to a

255

neighbouring town whence he either continued to carry on his work in the village personally, or leased it in some form or other to a second person for a yearly rent. Finally, the increase one observes in the flow of rural population to the towns which has been manifesting itself for half a century in a remarkably rapid rise in urban, and at some points in a stationary or even declining rural, population. With all these circumstances in mind, many consider themselves justified in speaking of the steadily advancing mobility of society.

How are these two series of phenomena to be reconciled? Is it a question of two principles of development mutually opposed? Or is it possible that modern migrations and those of past centuries are of essentially different types?

One would almost be inclined to believe the latter. The migrations occurring at the opening of the history of European peoples are migrations of whole tribes, a pushing and pressing of collective units from east to west which lasted for centuries. The migrations of the Middle Ages ever affect individual classes alone; the knights in the crusades, the merchants, the wage craftsmen, the journeymen hand-workers, the jugglers and minstrels, the villeins seeking protection within the walls of a town. Modern migrations, on the contrary, are generally a matter of private concern, the individuals being led by the most varied motives. They are almost invariably without organization. The process repeating itself daily a thousand times is united only through the one characteristic, that it is everywhere a question of change of locality by persons seeking more favourable conditions of life.

Yet such a distinction would not be fully in accord with the nature of either modern or mediaeval migrations. If we would grasp their true importance in historical evolution we must first thin out the tangled thicket of confused contemporary opinions that still surrounds the whole subject despite all the efforts of statistics and political economy.

Among all the phenomena of masses in social life suited to statistical treatment there is without doubt scarcely one that appears to fall of itself so completely under the general law of causality as migrations; and likewise hardly one concerning whose real cause such misty conceptions prevail.

Yet, not merely in popular circles and in the press, but even in scientific works, migratory *instincts* are spoken of; and thus those movements of men from place to place are put without the pale of

deliberate action. Indeed, a statistician once entitled an article in the
Journal of the Prussian Statistical Bureau of 1873 "The Affection for
the Homestead and the Migratory Instinct of the Prussian People,"
just as if home-keeping depended merely upon natural disposition,
and the abandoning of it upon an irresistible instinctive impulse
stronger with one race than another!

In strange contradiction to this, to be sure, is the fact that, while
the great bulk of official statistical compilations remains unheeded
by wider circles, the publication of the emigration returns generally
excites a most active expression of public opinion. The rising and
falling of the figures bring fear and hope, approbation and disappro-
bation, editorial leaders and speeches in Parliament. Here naturally
we hear less about migratory instincts and the love of home; people
have avague feeling that behind those fluctuating phenomena stand
very concrete causes. But how little they comprehend the nature
of these causes is evident when we recall, for example, that a few
years ago it was a matter of grave debate in the German Reichstag
whether people emigrated because they were getting along well or
because they were not.

With regard to this problem one cannot say that as yet statistics have succeeded inescaping from the turbid waters of confused
popular opinions to the firm conclusions of exact observation. From
the statistical standpoint migration is above all an economic and
social phenomenon of masses; and statisticians, in our opinion, have
been precipitate in abandoning the attempt to discover with their
peculiar machinery the causes of these migrations and turning to investigation by inquiry before the resources of the statistical method
were exhausted.

A perusal of the perfunctory remarks that Quetelet[314] devotes
to the phenomenon of emigration will readily convince anyone that
his exposition of the subject hardly rises above the prosaic common-
place. True, one finds on going through the official publications of
recent date that detailed systematic interrogations on the "causes"
and "grounds" of emigration, which would not even perplex the less
intelligent of the communal officials consulted, are by no means infrequent. But one immediately feels that such suggestive questions
mean the substitution of a series of subjective presumptions for the
objective results of investigation.

Before resorting, however, to a means of information that reads

---

[314] *Du système social et des lois qui le régissent*, pp. 186—190.

into the numbers only a strained interpretation not following of it-self, we should rather try to determine the phenomena of migrations themselves. We should classify them according to numerical reg-ularity, and connect them with other mass-phenomena of different times and places accessible to statistics (for example, the density of population, its division into trades, the distribution of landed prop-erty, the rate of labour wages, the oscillation in food prices); that is, undertake the statistical experiment of drawing up parallel lines of isolated series of figures.

From even these first steps on the road to an exact method we are, however, still far removed. The whole de-partment of migrations has never yet undergone systematic statistical observation; exclusive attention has hitherto been centred upon remarkable individual oc-currences of such phenomena. Even a rational classification of mi-grations in accord with the demand of social science is at the present moment lacking.

Such a classification would have to take as its starting-point the result of migrations from the *point of view of population.* On this basis they would fall into these groups:—

1. Migrations with continuous change of locality.
2. Migrations with temporary change of settlement.
3. Migrations with permanent settlement.

To the *first* group belong gypsy life, peddling, the carrying on of itinerant trades, tramp life; to the *second*, the wandering of jour-neymen craftsmen, domestic servants, tradesmen seeking the most favourable spots for temporary undertakings, officials to whom a definite office is for a time entrusted, scholars attending foreign in-stitutions of learning; to the *third*, migration from place to place within the same country or province and to foreign parts, especially across the ocean.

An intermediate stage between the first and second group is found in the *periodical* migrations. To this stage belong the migra-tions of farm labourers at harvest-time, of the sugar labourers at the time of the *campagne,* of the masons of Upper Italy and the Ticino district, common day-labourers, potters, chimney-sweeps, chestnut-roasters, etc., which recur at definite seasons.

In this division the influence of the natural and political insula-tion of the different countries is, it is true, neglected. It must not, however, be overlooked that in the era of nationalism and protec-tion of national labour political allegiance has a certain importance in connection with the objective point of the migrations. It would, therefore, in our opinion, be more just to make another division, taking as a basis the politico-geographical extent of the migrations. From this point of view migrations would fall into *internal* and *foreign*.

Internal migrations are those whose points of departure and destination lie within the same national limits; foreign, those extending beyond these. The foreign may again be divided into *continental* and *extra-European* (generally transmaritime) emigration. One can, however, in a larger sense designate all migrations that do not leave the limits of the Continent as internal, and contrast with them real emigration, or transfer of domicile to other parts of the globe.

Of all these manifold kinds of migration, the transmaritime alone has regularly been the subject of official statistics; and even it has been but imperfectly treated, as every student of this subject knows. The periodic emigrations of labour and the peddling trade have occasionally been also subjected to statistical investigation— mostly with the secondary aim of legislative restriction. The Government of Italy alone has long been endeavouring to clear up the subject of the periodic migration of a part of her population to other European lands through local investigations, exchange of tabulation-cards and consular reports.

The migrations involving permanent and temporary transfer of settlement between the different European countries are but very imperfectly noticed in the publications of the population census by means of the returns of births and of nationality. As for internal migrations, they have only in rare instances met with serious consideration.

Yet these migrations from place to place within the same country are vastly more numerous and in their consequences vastly more important than all other kinds of migration put together[315]. Of the total population of the Kingdom of Belgium there were, according to the results of the census of 31st December, 1880, not less than 32.8 per cent, who were born outside the municipality in which they had their temporary domicile[316]; of the population of Austria (1890), 34.8 per cent. The actual population of Prussia on the first of December, 1880, was divided as follows:—

---

[315]Comp. now also G. von Mayr, *Statistik u. Gesellschaftslehre*, II, pp. 116 ff., 354 ff.

[316]Annuaire statist, de la Belgique, XVI (1885), p. 76.

Place of Birth.	No. of persons	Per cent of population
1. In the municipality where enumerated	15,721,588	57.6
2. Elsewhere in census district (*Kreis*)	4,599,664	16.9
3. Elsewhere in enumerated province	4,556,124	16.7
4. Elsewhere in Prussia	1,658,187	6.1
5. Elsewhere in Germany	526,037	1.9
6. In foreign parts under German flag.	212,021	0.8

Of 27,279,111 persons, 11,552,033, or 42.4 per cent., were born outside the municipality where they were domiciled[317]. More than two-fifths of the population had changed their municipality at least once. Of the population of Switzerland on the first of December, 1888, there were born in the commune where then domiciled 56.4, in another commune of the same canton 25.7, in another canton 11.5, in foreign parts 6.4 per cent[318]. The commune in this enumeration is an administrative centre, which in many parts of the State embraces several places of residence. The figures here given thus exclude altogether the numerous class of migrations from locality to locality within the commune itself.

This latter class of internal migrations, as far as we are aware, has been but once a subject of investigation. This was in connection with the Bavarian birth statistics of 1871[319]. According to these the total actual, population of Bavaria was divided as follows:—

Place of Birth.	No. of persons	Per cent of population
1. In the municipality where enumerated	2,975,146	61.2
2. Elsewhere in census district (*Kreis*)	143.186	3.0
3. Elsewhere in enumerated province	677,752	13.9
4. Elsewhere in Bavaria	944,101	19.4
5. Elsewhere in Germany	78,241	1.6
6. In foreign parts	44,150	0.9

The Bavarian population of 1871 thus appears somewhat more settled than the Prussian of 1880 and the Swiss of 1888, a circumstance perhaps due to the earlier year of the census. Nevertheless, two-fifths of the inhabitants (1,888,000 out of 4,863,000) were not

[317]Ztschr. d. k. preusz. statist, Bureaus, XXI (1881), Beilage I, pp. 46. 47.
[318]Statist. Jhrb. d. Schweiz, II (1892), p. 57.
[319]*Die bayerische Bevölkerung nach d. Geburtigkeit.* Bearbeitet von Dr. G. Mayr (No. XXXII of *Beiträge z. Statistik d. Konigr. Bayern*), p. 10.

native to the place in which they were living; that is, had migrated thither at some time or other. In the larger cities the number of people not of local birth amounted to as much as 54.5 per cent., in the small rural towns 43.2 per cent.; even in the communes of the open countiy it sank to merely 35.6 per cent.

These are colossal migrations that we are dealing with. If one may venture an estimate, the data for which cannot be given in detail here, we believe ourselves justified in maintaining that the number of the inhabitants of Europe owing their present place of domicile not to birth, but to migration, reaches far over *one hundred millions.* How small do the oft-cited figures of transmaritime emigration appear in comparison![320]

That such enormous movements of population must draw after them far-reaching consequences is obvious. These consequences are chiefly economic and social.

The *economic result* of all kinds of migrations is a local exchange of labour and, as people cannot be dissociated from their economic equipment, a considerable transfer of capital as well. Or we may say, since we must presume that in these matters also men's actions have definite purposes behind them, that they bring about more effective distribution and combination of labour and capital throughout the whole inhabited world. In this regard it is indifferent whether labour follows capital or favourable natural conditions, or capital seeks unemployed hands.

Their *social result* is great shiftings of the population, which with an endless, undulatory motion seeks to preserve the equilibrium between itself and existing advantages for trade. These shiftings retard the increase in population at certain points, and accelerate it at others,— at once a thinning out and a concentration. The local distribution of the population, which is ordinarily determined by natural organic increase, through surplus of births over deaths, is broken through.

But in this very respect there is for the individual State an important difference between internal migration and emigration.

The immediate effect of emigration upon the mother country shows itself in only one way: it thins out the population and gives elbow-room to the remainder. That at the same time the settlement and development of thinly peopled colonial territories is accelerated

---

[320]In the seventy years, 1821-1891, the United States of America received from all countries of Europe 13,692,576 immigrants, v. Mayr, as above, p. 344.

only indirectly affects the mother country when ultimately by the practice of agriculture on a virgin soil the emigrants create a dangerous competition for home agricultural products, or by the transference of industrial skill and means of production into foreign lands cut off the market of home industry.

The effects of internal migrations, on the other hand, are always of two kinds: those displaying themselves at the points of departure; those perceptible at the objective points. In the one case they reduce, in the other they increase, the density of the population. They thus cause, as it were, a division of the population centres and districts into those producing and those consuming human beings. Our producing centres are generally the country places and smaller towns; our consuming centres, the large cities and industrial districts. The latter increase in population beyond the natural rate of the birth surplus, while the former remain noticeably behind it. Taking a yearly average for the period of eighteen years from 1867 to 1885, the total population of the German Empire has increased by 0.86 per cent, of the mean population[321]. Yet when we look at the details we see that the average yearly increase amounted:

In the large cities (pop. 100,000 and over) to 2.6 per cent.

In the medium-sized cities (pop. 20,000 to 100,000) to 2.4 per cent.

In the small cities (pop. 5,000 to 20,000) to 1.8 per cent.

In thecountry towns (pop. 2,000 to 5,000) to 1.0 per cent.

In the villages (below 2,000) to 0.2 per cent.

But of course the phenomenon of inland migrations is really not so simple and clear as this row of figures would seem to indicate. It certainly vividly illumines the much talked-of *"influx to the cities."* This expression, however, tells only half the truth. It overlooks the great number of internal migrations that counterbalance one another, and therefore find no expression in a change in the number of inhabitants of individual localities.

If we take a collective view of the internal migrations of a *large country*, without regard to their effect on the distribution of the inhabitants over the surface, their routes appear to us as a close variegated web in which the interwoven threads cross and recross continually. Into the rather simple warp stretched from the country places and towns to the large cities and industrial centres is woven a many-coloured woof whose threads run hither and thither between

---

[321] According to Schumann in Mayr's Allg. statist. Archiv., II (1890), p. 518.

the smaller centres of population. Or, to use a different figure, the broad and majestically surging surface-current, which alone we see, is not the only one; beneath it numerous lesser currents sport at will. Up to the present these latter have received scarcely any attention, certainly not so much as they deserve, even in cases where they happen to have been statistically ascertained. The Bavarian census of 1871 shows the following situation:

	Residents native to the locality of enumeration	Born elsewhere	Total
In the self-governing cities	301,494	361,899	663,393
In other places over 2,000 population	205,887	157,000	362,887
Total	*507,381*	*518,899*	*1,026,280*
In the rural municipalities	2,467,765	1,357,981	3,825,746
Grand total	*2,975,146*	*1,876,880*	*4,852,026*

From these figures it is plainly evident that the absolute number of persons who during the last generation migrated into rural municipalities is far more than twice as great as the number who had migrated to the cities. The same relation probably holds good for all larger countries.

But the significant feature in this connection is not that the country places receive as well as give in this interchange of population; it lies in two other considerations. The one is that they give out a larger population than they receive; the other, that their additions are made chiefly from the rural municipalities, while those leaving them find their way in part to the more distant cities. The excess of decrease over increase thus accrues to the benefit of communities of higher order; so much of the population enters into a sphere of life economically and socially different.

If we call the total population born in a given place and domiciled anywhere within the borders of the country that locality's *native population,* then according to the conditions of interchange of population just presented the native population of the country places is greater than their actual population, that of the cities, smaller. Thus in Bavaria, according to the census of 1871, the native population

263

of the rural municipalities amounted to 103.5 per cent, of the enumerated population, that of the cities to only 61 per cent[322]. In the Grand Duchy of Oldenburg[323] according to the census of December ist, 1880,

The influx from other places amounted in the cities to 25,370 persons
The exodus to other places amounted in the cities to 10,208 persons
The influx from other places amounted in the country to 57,366 persons
The exodus to other places amounted in the country to 72,528 persons

A balancing of the account of the internal migrations thus gives the cities a surplus, and the country municipalities a deficit, of 15,162 persons. In the economy of population one is the complement of the other, just as in the case of two brothers of different temperament, one of whom regularly spends what the other has laboriously saved. To this extent then we are quite justified from the point of view of population in designating the cities man-consuming and the country municipalities man-producing social organisms.

But the total remaining loss of population of the country municipalities exceeds the surplus that they furnish to the cities, even in the example here given from a small State, by almost four times. And the amount that they receive from one another is just as great. However large this mutual exchange of population by the country places may appear, only a relatively limited scientific interest really attaches to it. For here we are dealing with a species of migration which arises from the social limitations of the rural places, and which accordingly gains in importance the smaller the communities. In the whole Grand Duchy of Oldenburg the number of persons not born where at the time residing amounted in:

Municipalities of less than 500 inhabitants to   55.0%
Municipalities of 500 to 1,000 inhabitants to   37.4%
Municipalities of 1,000 to 1,500 inhabitants to   41.7%
Municipalities of 1,500 to 2,000 inhabitants to   40.4%
Municipalities of 2,000 to 3,000 inhabitants to   28.7%
Municipalities of 3,000 to 4,000 inhabitants to   22.2%
Municipalities of 4,000 to 5,000 inhabitants to   20.6%
Municipalities of over 5,000 to   29.4%

From this we notice that in the smaller municipalities (up to 4000 inhabitants), as the absolute size of the municipality increases the

---

[322]Mayr, as above, pp. 53, 54 of the introduction.
[323]Comp. Statist. Nachrichten über d. Groszh. Oldenburg, XIX, p. 64.

influx from other places decreases relatively to the native population, while in the larger places it increases.

Mayr has shown that the same holds for Bavaria. There in the year 1871 in the larger rural municipalities (of 2000 and more inhabitants) the number of those resident in the place of birth was 66.9 per cent., but in the smaller municipalities only 64.4 per cent.[324], while in the cities the exact opposite was the case. For in the self-governing cities 45.5 per cent, of the population were found to have been born where enumerated, but in the other (smaller) towns 56.8 per cent. Mayr accordingly sets up the proposition that *in the cities the proportion of persons born where residing decreases with the size of the place, while in the rural municipalities, on the contrary, it increases*[325].

There is a very natural explanation for this condition of affairs in the country. Where the peasant, on. account of the small population of his place of residence, is much restricted in his local choice of help, adjoining communities must supplement one another. In like manner the inhabitants of small places will intermarry more frequently than the inhabitants of larger places where there is a greater choice among the native population. Here we have the occasion for very numerous migrations to places not far removed. Such migrations, however, only mean a local exchange of socially allied elements.

This is again clearly shown by the work, already frequently referred to, on the native-born population of Oldenburg. In it the foreign-born population of Waddewarden, Holle and Cappeln, three communities chosen at random, is arranged according to zones of distance from the place of birth. The figures are as follows[326]:

[324] *Die bayer. Bevölkermg nach d. Gebürtigkeit.* Introduction, p. 15.
[325] This proposition has been corroborated by the Austrian census of 1890. According to the excellent treatise on it by H. Rauchberg, *Die Bevölkerung Oesterreichs auf Grund d. Ergebnisse d. Volksz. v. 31. Des. 1890* (Vienna, 1895), p. 105, of every 100 persons born where enumerated there were in places:
Of less than 500 inhabitants 65.7%
" 500 to 2,000 " 73-5%
" 2,000 to 5,000 " 699%
" 5,000 to 10,000 " 55-6%
" 10,000 to 20,000 " 464%
" over 20.000 inhabitants 43.1%
[326] *Statist. Nachrichten uber d. Groszh. Oldenburg*, p. 65 [1 German mile is taken = 45 English miles, although actually = 4.6.—ED].

	Waddwarden	Holle	Cappeln
Total population	861	1298	1423
From other places	270	445	388
Of these latter from places up to			
9 miles distant (absolute)	258	267	324
Of these latter from places up to			
9 miles distant (per cent)	95.6	60.1	83.5
From greater distances (absolute)	12	178	64
From greater distances (per cent)	4.4	39.9	16.5
Migrated to other places	400	544	387
Of those up to a distance			
of 9 miles (absolute)	332	490	332
Of those up to a distance			
of 9 miles (per cent)	83.0	90.0	85.9
Migrated to a greater distance (absolute)	68	54	55
Migrated to a greater distance (per cent)	17.0	10.0	14.1

How entirely different are conditions in this regard in the capital, Oldenburg, which with its 20,575 inhabitants is after all to be looked upon as only a small city. Of its total foreign-born population (13,364 persons, or 64.9 per cent.) there come:

From a distance of	Persons	Per cent
Less than 9 miles	2916	21.8
From 9-45	5625	42.1
Over 45	4823	36.1

Here the greater part of the influx of population is from a distance; the entry of the stranger-born into a new community means at the same time an entry into new social and economical conditions; and this urban community does not give as many of its native inhabitants to other districts as it receives from them[327]. On the contrary, it absorbs from a wide region round about the surplus of emigration over immigration, and repays it only in very small part.

This is the characteristic of modern cities. If in our consideration of this problem we pay particular attention to this urban characteristic and to a like feature of the factory districts—where the conditions as to internal migrations are almost similar—we shall be amply repaid by the discovery that in such settlements the result of internal

---

[327]The city of Oldenburg in the year 1880 received from other municipalities of the Grand Duchy 8,725 inhabitants, and gave up to them only 1,925. See, as above, p 212.

shiftings of population receives its clearest expression. Here, where
the immigrant elements are most numerous, there develops between
them and the native population a social struggle,—a struggle for the
best conditions of earning a livelihood or, if you will, for existence,
which ends with the adaptation of one part to the other, or perhaps
with the final subjugation of the one by the other. Thus, according
to Schliemann[328], the city of Smyrna had in the year 1846 a population of 80,000 Turks and 8,000 Greeks; in the year 1881, on the
contrary, there were 23,000 Turks and 76,000 Greeks. The Turkish
portion of the population had thus in 35 years decreased by 71 per
cent., while the Greeks had increased nine-fold.

Not everywhere, to be sure, do those struggles take the form of
such a general process of displacement; but in individual cases it
will occur with endless frequency within a country that the stronger
and better equipped element will overcome the weaker and less well
equipped.

In the year 1871, for instance, there were, in round numbers,
86,000 Bavarians living in Munich not born in the city; and at the
same time some 18,000 natives of Munich were to be found in other
places in Bavaria. In the year 1890 55.3 per cent, of the population
of the twenty-six largest cities of Germany was found to have been
born in other places, while 22.3 per cent, of their native population
was living in other parts of the empire[329]. Still more striking is the
fact shown by the English census of 1881, that there were living in
England and Wales (outside of the metropolis) just about half as
many persons native to London as England and Wales had supplied

---

[328] *Reise in d. Troas im Mai 1881*, pp. 29 ff.
[329] Comp. von Mayr, *Statistik u. Gesellschaftslehre*, II, pp. 122 ff.

to that city[330].

Thus we have here a case similar to that occurring so frequently in nature: on the same terrain where a more highly organized plant or animal has no longer room for subsistence, others less exacting in their demands take up their position and flourish. The coming of the new is in fact not infrequently the cause of the disappearance of those already there and of their withdrawal to more favourable surroundings.

This process need not, however, in the world of human society necessarily be a process or displacement, a consequence of the imperfect equipment of the native elements and of the superiority of the foreign ones. The reverse will perhaps occur quite as frequently, and in the examples cited is probably the rule. On account of the endless differentiation of labour in modern national economy it is the skilled labourers who experience most trouble in finding suitable employment and compensation for their labour where they live and have received their training, because it is there that the competition is keenest. They emigrate and seek more favourable surroundings, better conditions of competition, while at these points less highly qualified labour may at the same time be in demand, which demand must be met by importation of labour from outside places. This less skilled labour may, on the other hand, however, form the stronger, better equipped element in its own locality; and though it may lack here the opportunity for a profitable utilization of its skill, its departure may, nevertheless, leave a void that it is impossible to fill.

Thus the emigration of more highly trained technical labour from the cities was perhaps never greater than in the period of the so-called industrial boom of the seventies. At the same time,

---

[330]London had in 1881, 3,816,483 inhabitants. Of these there were born:

	Persons	Per cent of the population
In London	2,401,955	62.9
In the immediate neighbourhood	384,871	10.1
Elsewhere in England and Wales	787,699	20.6
In Scotland	49,554	1.3
In Ireland	80,778	2.1
In other countries	111,626	2.9

On the other hand, 584,700 natives of London were counted in other parts of England and Wales. For every 100 persons from these territories who had settled in London, 51 natives of London had left the metropolis.—According to the Ztschr. des preuss. statist. Bureaus, XXVI (1886), Statist. Correspondenz, p. xviii.

however, those same cities received an immense influx of labouring
population from the country; and the departure of the latter again
caused in the districts of great landed estates a serious dearth of
agricultural labourers, an advance in wages, and in some places a
lamentable condition of agriculture. Here, in every case, it was the
relatively stronger that had emigrated, the relatively weaker that
had remained; there could be no question at all of mutual displacement.

Still less is there ground for such a view with regard to those internal migrations that have their origin not in the effort to find a better place for carrying on work, but in the search for more favourable
conditions of living. The pensioned civil servant or military man
who leaves the expensive metropolitan city for the country or a
cheaper rural town; the speculator who has become suddenly rich
and exchanged his fluctuating stocks for a solid country estate; the
Parisian shopkeeper who enjoys his more laboriously earned income
in the quietude of his modest country cottage; and also, on the other
hand, the Jewish cattle-dealer who has become wealthy and seeks
the city in order to speculate on the exchange; Fritz Reuter's excellently portrayed Mechlenburg *"Fetthammel"* or rich farmer, who
after disposing of his farm will enjoy the pleasures of city life; the
poor clergyman's widow who moves into the city in order to give
her children a better education and supplement her scant pension
by keeping boarders;—none of these in their new places of residence
enters into dangerous competition with the native labouring population.

And yet at the objective points of the migration, even where
the danger of displacement cannot enter into the question, there
are innumerable struggles and endless friction, all originating in the
process of social amalgamation which is here always going on between the native population and the new-comers. The stranger has
to adapt himself to his environment, to the peculiar local economic
methods, to customs, speech and the political, religious and social
institutions of his new abode. And the inhabitants of the latter
place again, however settled in character and peculiar in type cannot altogether escape the influences that rush in upon them from
without. Though these influences often mean for them an increase
of working energy, an expansion of the horizon, a breeze bringing
freshness into corrupt local conditions, yet perhaps much more frequently they result in a loss of good old customs, of solid business

qualities, of interest in the common weal, and, above all, of social characteristics.

Now there can be no doubt that these struggles for mutual adaptation will take a vastly different form and course when waged between similar and between divergent elements. For this very reason the division used in municipal statistics for marking the distinction between native and resident population does not suffice for more exact socio-statistical investigations.

For if, for example, it has been ascertained that the native-born inhabitants of the city of Munich in 1890 amounted to 36 per cent, of the whole, while in Hamburg they constituted 47.5 per cent., the mere fact that in the former city there are 11.5 per cent, more citizens of extra-mural birth is far from proving that the population of Munich is to this extent more heterogeneous than that of Hamburg, and that in the former the process of mutual social adaptation is attended with more violent friction and struggles than in the latter. In like manner the fact that two cities—for example, Dresden and Frankfurt-on-Main—show the same proportion of non-native to native-born citizens does not mean that this process takes the same course in both. It is easy to conceive that the strangers in one city may show a greater homogeneity of customs and speech, economic energy and social habits amongst themselves and with the native population on account of coming from a neighbourhood more nearly akin, while in the other city heterogeneous elements from more distant localities are mingled together.

The final result of the mutual adaptation of non-native and native population will be altogether different in each of these cases. While in the former individuals and groups of persons of approximately like economic equipment and similar social character enjoy peacefully together the existing conditions for business, in the latter perhaps the more robust, energetic, easily contented race will vanquish the decrepit, weaker and more pretentious in its ancient home, or at least eject it from the most favourable fields of industry. Especially is it true that a lower standard of living can give the incomers a superiority over the native labour in the competitive struggle, which involves the latter in the most deplorable consequences. The immigration of the Polish labourers into the provinces on their west, of the Italians into Switzerland and south Germany, and of the Chinese into the cities of the North American Union are wellknown examples of this.

But even when the economic and social assimilation takes place without severe struggles there may persist between incomers and natives differences that simply cannot be removed, invading and disturbing the original homogeneity of the population. We have especially in mind differences of creed, of language and of political allegiance. The two largest cities of Switzerland, Geneva and Basel, both of which we are accustomed to look upon as strongholds of Protestantism, have today, in consequence of influx from without, a population of which over a third is foreign. In Geneva about 20 per cent, of the population have a mother tongue other than French. Finally, since 1837 the Roman Catholics have increased in Basel from 15 up to 30 per cent, of the population, while in Geneva they have reached 42 per cent. Even he who has no detailed knowledge of the internal history of these small municipalities will be obliged to admit that such differences are not void of danger.

If these considerations show that by no means the majority of internal migrations find their objective point in the cities, they at the same time prove that the trend towards the great centres of population can in itself be looked upon as having an extensive social and economic importance. It produces an alteration in the distribution of population throughout the State; and at its originating and objective points it gives rise to difficulties which legislative and executive authority have hitherto laboured, usually with but very moderate success to overcome. It transfers large numbers of persons almost directly from a sphere of life where barter predominates into one where money and credit exchange prevail, thereby affecting the social conditions of life and the social customs of the manual labouring classes in a manner to fill the philanthropist with grave anxiety.

This mighty flow of the country population into the cities and the universally rapid rise of the latter in volume is looked upon by many as an entirely modern phenomenon. In a certain sense this is true. The eighteenth century knew nothing of it, at least in Germany, The famous founder of population statistics, J. P. Süssmilch, did not succeed in discovering any regular law governing the movement of population in cities. He is of the opinion that they rise and fall in size according to the will of God[331]. J. H. G. von Justi

---

[331] "Thus does the mighty ruler of the universe impart to states and cities might, riches, and glory. He takes from them again and gives to others according to his good will. He pulleth down the mighty from their seat and exalteth them of low degree."—*Göttliche Ordnung*, II, § 546 (ad ed., pp. 477, 478).

deems it hardly possible that a city should increase unless special privileges be granted to the incoming settlers[332]. This is in accord with such population statistics as we have been able to collect for individual cities from the second half of the seventeenth century to about 1820[333]; these show retrogression and growth in irregular alternation. In France, on the other hand, the modern movement seems to have begun about one hundred and fifty years earlier; and men already spoke in the eighteenth century, according to familiar phraseology, of the "depopulation of the open country."[334]

If on the other hand we go farther back into the history of man in Europe we find two periods showing the same phenomenon on a grand scale: ancient times, especially the era of the Roman Empire; the later Middle Ages, in particular, the fourteenth and fifteenth centuries. Between them lie great epochs of quiescence, if not of retrogression and decay.

How are these earlier periods of migration to the cities to be regarded from the standpoint of the history of their evolution? Are they premature starts toward a goal whose attainment was reserved for our own time and its perfected means of communication? Or are they the outflow of other impulses than those behind the corresponding movement of the present, and did they on that account also lead to other results? Above all, was their influence upon population and their economic character the same?

As concerns *ancient times* it would seem as if we must assume, in spite of the uncertainty of the population record handed down to us, that a consequence of the influx of the rural population was the inordinate growth of the cities[335]. But it must not be overlooked that only a part of that population migrated of its own free will, namely, the free-men. The remaining and much larger portion, the slaves, were collected by their masters in the cities, or brought thither by the slave trade.

---

[332] *Grundsätze d. Polisziwiss.*, § 54. Comp. also *Gesammelte polit. u. Finanzschriften,* III, pp. 449ff.

[333] Much material relating to the subject has been collected by InamaSternegg in the Handwört. d. Staatsw., II, pp. 433 ff.

[334] Evidence collected by Legoyt, *Du progrès des agglomérations urbaines et l'émigration rurale* (Marseilles, 1870), pp. 8 ff.

[335] On what here follows compare particularly R. Pohlmann, *Die Uebervolkerung d. antiken Grossstadte im Zusammenhange mit d. Gesamtentwick. stadtischer Civilisation* (Leipzig, 1884); also Roscher, *System d. Volksw.,* Ill, Introduction, and Bücher, *Die Aufstande d. unfrei. Arbeiter 143-129 v. Chr.*

Where freemen moved in from the country they usually came not because a better prospect of economic advance in the cities beckoned them, but because they were deprived of their lands through the growth of the great slave estates. In the cities, it is true, they found all the lucrative branches of trade in the hands of slaves and freedmen; but they were here in less danger of starvation, inasmuch as the proletarian masses of the cities in whose midst they settled were supported by public and private largesses.

The large cities of antiquity are essentially communities for consumption. They owe their size to the political cen-tralization which collected the surplus products of the extensive areas cultivated by individual husbandry at one point where the governing class was domiciled. They are imperial, or at least provincial, capitals. Accordingly they first arise in the time of the successors of Alexander and reach their height under the Roman Empire. The capital, Rome, itself depends for its food-supply upon the taxes in kind from the provinces; and the same is later on true of Constantinople[336]. It is a communistic and imperialistic system of provisioning, such as the world has not seen a second time. The extortions of the officials, the farming of the revenues, the usurious practices, the great estates of wealthy individuals worked by slaves, the state-recognised obligation to supply largesses of bread, meat and wine to the masses—all these placed the productive labour of half a world at the service of the capital city and left open to the private activity of its inhabitants nothing but the sphere of personal services. From„ what we know of the larger provincial cities we may conclude that in them similar conditions prevail[337].

A favourable market for free labour, a place for the skilled production of goods on a large scale for export, the ancient metropolitan city was not[338]. Anything resembling factory work rests, as does the extensive agricultural production, upon slave labour. Accordingly among the motives mentioned by the ancient writers as impelling.the

---

[336]Krakauer, *Das Verpflegungswesen d. Stadt Rom in d. später. Kaiserzeit* (Leipzig, 1874), and E. Gebhardt, *Studien über d. Verpflegungswesen von Rom u. Konstantinopel in d. später. Kaiserzeit* (Dorpat, 1881). Also Rodbertus, *Zur Gesch. d. röm. Tributsteuern* in the Jhrb f. N.-Oek. Oek. u. Stat., VIII, especially pp. 400 ff.

[337]E. Kuhn, *Die stadtiscke u burgerliche Verfassung d. Röm. Reichs,* I, pp. 46 ff., points to an organization of the *cura annonœ* similar to that in the capital.

[338]Francotte, L'*Industrie dans la Grèce ancienne*, I, esp. pp. 149-158, has now established this for the Greek cities.

free rural population toward the cities the very one that is common-est today—the prospect of higher wages— plays no part. "Consider this body of people," writes Seneca[339] to his mother; "the houses of the immense city are scarcely sufficient for them. From municipia and colonies, in short from the world over, have they come together. Some have been drawn hither by ambition, some have come on pub-lic business, others as envoys, others again have been attracted by luxurious tastes seeking an apt and ample field for indulgence, others by fondness for liberal studies, others by the shows; some have been led by friendship, others by enterprise, which here finds extended fields for displaying personal merit[340]; some have brought their per-sonal beauty for sale, others their eloquence. There is no class of people which has not streamed to the city, where the prizes are great for virtue and vice alike."

Quite different was it with the town-ward flow of population in the *Middle Ages*. Taken as a whole, it is perhaps not less voluminous than that at the time of the Roman Empire. It did not result, how-ever, in the formation of a few central points of consumption, but in the construction of a large number of fortified places distributed pretty evenly throughout the country, uniting within their walls all the organized industrial activity of the nation which was not at-tached to the soil. The mediaeval towns are originally mere places of refuge for the surrounding rural population[341]; their permanent inhabitants are the burghers, or people of the burg. Everything else—the market, the prosecution of trade, monetary dealings, the personal freedom of the town inhabitants and their special privileges before the law—is only a later consequence of this extra-mural mil-itary relationship. The defensive union became in course of time a territorially circumscribed economic union, for which the town or city was the trade centre and the seat of all specialized labour.

The mediaeval cities[342] accordingly bear a great similarity to

---

[339] *Ad Helviam,* 6.

[340] *Quosdam industria latam ostendendæ virtuti nacta materiam.* It is compe-tition that is meant, not "industry," as Pohlmann, cited above, p. 17, translates it.

[341] Comp. above, pp. 116 ff.

[342] That is, so far as they really deserve the name. It is a peculiar inconsistency to attempt today to demonstrate the character of the mediaeval city by taking as examples places which never arrived at a true city status and which can bring forward no better claim to the name of city than that they were endowed with city privileges.

each other in the social and economic organization of their population, and differ, as far as we can see, only slightly in the number of
their inhabitants. At their original founding the influx of the rural
population seems often to have been far from voluntary. Later on
the chief factor determining their growth was the greater security of
person and property and the more varied opportunities for earning
a livelihood which they afforded landless freemen and serfs. Their
whole development, economically and numerically, came to an end,
however, the moment all the handicrafts that the limited extent of
the city-market areas was capable of sustaining were rep-resented
and supplied with a sufficient number of master workmen. Up to
this point the cities offered complete freedom of movement and almost unimpeded access to guild privileges and burgess rights, while
the rural land-owners, on the other hand, sought through limitations of the right of removal to secure themselves against the loss
of their serfs. When, however, the cities were able to supply all
branches of trade from the internal growth of their population, they
also exhibited a willingness to check accessions from without, and
hence brought about those numerous obstacles to settlement and to
entry upon a trade which have persisted into modern times. There
arose a sharp division between city and country. Migration to and
fro naturally continued to a certain extent, but it was confined in
the main to an exchange of labourers among the cities themselves.
City development had fallen, as it were, into a condition of numb-
ness from which it could be roused only through transition to a new
economic order. We are in a position to prove statistically for a few
localities the statement just made. There have been instituted exhaustive investigations into the origin of the mediaeval population
of Frankfurt-on-Main[343], and recently also regarding certain sections
of the population of Cologne[344]. From these it appears that the majority of the persons received by these two cities as burghers during
the fourteenth and fifteenth centuries migrated from the country. Of
every 100 new burghers there came to:

---

[343] Bücher, *Bevölkerung von Fr.*, pp. 163 If., 304 ff., 422 ff., 521 ff., 591 ff., 627
ff.

[344] A. Doren, *Untersuchungen z. Gesch. d. Kaufmannsgilden d. Mitlelalters*
(in Schmoller's Forschungen, XII, 2), Appendix I; and now also H. *Bunger's
Beiträge z. mittelalt. Topograph., Rechtsgeschich. u. Sozialstatistik. d. Stadt
Köln* (Leipzig, 1896), Sec. 3.

	In the Period	From Cities	From Villages and Hamlets
Cologne	1356-1479	37.4	62.6
Frankfurt	1311-1400	28.2	71.8
Frankfurt	1401-1500	43.9	56.1

We see from this that in the last two centuries of the Middle Ages the movement of population from the country to the cities, though it continued, was on the wane, while the admixture of town elements among the new burghers increased. Thus as early as the fifteenth century certain strata of the population of Frankfurt received their chief increment through emigration from other cities. Of the incoming Jews, for example, 90 per cent., and of the members of a fraternity of journeymen metal-workers 79.3 per cent., came from cities. The material from which the last percentage is deduced also covers, it should be said, the first quarter of the sixteenth century.

Unfortunately, further figures regarding the sixteenth and seventeenth centuries are not available. But for the period from the beginning of the eighteenth till after the middle of the nineteenth century we can offer some figures which serve to show that there was an epoch when the urban handicrafts received their workers almost exclusively from other towns. The Frankfurt municipal archives contain a number of books regarding the lodging-places of the bookbinders, in which are recorded the names and places of origin of all the journeymen of this craft who came to Frankfurt between 1712 and 1867 (14,342 persons in all). Some years ago we worked over this extremely valuable statistical material and found that of every 100 incoming journeymen bookbinders there came:

Periods	From Cities	From Villages and Hamlets
1712-1750	97.5	2.5
1751-1800	94.3	5.7
1801-1835	89.2	10.8
1836-1850	86.0	14.0
1851-1867	81.2	18.8

We see here how, in a trade of a specifically urban character, within a period of rather more than a century and a half, the proportion of workers drawn from the country has continuously increased. Had it been possible to continue the investigation for the period from 1867 down to the present time, we should undoubtedly have found that the balance has inclined more and more in favour of the journeymen from rural localities.

In the contemporary migrations to the cities a fusion of town and country strongly resembling that established by us for the fifteenth century seems to have set in[345]. Of every 100 of the inhabitants born in other places there were in:

	Year	Of City Birth	Of Country Birth
Leipzig	1885	50.6	49.4
Basel	1888	23.5	76.5

As in the Middle Ages, the city element relatively increases and the country element decreases according to the distance of place of birth from place of settlement. The various classes of the population show but slight differences in this regard. Generally speaking those occupations that demand a special training have a stronger admixture of city elements than the spheres of simple manual labour.

It is greatly to be regretted that similar statistical investigations have not been carried out for a larger number of modern cities. From the evidence at present to hand we are apparently driven to conclude that the number of incomers of city origin is relatively greater in the large cities than in the medium-sized and smaller ones[346]. The explanation of this phenomenon is a simple one. A large city exercises upon the population of the smaller cities the same power of attraction that the latter have for the population of the country. In this way the transitions from one social and economic sphere to another are rendered less violent. Thus a gradual elevation of the migrating masses takes place, as also from generation to generation a continuous preparation for the demands of life in a great city, which must render less violent the conflicts inevitable to the process of mutual adaptation within the new sphere.

But if the cities of today exhibit a process of redistribution of population similar to that of their mediaeval prototypes, the resemblance is only superficial. In the fourteenth and fifteenth centuries we have to do with the last stages of an evolution whose ultimate

---

[345] Only the simplest results of these investigations can be given here. Details may be found in my *Bevolkerung d. Kantons Basel-Stadt am I. Dez. 1888,* pp 62 ff. We may also refer to Hasse's *Ergebnisse d. Volkszahlung vom I Dez 1885 in der Stadt Leipzig,* Pt. II, pp. 7 ff. The higher figures in the rural accessions for Basel are explained by the fact that in the above work the city limits are made to include only 3,000 inhabitants.

[346] Besides the work on Leipsig already mentioned, a later exhaustive treatise on the accessions to, and losses of, population in Frankfurt-on- Main in the year 1891, published by Dr. Bleicher in the *Beitr. z. Statistik d. St. Frkf.*, II, pp. 29 ff., gives interesting information regarding this point.

result was the formation of numerous small autonomous spheres of economic activity, each of which exactly resembled the other in its harmonious development of production; in the nineteenth century we have to deal with an increasing differentiation of the individual centres of population, in accord with the designs of a greater whole, namely, of a state-regulated national economy.

This process begins with the development of the modern State and modern national administration. Hitherto each city had developed within itself all the branches of city life not forbidden by local conditions; now one city becomes a permanent royal residence, others become seats of district and provincial administrations, of prisons, of higher educational institutions and of all kinds of special branches of administration, while still others become garrison cities, border fortresses, fair-towns, watering-places, junction-points of commercial routes, etc. They take over definite functions for the whole country and for all other places, though these functions are not always specifically urban. The cities may also form alliances with rural residence centres. This process has been especially prominent since the fuller development of city industry on a large scale and the extraordinary increase and perfection of the means of communication. In this new national era the total national production endeavours so to distribute itself over the territory controlled by it that each of its branches may find the location best suited to it. Factory and house-industry districts arise, and separate valleys and whole regions take on a semi-urban character. Certain cities develop special branches of industry and trade reaching out far beyond the local, and often even the national, demand. In others, again, all industry and business life decline; they sink down to the level of villages, so that the historical rights of burgess that still attach to their name appear in striking contrast with their position as places of trade and with the number of their inhabitants. The distinctions between city and country are blotted out. This happens in the neighbourhood of rising industrial cities through the planting of factories and workmen's dwellings in the suburbs and beyond; in the neighbourhood of the declining "rural cities" through the approach of the latter to the condition of surrounding country places, and through the rise of populous industrial towns. On the whole, however, the number of centres of population and of objective points for internal migrations is today relatively much smaller than in the second half

278

of the Middle Ages[347].

But in still another respect does the redistribution of population resulting from the internal migrations of the present time differ from that witnessed by our ancestors from the tenth to the fifteenth centuries. In consequence of the greater certainty of a living and of far-reaching measures for the health of the people the increase in population is today more rapid than in mediaeval times. It is safe from those heavy reverses so frequently resulting in those ages from harvest failure, feuds and plague. On that account the modern migrations into the large cities and industrial districts in many cases absorb only a surplus population that would not find sufficient room for earning a livelihood in the places of its origin. At these points they retard or completely check the congestion of population; while on the other hand at the points of agglomeration no economic obstacles bar the way to a continuous and rapid increase.

In mediaeval times, on the contrary, the migratory accession of population was distributed among a multitude of walled places scattered at fixed intervals over the whole country. The increase in many cases continued only until the city was full. When once it had as many inhabitants as it needed to man its walls and towers and supply all the branches of industry, there was no room for more. Extensions of the city limits often did take place in mediaeval times, it is true; they are the result of the increasing formation and subdivision of

---

[347]The German Empire had in 1890 a total of 2,285 "cities." Of these there were 26 with more than 100,000 inhabitants, 22 with from 50,000 to 100,000, 104 with from 20,000 to 50,000, and 169 with between 10,000 and 20,000. Besides these there were 56 villages and suburban municipalities with from 10,000 to 50,000 inhabitants, 11 of them with more than 20,000.—In Prussia there were in that year 46 "cities" with less than 1,000 inhabitants, 14 of these being in the Province of Posen, 12 in Silesia, 10 in Hesse-Nassau, 3 in Brandenburg, 2 each in West Prussia and Westphalia, 1 each in Saxony, Hanover and the Rhineland (Schleiden with 515 inhabitants). Alongside these dwarflike cities there were 37 rural municipalities with more than 10,000 inhabitants.—How far some of the old cities have declined is shown by the following figures for the Grand Duchy of Baden. There the census of 1885 gave 114 "cities," only 63 of these having a population of over 2,000, and 9 with over 10,000. Of the remaining 51 "cities" 42 had from 1,000 to 2,000 inhabitants, 4 had from 500 to 1,000, and 5 below 500 (among these last being Kleinlaufenburg with 441, Neufreistett with 427, Blumenfeld with 349, Fiirstenberg with 341, Hauenstein with 157). For every city there were on an average 14 villages. On the other hand, there were altogether 129 municipalities with over 2,000 inhabitants, 66 of these being "villages." Of the old cities only 55 are thus cities according to the modern idea, and of the villages four per cent are from the point of view of population to be reckoned in with the cities.

special trades. But the Middle Ages developed no large cities; the mediaeval economic and commercial system forbade it. The country was often deprived of the population necessary for the cultivation of the soil; yet even with such accessions the frequency of extensive losses kept the city populations stationary.

From these remarks it will indeed remain uncertain whether or not the internal migrations that accompanied the development of the industrial life of the mediaeval town were relatively more extensive than the corresponding territorial movements and shiftings of population that result today from the more national character of settlements. On the other hand, it cannot be doubted that the attraction of the great cities of modern times for the population of the smaller towns and the country is exerted over greater expanses of territory than the mediaeval towns held within the circle of their influence. One is not in a position to say, however, that the recruiting territory for the population of a city has expanded since the beginning of modern times in direct ratio to the number of its inhabitants. On the contrary, one is astonished to find what a slight effect the perfecting of the means of com-munication and the introduction of freedom of movement have had upon the extent of the territory covered by the regular internal migrations.

A few figures will make this clear. Of every hundred new settlers coming to Frankfurt, Oldenburg and Basel the numbers according to distances are as follows:

City	Class of Population	Period	0-9 Miles	9-45 Miles	Over 45 Miles
Frankfurt	New citizens	14th century	46.7	39.3	14.0
Frankfurt	New citizens	15th century	23.1	52.7	24.2
Frankfurt	Metal workers	15&16th century	2.7	45.0	52.3
Oldenburg	Citizens born in other places	1880	21.8	42.1	36.1
Basel	Citizens born in other places	1888	16.7	50.2	33.1
Basel	Journeymen craftsmen	1888	13.9	40.0	46.1
Basel	Factory laborers	1888	17.1	59.6	23.3

Of the three recruiting zones distinguished here the outermost at present contributes more to the *total population* and the inner less than in mediaeval times. The reason probably is that today the population in the more immediate neighbourhood of a city takes advantage of the city's labour market without settling in the city itself, whether it be that they go daily to their places of work in the city by special workmen's trains or other convenient means of transportation, or that the great industries of the towns erect their workshops in neighbouring places. The recruiting territory for *journeymen* has rather contracted as compared with mediaeval times. With this is linked the circumstance that at present three fourths of this class of workmen are drawn from the country, while at the close of the Middle Ages less than one quarter of them came from villages and hamlets. Of the Frankfurt journeymen metal-workers in the fifteenth and sixteenth centuries only 20.7 per cent, were born in the country; of the Basel bakers and butchers in 1888, on the contrary, 78.7 per cent, and of the journeymen of other handicrafts 75.2 per cent, were of country birth. Even today journeymen craftsmen still migrate in much larger numbers and to greater distances than the typical workman class of the present, the *factory hands.* Of the factory workingmen in Basel in 1888, 25.8 per cent, were born in the city itself; of the handicraft journeymen, only 16.3 per cent. How many of them were born and still domiciled in the immediate neighbourhood the statistics unfortunately do not show. But all modern industrial development tends in the direction of producing a permanent labouring class, which through the custom of early marriage is already much less mobile than the journeymen of the early handicrafts, and which in future will doubtless be as firmly attached to the factory as were the servile labourers of the mediaeval manor to the glebe.[348] If this is not very noticeable at present it is because the majority of large industries have not yet attained their growth, and because it is necessary for them, as long as they extend their works, to meet the increased demand for labourers by drawing further upon the surplus population of the rural districts.

These remarks point to the conclusion that we are not justified in attributing a growing migratory character to society as a result of the closer network of commercial routes and the invention of perfected means of communication. Rather should we say that at present we are in the midst of a *transition period* in which the yet uncompleted transformation of the town and territorial economic structure into

---

[348]The construction of workingmen's dwellings by the great manufacturing establishments, whether these pass over into the possession of the labourers or are rented to them, is even now begetting a sort of factory bondage, which has an appalling resemblance to the old bondage to the soil. Comp. my article on the Belgian social legislation in Braun's Archiv. f. soz. Gesetzg. u. Stat, IV, pp. 484, 485.

a national one involves a continuous displacement of the boundaries of division of labour and of the centres of the various branches of production, and consequently displacements of the labouring population.

After a period of economic and social ossification extending over centuries, in which all sorts of limitations upon migration and settlement held the population fast to the original ancestral seats, it is not surprising that many view with anxiety the great movements of population which today extend over whole territories. It seems almost as if the early times of universal migration were returning. But in this they forget that it is only a part—the rural part—of the population that has become more migratory; that up to the early years of last century a great number of these were bound to the soil. The merchant, the craftsman and the scholar are today much less mobile than, for instance, in the time of the Reformation; and the industrial labourers move relatively less often and to shorter distances than they did even a century ago. Only their number has become much greater and is still steadily increasing. This growth of industry displaces a part of the rural labouring population from their usual places of abode, to which nothing now holds them but the interests of those who profit by their helplessness. The further progress of this movement will probably show, even in a few decades, that the human race in the course of its evolution has on the whole become more stationary.

We may thus say in conclusion: In this general influx to the cities and their suburbs we are to-day undergoing what our ancestors experienced in the second half of the Middle Ages, the transition to a new economic and social order and a fresh distribution of population. At that time the movement inaugurated the period of town economy and of sharp separation of town and country; the movement in the midst of which we now live is the outward sign that we have entered upon a new period of development,—the period of organic distribution of population, the period of national division of labour and of national satisfaction of wants, in which the distinctions between city and country as places of abode are being obliterated by numerous transitional formations. This fact has long since been recognised by statisticians who have dropped the historico-juridical conception of city and substituted a statistical one in which places are distinguished according to the number of their inhabitants.

Every transitional epoch has its inconveniences and its suffering.

But the modern movement of population, in so far as it is expressed in the influx into the cities, will, like that of mediaeval times, reach its goal and then subside. This goal can be none other than to assign to every individual capacity and to every local group of persons that place and that role in the great national life in which its endowments and the altered technical conditions of economic activity best fit it to contribute to the general welfare.

Thus from a consideration of internal migrations, despite the fact that the conditions accompanying them are often far from pleasant to contemplate, we may gain the assurance that they too mean, from the wider standpoint, an advance towards higher and better forms of social existence, both for the individual and for the race.

Index

Oecolampadius, 164

periodical migrations, 258
personal casual element in divi-
    sion of labour, 220
personal transportation, 57
Pius V, 167
polygamy, 24, 26, 28, 41, 186
Prague, 167, 169
principle of nationality, 103
property, ancient Greeks and Ro-
    mans, 243
Protestant Germany, 247
Prussia, 139, 152, 165, 257, 260

railway, 107
repair trade, 145
Robinson Crusoe, 65
Romans, 71
Rome, 273
Russians, 69, 125

scrittori d'avvisi, 166
Serbs, 70
Shakespeare, 240
shifting of demand, 149
Siberian nomad, 212
Silesia, 118
slavery, 41, 71
Smyrna, 267
social mobility, 252
social outcome of migration, 261
specialization in science, 238
specialization or division of trades,
    212
Switzerland, 163, 169

telegraph, 107, 178
telephone, 107, 178
telephonic contrivance, 58

temporary community of produc-
    tion, 226
Thünen, 65
the Hague, 170
town economy, 66, 84
tribe of the Osakas, 54
tscheta or družina, 70
Turkey, 58
Turks, 165, 267

Uaupes of Brazil, 40
unfree houseworker, 130
union of labour, 189, 234
use of time, 30
usury, 84

Venice, 165
Vienna, 167, 169, 170, 172
Vienna furniture, 148
Voigtland, 126

W. H. Riehl, 241
West Prussia, 121

Zeit, 162
Zurich, 128

*9 781622 730056 *